HOW **NOT** TO BE A
FOOTBALL
MILLIONAIRE

KEITH GILLESPIE
MY AUTOBIOGRAPHY

HOW NOT TO BE A
FOOTBALL
MILLIONAIRE

KEITH GILLESPIE

MY AUTOBIOGRAPHY

Sport Media

To Mum, Dad, Claire, Angela, Heather,
Madison, Lexie and Nico

Sport Media

HOW NOT TO BE A FOOTBALL MILLIONAIRE

By Keith Gillespie with Daniel McDonnell

Copyright: Keith Gillespie

Published by Trinity Mirror Sport Media
Executive Editor: Ken Rogers
Senior Editor: Steve Hanrahan
Editor: Paul Dove
Senior Art Editor: Rick Cooke
Production: Alan Jewell, Adam Oldfield, Gary Gilliland, James Cleary
Design: Colin Harrison, Jamie Dunmore, Adam Oldfield
Senior Marketing Executive: Claire Brown
Senior Book Sales Executive: Karen Cadman

First Edition
Published in Great Britain in 2013.
Published and produced by: Trinity Mirror Sport Media,
PO Box 48, Old Hall Street, Liverpool L69 3EB

ISBN: 9781908695192

Photographic acknowledgements:
Keith Gillespie personal collection,
Trinity Mirror (Daily Mirror, Newcastle Journal & Evening Chronicle)
PA Photos, INPHO Photos, Tony Woolliscroft

With thanks to Phil Munnelly and Guy Rose

Printed and bound by CPI Group (UK) Ltd, Croydon, CR0 4YY

Contents

Acknowledgements

MY family have shared in my trials and tribulations and I cannot stress enough how grateful I am for their continued support.

Thanks to Mum and Dad for being there through the ups and downs, especially when the downs were more frequent. It meant a lot to have you there whatever happened. Angela and Heather are great sisters and great friends, and deserve all the happiness in the world with Davy, Stephen and the kids.

Claire Munn only came into my life as I started working on this project so, while she might only feature in the latter chapters of this book, I know she is going to be a huge part of the years ahead. Without Claire's support and love, I wouldn't have been able to open up and become a better person. I don't know where I would be without her.

Madison, Lexie and Nico are the three best things to ever happen to me. Every day is a joy and I look forward to watching you grow. You are my everything.

I will always be eternally grateful to Eddie Coulter, the great Manchester United scout, who passed away in 2011. Without his backing, I may never have got the chance to spend time at such a wonderful club.

My grandad Bob was a constant presence on the sidelines in my early years and I miss him dearly. I should also mention the living legend, Joe Kincaid, 'Mr St Andrews' who gave me an opportunity at a great club to start my journey.

Like football, putting a book together is a team game and there are plenty of people I need to thank. Without the perseverance, help and support of Phil Munnelly this book simply wouldn't have happened. As an agent, he is a one-off. Some agents desert a player when he's of no value to them anymore, but Phil continually places his client first and has become a great friend.

Thanks to Daniel McDonnell for his hard work and graft in putting my thoughts on paper. We've spent many, many hours together but it's been easy for me because of the rapport we struck up; I'll always appreciate it.

Caroline Rhatigan has helped me in the PR department in recent years and was the key player in bringing me to Longford Town which has given me purpose for the last few seasons. My thanks also to the players, management, officials and fans of the club for their support.

Sarah Munnelly was instrumental in lining up the publisher for the book when we sought to get the project off the ground, and thanks also to Guy Rose from Futerman/Rose Associates for his assistance and Paul Dove and the staff at Trinity Mirror for their guidance in the final months.

Keith Gillespie, September, 2013

WHEN I first met Keith to discuss working together on the book, I was a little apprehensive.

My view was that there are too many football autobiographies where the subject's primary goal appears to be crafting the image of themselves they would like the world to see rather than providing an actual insight into who they are. Within a minute of speaking to Keith, I was reassured. He listed examples of books that he disliked for that reason and stressed that he was keen to do things differently and portray the reality of life as a professional footballer, even if the truth isn't always flattering.

ACKNOWLEDGEMENTS

When we started plotting a way through his eventful career, I didn't realise there were still a lot of things going on with his life that any man would struggle to deal with. They are reflected in the final chapters, particularly with regard to the impact of financial setbacks on his day to day wellbeing. I respect his honesty in opening up on a difficult subject. I hope it encourages others to do the same. Pride should never be an obstacle.

It's taken us a while to finish the story and I must thank my sports editor David Courtney and the staff at the Irish Independent who allowed me to say yes when the opportunity arose. I'm also indebted to a variety of journalists who covered various stages of Keith's career and pointed me in the right direction when I needed help; if I start listing them I'm afraid I'll forget someone. Paul Dove and the staff of Trinity Mirror have done a thoroughly professional job, and cheers also to Barry Landy for the assistance with the transcribing. Thanks and apologies are also due to my parents Derek and Anne and the unfortunate friends who didn't always get a short answer when they asked how things were going, especially the Stateside contingent who had to put up with my 'writing visits'; I promise I'll stop talking about it now.

Phil Munnelly and Caroline got me involved with the project and I'm grateful you made the call. We've had plenty of laughs along the way and your hospitality is appreciated. The research was made easier by the scrapbooks and newspaper cuttings which his mother, Beatrice, has studiously maintained, aided by Keith's remarkable memory of the little details. It's been a pleasure to help construct this story. I sincerely hope you enjoy it.

Daniel McDonnell, September, 2013

Prologue

THE phone is ringing. Number withheld.

It can run to voicemail, like most callers have for the past month. If the digits are unfamiliar, it's probably something to do with the bundle of unopened letters gathering dust in the corner of the room.

I don't like opening letters very much. Don't like answering the phone to strangers either. But if they follow up with a few words after the tone, I listen.

"You have one new message," says the automated voice that I know so well. I wait, and then a human takes over. A journalist, from the Belfast Telegraph.

"Keith, I'm just looking for your reaction to the news today..."

I stop listening, delete it and sit down on the couch So, this is it then. Finally, the day had arrived.

The main evening TV news confirms it. I flick over to find that my plight is the lead item. Clearly, October 1, 2010 is a slow day in Northern Ireland. The announcer reads in a sombre tone over a montage of clips from my career:

'The news that football star Keith Gillespie had been declared bankrupt came in the High Court today.

'An order was made against the former Manchester United and Newcastle United winger following a petition by HM Revenue and Customs Commissioners over a tax bill. The High Court document confirmed that the decision was taken on the basis of evidence from a solicitor from the petitioning creditor.

'It said that Keith Robert Gillespie from Bangor was adjudged bankrupt on the 22 September. The statement also revealed that the official receiver had been appointed manager of his estate.

'The 35-year-old spent much of his career in England, having also played for Blackburn Rovers, Leicester City and Sheffield United. He also won 86 caps for Northern Ireland. Mr Gillespie left Irish League side Glentoran in June after failing to agree terms.'

At least I'd warned Mum. On her last visit, she'd asked when I was going to deal with the stockpile of stuffed envelopes. I've always needed a kick up the arse to sort things out, and she is usually the instigator. But this problem is different.

Once it entered the legal realms, there could be no escaping the truth. Returning calls from accountants and solicitors serves no purpose. It isn't going to change anything, so why bother?

I don't have £137,000. Simple as that.

Another phone call. This time, from a number I do recognise. My agent, Phil Munnelly.

"What the fuck is going on Keith?"

He'd heard the news on the radio.

I should have given Phil the heads-up. We're good friends, we speak often. He's bollocking me for keeping him out of the loop, and I struggle to explain why. Maybe I was embarrassed. Maybe I didn't want the hassle.

He's annoyed. By now, he's aware of the quirks of his client. My trademark response to a crisis is to say nothing and hope that it goes away. Decide there's nothing to worry about, and press on with things.

But he expected more of me this time. Phil knew I was in trouble. After all, I've been without a club for over three months. He just didn't realise the full extent of it.

I apologise to Phil and hang up.

Certainly, I've had better days.

Part of me hoped that nobody would notice. Other former Premier League footballers had gone through bankruptcy, and their shame slipped under the radar. I should have known it would be different in Northern Ireland. Big fish, small pond.

I pick up the phone one last time before switching it off and call my brother-in-law, Davy, to check that the usual team is in place for the following night's table quiz down in our local pub.

"Are you on for it?" he said.

"I'll be there."

I don't know if anyone is surprised when I walk through the doors of the Groomsport Inn, but nothing was going to stop me. My face might have been plastered all over that day's papers, but I had a lifetime's practice of dealing with controversy. Another smidgeon wasn't going to hurt. In my mind, I've experienced far worse than this.

I anticipate a few comments but the teasing is gentle. Heads turn in my direction when one of the boys asks whose round it is. "Well, I'm skint lads..." Cue loud laughter.

They know me well enough to leave it there, and change the subject. We have a quiz to win.

I'll deal with this my own way. Look in the mirror, face the day. Get over it, and get on with it.

It's an attitude that has a shelf-life.

$$\textbf{1}$$

Best Laid Plans

"WHERE did it all go wrong?"

Isn't that what a hotel porter once said to George Best? I've been asked the same question more than once but, unlike George, I don't have Miss World and stacks of cash lying next to me. It's usually posed by a drunken stranger in far less glamorous surroundings.

I never spoke with George, even though his name is interwoven with my life. We shared a dressing room for Billy Bingham's testimonial when I was a teenager, but shyness prevented me from saying hello. What would I have said anyway? "Hi, I'm Keith, I'm a winger from Northern Ireland who plays for Manchester United, and the newspapers say I'm going to be the next George Best."

At Blackburn, the dressing room comedians christened me

KEITH **GILLESPIE**

'Bestie' alright, but that was more a reference to my roguish tendencies than the playing ability. The name stuck with me, up to and beyond George's death in 2005.

I've led a colourful life. I doubt that anyone who crossed my path would describe me as a clean living, model pro. I liked a drink, learned to smoke, and swear by an unhealthy diet. No veg, no eggs, nothing unfamiliar. Nutritionists tried to change that, prescribing a list of foods and giving me a chart to fill out my daily intake. After a couple of days, I ripped it up, and went back on the cheese and ham toasties. I couldn't be arsed with all that hassle.

I've taken a single-minded approach to looking after my body and I insist to this day that it never caused any of my problems. I'm 38 now, and feeling good. I haven't put on weight. At my peak, my body fat percentage was seven per cent. Today, it's 10 per cent, well within the ideal range for an athlete.

Club doctors always thought I was a freak. My inability to put on the pounds no matter how I lived baffled them, and tormented less fortunate team-mates. I remember the reserve keeper at Newcastle, Mike Hooper, coming back for pre-season weighing 17 stone. The club put us on the scales every Friday so, in order to shed the pounds, Mike would spend early morning in the sauna and then run to training. On the bus home from away games, we'd stop for chicken and chips, and he'd sit there, looking at it, wanting it, but knowing it was wrong. I could eat a bucketload and report the next day to find I'd lost a pound.

Beer is a similar story. It's no secret that I've always liked a night on the town. The strange thing is, I played the best football of my career when I drank the most. I was out three times a week in Newcastle, boozing as much if not more than the average bloke my age. In hindsight, not a wise move for a public figure. In my younger days, it led to rows, bad publicity, and, inevitably, amateur shrinks put two and two together and came up with the conclusion that I had a drink problem. Incorrect. Let's make that clear early. Alcohol was the catalyst to mischief in town, but I seldom drank at home, and never needed it to get out of bed in the morning, nor will I in the future. I've read what alcoholism did to footballers like George and Paul Mc-Grath, and I'm grateful to have avoided the affliction of that terrible disease.

This man was susceptible to other urges. They didn't cost me my health, but they almost cost me everything else.

How much money did I blow? One afternoon, I sat in Phil's apartment to figure it out, once and for all. It's the closest I've come to therapy until I realised that I actually needed therapy.

He scribbled down my recollections, correcting me on a figure or two along the way.

Working out the bonuses was the hard part. The signing-on fees, the appearance money, the inducements. At Newcastle, we received £50,000 a head for coming second in the league, which was huge money in 1996.

By the time I moved onto Blackburn, the globalisation of the Premier League had inflated the wages and the incentives. We earned £1,500 per league point, so two wins on the trot could be worth an extra £9,000. And if you scored a few goals along the way, it helped.

So, the calculations took a while. Eventually, we reached a club by club consensus.

It went like this...

Manchester United £60,000
Newcastle United £1,102,000 [+£250,000 in bonuses]
Blackburn Rovers £3,510,000 [+£400,000 in bonuses]
Leicester City £1,050,000 [+£40,000 in bonuses]
Sheffield United £670,000 [+£75,000 in bonuses]
Bradford City £15,000
Glentoran £43,875

Total £7,215,875

A substantial amount of cash, eh? And that's only a conservative sketch of the incomings. It doesn't include boot deals, promotional appearances, Northern Ireland match fees, libel settlements, and all the other elements that come with the territory.

Not that the libel settlements could be classified as a perk of the trade. The £150,000 or so I've made from that avenue does not compensate for the loss of earnings from the negative publicity, particularly the episode in La Manga that etched a black mark next to my name. Without the media driven set-up that unjustly landed me in prison – we'll deal with the details later – my total earnings might have reached the £10 million mark although, as my friends point out, I'd have probably blown the extra £2 million anyway.

I always tended to spend what I had in my possession. My relationship towards money probably mirrored my attitude towards life when the going was good. Impulsive, reckless, unthinking. When it came to real responsibilities, I always veered towards the 'why do today what you can do tomorrow' school of thought. The brain switched off.

With cash, there was no tomorrow. All that mattered was having enough for the next race, the next round, the next taxi home with the girl I just met ten minutes ago.

Gambling emptied my pockets, decimated the short-term cashflow. Truly, I haven't a notion how much I squandered. There's no way I can put a figure on it. Between all the lost afternoons in the bookies, the ill-advised phone bets, and the multitude of opened and closed accounts, there's no coherent paper trail to reach a definite conclusion.

I didn't gamble away all of my money, however. If only it was that straightforward. While I had an unbelievable ability to back the wrong horse, that poor judgement extended from the racetrack to the decisions I made in day-to-day life.

My savings were directed towards people that I shouldn't have trusted. It was too late when I realised I'd done my money. My race was run. The taxman caught up far too easily.

This is my 2013. It's leaving home in Bangor, County Down, on the north-east coast of Northern Ireland, at lunchtime, and embarking on a 149-kilometre journey to my place of work. Longford Town is a semi-professional club in the midlands of the Republic of Ireland, vying for promotion from the second tier, the graveyard of Irish football. A good home gate is 500 supporters, although our 4,000 all-seater stadium is above average for our division, a reminder of better times at the turn of the century when they won a few trophies.

I knew nothing of their existence when Phil mentioned them as I sought to rebuild after bankruptcy. Now, my football life revolves around this small, community club.

The straightforward route from Bangor to the City Calling Stadium takes me down a variety of country roads. Sometimes, I take the long way around to get some extra time on the motorway but, usually, I negotiate my way through the towns of Armagh, Monaghan and Cavan until I reach the N55 at Granard, which brings me into the county of Longford, just 30 minutes away from my destination. I arrive at the ground over two hours before kick-off, and head straight for the dressing room to change. At this level, we don't have the budget to gather in a hotel for a pre-match meal before a home game. I'm expected to have eaten earlier in the day. Afterwards, a local pizza company might dispatch some of their produce to the ground, and I grab a slice before throwing the gearbag into the back seat, and starting on the return journey through the night.

I break my trips by making phone calls. On the way down, I'll call my daughters, Madison and Lexie, who live in England with their mother. Madison, the eldest, is five and quick as a flash.

"Where are you?" I ask.

"But you know where I am, Daddy, I'm talking to you," she'll say.

After the match, I might call Phil to talk it over. I don't know any footballer who can switch off after a game. If I'm lucky, I reach my house at 1.30am and then it takes me a couple of hours to shut down, although I know I'll be woken by my baby son, Nico, when the sun comes up.

Before I put my head down, I remember to reach into my gearbag for the package I take with me everywhere and pour a glass of water from the tap. I pop a couple of green and gold

Prozac tablets into my mouth and wash them down. This is my daily dose of medication, a regular routine when you suffer from depression. It's a recent development, and a secret to all but a few people. Two and a half years of stress since the bankruptcy wore down the tough exterior, the shield of denial that I brought everywhere. I'll be seeing a psychologist until they decide I don't need these pills anymore.

I can always trust the body to look after itself, but will never be sure of the mind. The grind of driving alone for hours leaves it vulnerable to all sorts of thoughts. To shut them out, I mostly switch the car radio to Talksport, catching up on the news from the world I once inhabited. Craig Short, an old colleague of mine, said I was one of the most knowledgeable footballers he'd ever met. Most people would expect that statement to be followed by a punchline.

But I've always loved quiz shows. Who Wants To Be A Millionaire, The Weakest Link, The Chase, Eggheads, whatever it may be. My idea of a good afternoon in the pub is sipping a pint and testing myself on the touch-screen brain teasers. My competitive instinct always drew me towards them. That's why I still love the buzz of the Thursday night table quiz down the local with my brother-in-law and the gang. We take it seriously, and it bugs me when I can't think of a fact that I should know.

When it came to my own affairs, however, I always pleaded ignorance to relevant questions for as long as possible. I preferred the distraction offered by useless information, the crucial distinction between intelligence and common sense.

I can recite all sorts of facts off the top of my head. I know that the origin of the phrase 'Bob's Your Uncle' dated back to 1887, when the British Prime Minister, Robert Gascoyne-Cecil

(Lord Salisbury) was accused of nepotism for appointing his nephew to the position of Irish Chief Secretary, but I don't know how a Premier League footballer, who considers himself to be a smart guy, managed to turn £8 million into nothing.

I wish I could adequately explain how he chose the wrong friends, failed in two marriages, and wound up in a Mental Health Assessment Centre, looking for solutions from a strange man in a white jacket.

So, back to the original question. Where did it go wrong?

Let me try and explain.

2

Having A Ball

FOOTBALL was my childhood. I grew up in a country ravaged by the violence of the Troubles and yet, long before my profession gave me a protective shell, I was unaffected by it. Some people don't believe that could be possible in Northern Ireland, but it was my reality.

My Dad, Harry Gillespie, worked as a prison officer in the Maze, the notorious home for paramilitary prisoners, during the height of the violence. A year before he got the job there were hunger strikes; a year after there was a prison break where one of the other officers died. But he never took the stress from work home with him; it must be in our genes. Sitting down and revealing our deepest thoughts to our loved ones is the last thing the Gillespie men are likely to do. Instead, we just try and block it out and move on to the next day. I think my Dad wanted his kids to have as normal a childhood as possible and I appreciate why he did that. I've no doubt that he encountered some terrifying people, but we barely talked about the pictures that were on the evening news every night.

It helped that Bangor, a wealthy Protestant town, largely escaped the unrest. There were a few incidents in the early '70s, long before we moved there, but while other parts of Northern Ireland constantly suffered, I led an idyllic existence by comparison. At least that's how I remember it anyway. We were 13 miles from Belfast and one day a bomb went off with such force that we felt the reverberations in our kitchen. Truthfully, I couldn't tell you when that happened. I could look it up and pretend I remembered every second, and suggest that it had a huge impact on me. But that wouldn't be honest. I occupied my own, happy world, aware of bad things without really paying too much attention. Sure, security checks were a way of life, and I knew I had to be careful on my trips to Belfast. Yet I was born into that environment, so this was normal. I never knew any different.

I spent my early years in Islandmagee, a quiet peninsula seven miles from Larne, a seaport on the east coast of Northern Ireland. Dad is from Larne. My mother, Beatrice Thornberry, hails from Kilrea in County Derry. When I was born on February 18, 1975, I already had a two-year-old sister, Angela. Three years later, Heather arrived.

Both my parents came from the Protestant community. Mum's father, Robert Thornberry, was in the police, the Royal Ulster Constabulary, and moved around a lot with his job. She lived on the same street in Kilrea as a budding Catholic footballer, a young Martin O'Neill. They weren't friends, although

I remember my Grandad speaking a lot about the O'Neill family – especially after the 1982 World Cup when, against all the odds, Billy Bingham took our wee country to the finals in Spain, with Mum's old neighbour right at the heart of it.

That tournament is my first vivid football memory. Before that, Dad watched football on Sunday afternoons and I used to cry because I wanted the Muppet Show so we had to rotate on a week to week basis until, all of a sudden, I tired of Kermit and wanted the football instead.

Dad was a Manchester United fan, going right back to his memories of the coverage of the Munich air disaster and the Busby Babes. Then, George Best came along and the connection between Northern Ireland and Old Trafford was strengthened. Dad passed his love for United onto me and Norman Whiteside, a 17-year-old from Belfast, became my hero in the summer of '82. He became the youngest player to feature in a World Cup, and I was captivated by him.

They were a magic couple of weeks. The win over Spain is the abiding memory. I can picture the goal clearly, with Billy Hamilton charging down the right wing and crossing, their goalkeeper Luis Arconada half clearing, and Gerry Armstrong smashing home the loose ball. Mum was in the kitchen and smacked her head on a cupboard door as she rushed to find out the cause of the big cheer from the living room.

We lived in a two-storey house, the last of a row in a working-class estate, a blessing as we had a big grass area next to us with a football pitch. On those long summer evenings, I ran around imagining that I was Whiteside, flying down the wing, dodging tackles. Dreaming that one day it would be me.

I collected my first goal bonus when I was eight. The occasion was my first 11-a-side for Rathmore Primary School, and I banged in a hat-trick. Dad had promised me 20p for every goal.

Football gave me an identity in my new school. Moving to Bangor was hardly a big switch; two of Mum's brothers lived within six miles and her parents eventually moved there. Dad's family in Larne were only 18 miles away. So I found settling quite straightforward, although my favourite sport helped a lot. While Dad had togged out at a high enough amateur level, there was no real football pedigree in our family. It turned out I was quite decent at it. I entered Rathmore at P4 level – P7 was the oldest – and I was instantly promoted to the school team. The teachers spotted me in the playground. Like any kid, I loved getting the ball and trying to dribble around others, and I seemed to have more success than most. I didn't know how good I was, but I copped that getting put in with lads three years older than me was a compliment.

It also introduced me to a lifelong friend, Jim Allen, who would later act as best man at my second wedding. He was in P6 and his back garden leaned onto the school grounds. Our house was nearby and I spent most evenings kicking the ball about with Jim and the other lads from the area. We've been best mates since. Jim has always looked out for me. There was a dark alley that linked our estates and, at night, when we finished playing, Jim would stand at his end and watch me sprint down it just to be sure that I made it to the other side safely. Through the years, I've trusted people that I shouldn't have, but Jim never let me down.

Our team started winning games and I was picked to play for our district. Soon, I was playing wherever I could, even with the Boys Brigade, effectively a Northern Irish version of the boy scouts, who only offered one thing that I was really interested in. My Dad and his friend Morris McCullough started a team called Bangor West, and started entering lads from our age group in tournaments. Even though we were basically formed from nothing, we went to Belfast and won the Northern Ireland Indoor Championships. They said I was the star player, but I didn't really think about that. As in later life, I tried not to think too hard about anything. All I wanted was to get the ball, and enjoy myself.

By the time I turned 12, teams from Bangor and beyond were regularly approaching Dad to ask about my availability. Joe Kincaid, a scout for Glasgow Rangers, came forward with the most attractive offer. He was part of a group that had set up a schoolboy team in Belfast called St Andrews. Joe knew where the best young players in the country were, and wanted to bring them together. I agreed to come on board, and linked up with a group of lads that would dominate the local scene all the way to U-14 level. It was the perfect way to get noticed.

One weekend, Dad was standing on the sideline watching us rack up another win when a guy sidled over and introduced himself as Eddie Coulter, a scout for Manchester United. He asked Dad if I would be interested in coming along to the Manchester United School of Excellence – a group of 16-20 players from Northern Ireland who trained together in Belfast every Wednesday night. It was a no-brainer – I think Dad was more excited than I was.

When I turned 13, Joe fixed me up with a week at Rangers, where I did enough to be asked back, but I eventually said no to that offer. That's because I spent the following week at Manchester United. No other club mattered.

The climax of my week in Manchester was the moment when Alex Ferguson called me into his office. I was terrified. It was during the school holidays so there were loads of us there trying to impress, plenty of games for the coaches to look at.

The first team were knocking around the place and I got to meet Norman Whiteside and have a treasured photo taken. But the most exciting part was looking over in the middle of a match to see the manager of the club standing on the sideline. Back then, Fergie was under pressure, with a winning reputation from Scotland that had failed to immediately translate to his new job. That didn't bother me. All I knew was that the manager of Manchester United was looking at me play, so I'd better do something.

He had watched me before, a specially arranged match involving the lads in the School of Excellence. I'd met him, and posed for a pic, but this was a completely different scenario. I was surrounded by top kids from around the UK, all of whom had the same ambitions. I concentrated hard. And I felt I was doing well. Dodging the tackles, scoring goals. Just like the Rathmore playground.

Still, when the week ended, and everyone was sat in a canteen waiting to go into the manager's office for an assessment, nerves crept in. Part of me couldn't believe that the first-team boss would have time to speak with every kid on trial, but he was very much involved. And the first thing that struck me was that he knew everybody's name.

"Come in, Keith," he said, with that familiar Glaswegian twang, as I gingerly pushed open the door after my name was called. He continued speaking, but the words were going over my head. All I wanted was the verdict. "You've done really well," he declared, "And we want you to come back." I walked out feeling ten foot tall, and desperate to tell everybody the news.

The process sped up from there. Eddie, a lovely man who sadly passed away in 2011, arrived at my house with a pre-contract agreement and a pen. Then, I was flown over with my folks for a game with Middlesbrough, where they gave us the red carpet treatment. The night before, Fergie and his wife Cathy came to our hotel to have dinner. That was intimidating. I can't imagine what it was like for my Dad, a lifelong Manchester United fan, but the grown-ups seemed to get on well and chat politely. I just tried to mind my manners and say very little. I can't even remember too much of what the conversation was about. What I do recall is Fergie reaching into his pocket at the end of the meal and producing a crisp £20 note for the waitress. I'd never seen a tip like that before. We knew that by coming out with us, he was obviously making a big effort and when Dad mentioned that we liked to go and watch Northern Ireland in Windsor Park, he promised to sort us tickets for the next home game. "Let me know if there's anything else you need," he stressed.

The following day, he allowed me into the dressing room before the match, and I was introduced to the rest of the players. Maybe new recruits were brought in all the time but, to this bright-eyed kid, it was the biggest thing in the world. Bryan Robson scored the winning goal, and I went home awestruck by the experience.

Concentrating in school on Monday morning was that little bit harder.

3

Making The Grade

THE real troubles of my youth took place within the four walls of Bangor Grammar School.

My relationship with that place is summed up by their reaction to my call-up into the Northern Ireland U-15 squad. There was a tradition that the school paid for their proud student's team blazer. Not in my case, however. The authorities at the Grammar refused, even though they could have afforded the £80 easily.

It was a wealthy school, with a good reputation for delivering a solid education but from the start it was clear I had a major problem. They hated football. Hated it so much that they went out of their way to deter me from progressing in it. Most schools would have considered it an honour to have a student representing their country, but they saw it differently. It was just one part of an ongoing struggle. And my strife was nothing compared to some of the sick stuff going on around that place.

Certain sports were tolerated. Rugby was king. The walls were lined with pictures and stories of Grammarians who excelled with the oval ball. David Feherty, the golfer, also schooled there, and that was acceptable. There was only a passing reference to Terry Neill, a former Northern Ireland football international who then managed Arsenal. What they didn't mention was that he only lasted six weeks in the Grammar, and I can understand why. The hostility towards my passion was remarkable.

In first year, we had one afternoon a week for sport, and the options were limited. Just one choice. Rugby. I'd never paid any attention to rugby. I like watching it now, but I detested it then and, on my first day, I decided to escape. But they caught me as I tried to sneak out the door when the teams were being assigned. The teacher stuck me into the 'C' team with the lads that were picked last. The rules were a mystery so I stood on the wing and just ran with the ball when I got it, and used my pace. A few tries later, I was promoted to the 'A' team. Which was fine until games were scheduled for Saturday morning, the same time when I was needed in Belfast by St Andrews. I always chose football, but it landed me in constant trouble.

I thought I'd found the solution in second year. Hockey was added as an option B, so I went for that. But their games were on Saturday mornings too. The meeting point was the bus station in Bangor, just across the road from the train station where I caught the service to Belfast. I'd creep quietly up the road, head buried in my jacket, and dart into the railway tracks hoping that the group standing on the other side of the street wouldn't notice. The no-shows became an issue, and the school decided to punish me by suspiciously choosing a Saturday morning detention. I had to let St Andrews know that I'd miss a game. My parents spent so much time down the school complaining, that the other kids started to think they were teachers.

The biggest obstacle was the headmaster, Tom Patton. He marched around in this big black cloak, with an air of superiority, looking down his nose at everyone. He seemed to enjoy the power of his position, being the boss of a school that's been around since 1856. A place that even has its own song, in Latin of course. Everyone had to jump to Patton's attention. 'Yes sir', 'no sir'. Mum found him unbearable. He refused to make eye contact with her and one day she'd had enough. "Mr Patton, when you talk to me, I look at you. When I talk to you, you bow your head. Please look at me."

She told him that I wouldn't be showing up if I was given any more of these Saturday morning detentions. He never listened. It was like he thought he was a god instead of a headmaster. And that was supposed to justify the petty behaviour, the pointless detentions and the refusal to fork out for a blazer. It felt like they were trying to make a student suffer for succeeding.

As it transpired, the decision makers in Bangor Grammar had more serious matters to be concerned with. In 1998, it emerged that the Deputy Head, Dr Lindsay Brown, my religion teacher, was a paedophile. Brown was always in charge of taking kids away on camping trips, and it came out that he forced himself on boys after pretending he forgot his sleeping bag. The victims showed bravery to come forward and say that he'd sexually abused them and he was sent down for seven years after being found guilty of nine counts of indecent assault, and two of gross indecency. I was stunned when I heard.

There were always stories about Brown going around the school, with other lads saying he was one to watch, but I'd never had a problem with him, although I only went to those religious camps once. I thought all the rumours were just kids spreading crap and having a laugh. In prim and proper Bangor Grammar I'd never have imagined that a teacher could get away with such despicable behaviour. A special report commissioned after the case found that Patton had failed to take complaints against Brown seriously. Imagine living with that on your conscience.

Despite the school's best attempts, they couldn't halt my path. The countdown to my departure from Northern Ireland was underway, and my face was starting to pop up in the local news-papers. The real catalyst was the Milk Cup, a youth tournament that attracts top teams from all over the world to the small town of Coleraine, just 40 miles outside Belfast. It's a big deal. In 1989, St Andrews were unable to participate and a team-mate from Northern Ireland, Rodney McAree, asked me to play for Dungannon Swifts. His father, Joe, was their manager. Nobody gave us a chance in the U-14 competition, but we progressed to the final, where we encountered a selection from the Dub-lin and District Schoolboys League, the biggest league in the Republic, who were the hot favourites to win the competition. We surprised them; I got the winner in extra-time. A local team winning made plenty of headlines, and a fair share of them were devoted to me.

The trips with Northern Ireland also helped my profile. Our U-15 group was decent, managed by the late, great Davie Cairns. We should have won the Victory Shield, the marquee tourna-ment for the Home Nations, after beating Wales and Scotland

and then leading England into injury time of a game that was played at Hillsborough in driving sleet and snow. Everyone was going down with cramp, and our legs went. They scored twice. I later heard that one of their goalscorers was over-age.

Still, it was a good platform for us, and the major clubs were represented. I received approaches too, even though the Manchester United deal was common knowledge. Liverpool made an enquiry, but it was politely refused. I belonged to United and, from afar, they were playing a bigger role in my life. It was set in stone that I would be going over in the summer after I turned 16. I spent all my holidays there during my final year, and was often flown in for games at the weekend. In the 1990 Milk Cup, I was in Manchester United colours, part of a team where the starring member was a winger called Ryan Wilson. I was still at school when he made his senior debut the following March under his mother's maiden name – Giggs.

For Dad, that tournament was a special thrill. The head of the youth set-up, Brian Kidd, and his assistant, Nobby Stiles, were legends he'd watched from afar. He was particularly excited about meeting Nobby, one of his favourite players from the 1968 European Cup-winning side. We stayed in Harry Gregg's hotel in Portstewart during the tournament. Harry is a Manchester United legend from Northern Ireland who survived Munich, and he loved catching up with Nobby and telling stories from the past. It gave us a sense of the club's history, but we didn't bring the magic onto the pitch. We exited at the group stage.

When I wasn't needed in Manchester, I lined up for Linfield Colts, the youth side of the most successful club team in Northern Ireland. Linfield had an arrangement with United which was convenient when I became too old for St Andrews.

This was a jump up to U-18 level and a physical test. My first appearance against Ballymena went so well that the Linfield first-team manager enquired about bringing me into their ranks. The Irish League was a demanding place and I'd have been coming up against hardened semi-pros 10 or even 20 years older than me. United got wind of the idea, and vetoed it straight away. I was only small at that point and fairly slight. The experience could have broken me, so it was the right decision, although the idea did make me curious.

So, I stayed with the Colts and waited for the summer. The coverage increased in the final months. From the day the United news went public, the local papers were constantly on the phone. Inevitably, they trotted out the 'next George Best' line, a tag that was also attached to Whiteside in his youth. That's the thing about being from a small country. The spotlight comes earlier than England, where promising kids can stay under the media radar until they reach the first team.

Dad handled the queries. "We've done all we can to help him," he'd say, "but from 16 to 18, it's up to him to make a go of it."

I think I was too young to know what pressure was. But I was wary of getting carried away. I knew what people were saying. All the reports were positive, and I was supposed to be the next big thing, tipped for stardom as though it was a formality.

You often hear footballers giving interviews and talking about proving people wrong. This was the opposite.

When I packed my bags to head for England, the mission was to prove everyone right.

4

Fergie Fledgling

ON July 9, 1991, the Gillespie family gathered at the airport to wave goodbye to a 16-year-old boy who was daunted by the prospect of leaving home.

There were tears, because it was an emotional time. A week earlier Mum's mother, Gladys, had passed away. She lived around the corner with Grandad Robert and it hit us hard. Mum was only beginning to come to terms with that and now her son was packing his bags for good. It was the sacrifice that came with my new life. There was no other option.

I'd made the same flight plenty of times before but, as I turned around to wave goodbye before going through the departure gates, I knew this was different.

The minute I landed at Manchester Airport, I raced to one of the payphones to ring home and they were barely in the door.

It's a bloody short journey after all.

My next stop was my new lodgings in Salford, a digs run by a welcoming maternal lady named Brenda Gosling. She'd been looking after apprentices from the club for quite a few years, including a young Lee Sharpe. Her location was ideal, less than two minutes walk from the Cliff. Perfect for an occasional late sleeper.

Brenda cooked all the meals, and made life easy for her tenants. The house was split into two. She lived on one side, and I shared the other with four others. There was Adrian Doherty and fellow St Andrews graduate Colin Telford from Northern Ireland, a Scottish lad, Colin McKee, and a vain Welsh boy called Robbie Savage. We weren't strangers. The cast of characters in my everyday life were familiar considering I'd been over and back since I was 13. But seeing each other 24/7 was a big change.

Robbie had plenty of quirks. He was my room-mate, which meant waking up to the sound of a hairdryer. His mop was shorter then, but he devoted a huge amount of time to it. I'd be hopping out of bed at ten past nine to report for training at a quarter past, and Robbie might have been up for an hour at that point, preening himself. And I was still usually ready before him.

I reported for duty on my first proper day as a professional footballer with a group of other fresh-faced apprentices. There were the Manchester lads like Gary Neville, Paul Scholes, Nicky Butt and Ben Thornley, and outsiders like John O'Kane from Nottingham, Chris Casper from Burnley, and a kid who went by the name of David Beckham. It was an exceptional group, although I don't think we'd copped it just yet.

Circumstances kept our feet on the ground. I was earning £46 a week, and Manchester United paid Brenda for my upkeep on top of that. The locals had a bit more cash because the rent money went to their parents, and they still had their mates from home about. So, the outsiders palled around together initially. We didn't have the money to go out and party and, besides, we were too young to really be able to do it properly anyway. Instead, we led quite a tame existence in our first year. We didn't see a lot of Manchester, bar the odd trip for a game of snooker or the cinema, but the five quid taxi fare from Salford to the centre of the city was an obstacle. I was saving my cash for the afternoons in the bookies. We'll come to that in a while.

I became good friends with Robbie. He was from Wrexham, which was only around an hour and 20 minutes away, and as soon as he passed his driving test, he used to commute regularly. I went down and stayed with his folks some weekends, just to break up the usual routine of sitting in. Becks lived with John O'Kane in a digs on Lower Broughton Road which was a bit further away. They were talented players with a different work ethic. John was a laid back type, probably too much so, whereas Becks was a real worker. He'd always spend time after training practising free-kicks and his ball striking. Off the pitch, he put the graft in as well. John used to call him the pretty boy, and reckoned I had it easy waiting around for Robbie in the morning. Long before the Spice Girl days, Becks was the first of the group to have a girlfriend. He bought an old Ford Estate off Ryan Giggs and I'm sure that helped. The lads with a car were always a step ahead with the ladies.

Gaz Neville had no interest in them at that stage. Football was his obsession. We had strong characters in our group, and he stood out. We called him 'Busy Bollocks' and with justification. On and off the pitch, he found it hard to relax. He used to come and play snooker with myself, Robbie, Becks and John O'Kane. Robbie and I were pretty decent, Becks was average, and Gaz was crap. Whoever his partner was, we generally had to give them a head start. But he still ended up on the losing side more often than not, and he hated it. There were other strong personalities. Chris Casper, Gaz's centre-half partner, was another talker. Nicky Butt was well ahead in terms of physique and stature, and it was no surprise when he rapidly moved up the ranks. You didn't mess with Nicky. I learned that when I wound him up in the showers one day, just messing about pinching him, and he decked me. By contrast, our other ginger midfielder, Scholesy, was a late bloomer, and therefore a peripheral member of the squad in that first year. He was a quiet lad with sharp wit; fame didn't change that.

There was no special treatment for us at that stage though. We trained twice a day in a competitive environment, and the intensity carried over to the changing rooms where the second-year apprentices ruled the roost. The newbies had to go through an initiation process, a series of dares that varied in levels of humiliation. Although he was a first teamer already, Giggsy was technically a second-year apprentice and the chief tormentor. The seniors would sometimes come down to enjoy the established tradition of the first years being put through hell.

I had to pretend to shag a physio bed in front of the mob. Other days, you might have to chat up a mop as though you were trying it on with a girl in a club, or else perform some kind of dance for everyone's entertainment. For shy teenagers, it was painful. I didn't have any real experience of the actions I had to impersonate. Robbie loved it though. He was the showman, and looked forward to his turn.

There was punishment if you refused a challenge. You might get smacked over the head by a football wrapped in a towel, or lined up for a flurry of punches that would leave you with a dead arm. Worst of all was getting stripped naked, and having the design of a United kit rubbed onto your body in boot polish with a sharp brush. Or getting thrown into the tumble dryer for a spin. A few years previously, Russell Beardsmore was left in the sauna with ten tracksuits on and had to fight to get them all off before he was let out. The club put an end to the rituals a few years later when it got out of hand.

At least, in hindsight, it was a laugh. Another rite of passage was far less entertaining. Thursday was school day. Continuing studies was part of the contract. I was in Manchester when Mum rang with my GCSE results. I remember them clearly. An A in History, Bs in English, English Lit and French, a C in Maths, Ds in German and Latin, and an F in Physics. Science never interested me and I didn't even bother with revising. My French grade was the regret; I was aiming higher.

Nevertheless, my results were respectable, and put me near the top of the apprentices' dressing room. For our day of learning, we were divided according to our results. I went to Accrington College, with Robbie, Gaz, Chris Casper and another lad, Mark Rawlinson. And the others? They went to a place in Manchester that we called the stupid college. I don't even know what they did.

That said, I don't really remember what we were doing either. It was some kind of BTEC in Leisure and Tourism, but it was boring. There were other apprentices from Man City, Burnley,

Blackburn and from around the north-west. I guess myself and Robbie were a bit disruptive. We were in class from 10am until 5pm and needed some amusement to pass the time. The girl in charge grew sick of our messing and punished us with six Thursdays together in the library away from the group. As if sharing a room with Robbie wasn't bad enough! The course was a waste of time although, somehow, I managed to pass.

Our real education was at the Cliff, where the blasé attitude we took to Accrington would never have been permitted. The tone was set from the top. Discipline and hard work was the mantra. It was no place for big-time charlies. Eric Harrison always told us that.

Eric was our manager, and the person who moulded the raw materials into a serious team. He had a modest playing career, predominantly with Halifax, but quickly made his name as a coach. Ron Atkinson hired him and, when Alex Ferguson arrived to sweep a broom through the club, Eric was retained. It was obvious why.

The youth-team supremo must instil discipline while gaining respect, and Eric found the balance. He was a tough Yorkshire man who could really flip when he was angry. You feared being on the wrong end of his bollockings.

Our games at the Cliff were surreal. Rather than watching from the sideline, Eric would be up in his office behind a glass window with an elevated view of the pitch. During a match, we would sometimes hear a relentless banging, and glance up to see an animated Eric losing the plot with his mouth moving at a million miles an hour. Or, worse again, you'd hear the noise and then look up and there's nobody there. That meant he was on his way downstairs to aggressively make his point to the culprit. I'd be praying that it wasn't me.

The attention to detail extended to everything. We all had our jobs to do around the club, and mine was to clean our dressing room. Sweep up the rubbish, mop the floor, all of that. We couldn't leave to go home until Eric came to inspect and gave the all-clear. If whoever was on duty in the first team dressing room had erred, it didn't matter if the apprentices' changing room was perfect. As a group, we were kept back, and the guilty one sure as hell heard about where they'd gone wrong.

Eric could be terrifying in full flight, but he was also considerate. Every couple of months, he'd organise these sessions that were like a parent-teacher meeting except we got the feedback individually. In that environment, he was understanding, and tried to point us in the right direction. At the same time each week, all our eyes would be trained on Eric as he made his way to the noticeboard to pin up the teams for the weekend. The apprentices were split into 'A' and 'B' teams. From the outset, I was a regular in the 'A's – in fact, the first years quickly became the core of the team – so I didn't get much chance to work under Nobby Stiles, who was in charge of the 'B' selection. I spent more time with Jim Ryan, the reserve manager, who drafted me in a couple of times not long after my arrival. Jim was mild-mannered compared to Eric, but he was a former Manchester United player, which gave him gravitas. He was assisted by Bryan 'Pop' Robson – no relation to the skipper – and together they removed the fear factor for a raw teenager encountering hardened professionals for the first time. The senior players on reserve duty were either on the comeback trail from a setback or simply out of favour. Jim had an ability to coax the best out of them, while acknowledging they would rather be somewhere else. "I know you senior lads don't want to be here," he would say, "but you have to put in a shift for the young players."

The experienced lads couldn't afford to switch off anyway, because there was always a chance that Alex Ferguson would be watching. He had a knack of keeping everyone at the club on their toes.

It could be a reserve match, a youth-team game, or just a routine training session, and the boss might suddenly appear unannounced.

Although we assembled at the Cliff, we trained at Littleton Road which was a five-minute bus ride away. The reasoning was to preserve the surface at the Cliff, but it also allowed the first team, reserves and the youths to train on separate pitches in close proximity to each other. It suited the gaffer perfectly. He could wander over and watch whoever he wanted.

Back at the Cliff, his office also overlooked the pitch, next to Eric's and Brian Kidd's. So, during a match, you might glance up to see Eric's reaction to something and then catch a sight of the gaffer as well.

Around the club, the apprentices were always wary when he was about. His mood was impossible to predict. Sometimes, if you walked past him in the corridor, he'd stop for a chat or give a good natured 'hello'. Other times, he would ignore you completely, so you'd just assume that someone was in trouble.

After winning the FA Cup in 1990, and the Cup Winners Cup in 1991, some pressure had been lifted from his shoulders but the Holy Grail was the league, which had eluded the club since 1967. My debut season in England was the last one before the

Premier League era. Leeds, managed by Howard Wilkinson, claimed the Division One trophy.

Despite the disappointment, there was a feeling around the club that the end of the long wait was imminent. And our crop was fuelling a lot of the optimism about the future. We had a big reputation.

A week after I left home, I was actually back in Northern Ireland for the Milk Cup, and in top form. That week, everything went right. We picked up the trophy, and I was awarded man of the match in the final and player of the tournament. That set us off and running and, as we carried that form into the new season, word spread fast.

Fans started to come and watch matches at the Cliff on Saturday mornings, and if the first team were at home that afternoon, the gaffer would be there until half-time. The injured senior players would come along as well. I remember the adrenaline rush when I spotted Bryan Robson standing on the sideline.

The old pros christened us the 'Dream Team' – I always remember Steve Bruce saying it – while the local newspapers called us 'Fergie's Fledglings'. The gaffer made sure we were well protected from the hype, but he laid the foundations to prepare us for what was coming down the line, like the day we were told to report to Old Trafford for a media training course. We went into a room where we took turns being asked questions by a man with a microphone. I remember being quite nervous because the rest of the boys were sitting there watching, giggling at any little mistake. It was all a bit strange.

Our mentors looked for signs that the attention was affecting us, but nobody was getting ahead of themselves. Yes, we had belief, and the fact that Giggsy was doing so well gave everyone in the youth ranks a boost. But we knew there was a long way to go, and with characters like Gaz and Butty around the place, complacency wasn't an option. They always raised the bar.

My own form dipped after Christmas. I don't know why. Right midfield was a confidence position. I always found the first couple of minutes in a game to be the most important. If you get on the ball early and roast the full-back, you're off to a flier. I started to find it difficult. Rather than bollock me, Eric was decent about it. He took me aside and told me not to stress, saying that it was common for a lad my age to go through a sticky patch.

There was so much quality in the ranks that I knew I would suffer for it. Sure enough, my difficulties opened the door for others. Becks, who was still developing physically, was taken out of centre midfield and placed on the right. Simon Davies joined Butty in the engine room, with Ben 'Squeaky' Thornley raiding the left flank.

The focal point of our campaign was the FA Youth Cup and, after booking a place in the semi-final against Spurs, Eric went with those four in midfield. Scholesy wasn't even considered ready for the bench at that stage. That was a good Spurs team, with Sol Campbell, Nick Barmby and Darren Caskey in their ranks, but they were no match for us.

A two-legged final with Crystal Palace was the reward. I was so out of sorts that I didn't even make the squad for the first leg in London which was nearly postponed due to a downpour in the hours before the game. Instead, I was in Manchester making up the numbers for the reserves, when the news came through that the boys had won 3-1.

Eric put me on the bench for the second leg at Old Trafford, which attracted a crowd of almost 15,000 people. Giggsy, who had been drafted in for the cup games to further strengthen Eric's hand, was already comfortable in that kind of arena. For the majority, the occasion was a new experience, both frightening and exciting at the same time. I was brought on as a sub in a 3-2 win on the night [6-3 on aggregate] and the buzz of being involved made up for the disappointment of the previous months. The reassuring words from Eric had removed any trace of worry anyway.

Giggsy lifted the trophy, and the 'Class of '92' danced around the pitch like idiots, drunk on the feeling of achievement. It was the start of something special.

(5)

Stepping Up

THERE was always a strict door policy at the first team dressing room in the Cliff. Young players went in there to clean but never to change.

The tradition was that you served your time before graduating to the big boys' area. I wasn't at the club long enough to make that leap.

Even when I became a part of the first team picture, I checked in at the reserves' room across the corridor because I wasn't established enough. The pegs on the main dressing room wall were highly sought after. Even when Giggsy broke through, it took him a few years to get one.

As much as the senior pros at the club were supportive of Fergie's Fledglings, the invisible barrier preventing a youngster from changing with the top men every morning was a reminder that a season or two in the first team didn't constitute making it. Still, when I reported back for my second year as a professional footballer in the summer of 1992, it became apparent that the Youth Cup-winning team were going to be spending more time around the elders. I was back in form – an end of season tour to Switzerland had got me back on track – and as a final-year apprentice, now was the time to impress Alex Ferguson. I got the chance when I arrived for training one morning and Eric simply said: "You're in with the first team today, Keith."

After admiring from afar, I was suddenly in the mix. Brian Kidd ran the session, and I was desperate to show I belonged. I started off afraid of giving the ball away, but I was a player who had to take risks and eventually I was able to relax in some illustrious company.

There was a real sense of purpose around the club. Foreign signings Peter Schmeichel and Andrei Kanchelskis were settling into their second full seasons, Paul Ince was growing into the midfield general role, while Paul Parker, Steve Bruce, Gary Pallister, and Denis Irwin were a rock solid and settled back four. With Giggsy getting better, Mark Hughes and Brian McClair providing goals, and a production line of talent, the vibes were good.

Gaz and Becks made first-team appearances in September. Gaz in a UEFA Cup tie at home to Torpedo Moscow, and Becks in a League Cup tie at Brighton. The promotions gave all the apprentices something to strive for. The Friday after the second leg of the UEFA Cup tie – which the lads had lost on penalties in Russia – Eric told me that I was training with the first team again, which was unusual considering they were travelling to Middlesbrough afterwards for the following day's fixture. I guess that was a strong hint. When the session finished, the kitman Norman Davies handed me a tracksuit; an unsubtle way of telling me I was in. I raced back to the digs to pack a bag, and hopped in a taxi to Old Trafford, pausing only to ring home but nobody answered.

I was the only young lad on the trip so I sat up the front and minded my own business, although I couldn't resist a look around to see what the others were doing. The gaffer was down the back in a card school with Ince, Bruce and Pallister. Paul Parker was forever chatting away on the mobile – he must have owned one of the first ones. Giggsy and a few of the others were listening to music. We reached the hotel and I was put in a room with Darren Ferguson, the gaffer's son. Darren took a bit of stick from the boys over that, and probably had to prove himself that little bit more, but he'd started that season well until injury checked his progress.

Being stuck with the new guy had its pitfalls for Darren. We came back from dinner to find crushed crisps in our bedsheet and a trail of crumbs all over the floor. Incey and Giggsy, of course.

Incey was the loudest and brashest of the group, with a flash car and his nickname 'The Guv'nor' carved into the back of his boots. Luckily, he was able to back it up on the pitch. Darren told me that Incey always answered the phone with a simple one word response: 'Speak'. When we rang the lads' room to see if they were the culprits, Incey answered with that very word. After that, all we could hear was the two boys cracking up.

Matchday was about learning the routine. Getting up early for light breakfast, then a long walk before the pre-match meal.

Up to the room to change. Down for a team meeting, and then into the bus and off to the game.

I sensed I was only along for the ride. 16 of us had travelled, but only three substitutes were allowed on the bench back then, so I missed the cut along with Neil Webb, an English international. Neil had played well in Moscow, and was pissed off about missing out. Not knowing what to do, I just ended up following him around. He went straight to the players' lounge and started sinking pints. I was underage, so I just sat there, feeling sorry for an unhappy bloke who I didn't know that well, and would soon be on his way out of the club.

My next taste of travelling was in December. I didn't make the subs, but I was sitting unchanged on the bench for a landmark moment – Eric Cantona's first goal for Manchester United. He was two weeks at the club, and his shock arrival from Leeds had given everyone a lift. Eric oozed charisma. When he walked into a room, heads turned. And when he crossed the white line, regardless of whether it was in training or a match, he was the centre of attention. By no means a shouter. Quiet actually. But with his swagger, he exuded authority, and led by example. Eric was a serious trainer. Brian Kidd always encouraged people to stay back after training to do some extra ball work, and Eric was always prominent. Incey as well. It was a chance to learn.

The senior lads were always mindful of us, even when it came to the financial side of things. If there were newcomers in a squad who didn't get stripped, Steve Bruce or Bryan Robson would go to the gaffer asking him to pool any bonus for the game so the young lad could get some of it.

We didn't immediately warm to everyone. Schmeichel was hard work when we started getting on the bench. The subs had to warm the goalkeeper up, and if you crossed a ball in that went astray, he'd bollock you. Proper pelters at times, which was embarrassing because there were people in the crowd that could hear it. You could hardly turn around and tell him to fuck off. Every time I was named sub, I'd be dreading it, and it was the same for the others. Before every cross, I'd pray that it landed in his hands. He was precious too, any minor knock was a drama. You'd hear grumbles. 'What he's done now? Broke his toenail?' But he was the best keeper in the land, and those annoyances were part of the package.

After spending a bit more time around the set-up, I was gasping for an opportunity. The first game of 1993 was my chance, a Tuesday night FA Cup tie with Bury at Old Trafford. I'd trained with the youth team on the Monday, so assumed I was just being invited along to the pre-match to make up the numbers. Giggsy had been struggling with a knock, but there was no hint that it was anything serious.

The gaffer walked past during the meal and Paul Parker asked if Giggsy was fit. "No," he replied, "but he can play." His finger was pointing in my direction.

Some moments live with you forever. That was such a big thing, so it was a strange way to find out. I didn't have time to tell anyone. Before I knew it, I was in the dressing room, with my hands trembling, tying up my bootlaces while senior players queued up with words of encouragement. Steve Bruce just told me to play my natural game. Brian McClair only ever really said one thing to me, both then and in the future. "Run fast, score goals." Choccy was always an odd one. The manager was relaxed, like he generally always was pre-match.

Certainly, there was no reason to be on edge for the visit of Bury, a team from the fourth tier of English football. He was fielding an experienced side with one obvious exception. Look at the names, listed 1-11: Schmeichel, Parker, Irwin, Bruce, Sharpe, Pallister, Cantona, Phelan, McClair, Hughes, Gillespie. I was in good hands. "Just do what you've been doing," he said.

I walked out, had a brief, 'Wow, what am I doing here' moment and got down to work. After a few nice early touches to relax, I collected a pass from Mark Hughes, and centred it for Mike Phelan to head the opener. The perfect start. Easy game, this.

We coasted through the rest of the game. Cantona was majestic, although his best piece of advice was from left field. I was running out of the tunnel at the start of the second half when he called me and gestured to take off the black armband we had worn for a bereavement; it was a bit uncomfortable, and I seemed looser without it. Bury weren't applying much pressure anyway, and I was set for a winning debut whatever happened. But the best was yet to come. Eleven minutes from the end, Eric played me into space and I veered inside and released a tame shot that slipped through the fingers of their keeper, Gary Kelly, and crept over the line.

My heart was still racing at the final whistle. I was just 17, barely 18 months out of school, and a Manchester United fan that had just scored on his debut at Old Trafford. Players I had grown up watching on television were queueing up to offer congratulations. I could have floated back to the digs, but a taxi would have to do.

I rang home to see if they knew and was met with a chorus of screams. My sister had heard on the news that I was in the team, so they were tuned into Radio 5. They were jubilant.

Robbie and the lads were delighted for me as well, and said I'd be all over the back pages in the morning. I was sceptical, but was out of bed quicker than usual to find out that the house-mates were right. My name was plastered everywhere, accompanied by some nice words from the gaffer, although he pointed out that I could have crossed the ball better and would be back in the youth team at the weekend. Bump.

It was a giddy few days though, a small taste of the trappings of fame. It was the little things. I was wearing Puma boots at the time and, courtesy of their rep Martin Buchan, an ex-United player, a big package arrived at the Cliff with free tracksuits and boots. That was a novelty and so was the attention of auto-graph hunters. The hours I'd wiled away at school practising my signature finally came in useful.

Later that month, I was given another chance in the next round of the FA Cup when I was summoned from the bench with half an hour left at home to Brighton. It was scoreless when I came on, and the gaffer said I did more in that 30 min-utes than in the entire 90 against Bury. Giggsy nicked a winner.

After that, I faded into the background. The business end of the season was approaching and the club was on course to finally be crowned league champions. Cantona was the miss-ing link, the man with the flair to complement a sturdy spine. When nearest pursuers Aston Villa slipped up against Oldham, the title race was over.

The youth team had their own celebration on the night when the trophy was lifted at Old Trafford, but our own year ended in disappointment. Against the odds, Leeds toppled us over two legs in the FA Youth Cup final. We had lost a bit of momentum with the earlier developers spending so much time with the first team and reserves.

Our two-year cycle had ended and I was an apprentice no more. In fact, the change of status was confirmed in the weeks after Bury. The club took the unprecedented step of handing out eight professional contracts in January, shortly before my 18th birthday. Gaz, Becks, Scholesy, Nicky, John O'Kane, Ben Thornley and Chris Casper were the other chosen ones.

We were invited down to Old Trafford to sign a four-year deal worth an initial £230 a week with a £20,000 signing-on fee split into four instalments. It felt like a lotto win.

They said we were the future.

My parents were delighted. In their eyes, it was a reward for all the hard work. I had a secure job, and a wonderful opportunity. The daydreams were closer to reality.

6

Joining The Party

ALL the time, strangers ask me if I am jealous of the boys I came through with at Manchester United who lasted the course and won everything the club game has to offer.

Gaz, Nicky, Becks, Giggsy and Scholesy were key components of the 1999 treble-winning side. Becks became a global superstar and moved on to crack Spain. Gaz eventually became club captain and, along with Scholesy, won the lot and stayed at the club for the rest of his career. Giggsy the same, and he's still bloody going.

Trust me, I'm not bitter or resentful of their success. I believe I was one of the lucky ones.

Perspective can always be found in the pictures of the teams I grew up with at the Cliff. Every so often, a newspaper will run shots of the Class of '92 and circle the heads of those who went on to be famous. But what about the others? MUTV ran a documentary to mark the 20-year anniversary of our Youth Cup win, and it made me appreciate my fortune.

Thousands of teenagers have come through the gates of Manchester United with dreams of glory. The vast majority leave without securing professional terms. When I put pen to paper on my contract, I was already ahead of the pack. When I was selected and scored for the senior team, I joined an elite group.

All was good in my world after I signed that four-year deal. For some of my pals, it was a different story. While I was moving up the football world, there was a steady stream of youths going in the opposite direction.

I think back to my first set of dressing room colleagues.

Colin Telford was always struggling with a back problem and was released within a year. Colin McKee made one first-team appearance, had moderate success in Scotland and hung up his boots in 2001. George Switzer, the left-back in the '92 cup-winning team, was in non-league football two years later. Football kicks you in the nuts sometimes. A four-year contract was no guarantee of luck. For many, 'Squeaky' Ben Thornley was the pick of the crop, a silky left winger with the world at his feet. His knee was destroyed by a tackle in a reserve match in the first year of his deal, and he was never the same.

Chris Casper found opportunities limited at Manchester United, secured a decent move to Reading and was retired by the age of 24 after sustaining a complicated double leg fracture. John O'Kane was a bit too casual and finished in senior football at 28.

Others, like Colin Murdock and David Johnson, stayed in the game for a long time, albeit below the top tier.

The saddest story of all is that of Adrian Doherty, my original housemate from Strabane, who was tipped for the top but never recovered from a cruciate knee problem. He drifted out of the game and tragically died in an accident in Holland in 2000.

Robbie Savage bucked the trend by fighting back from rejection and establishing himself in the Premier League. He rebranded himself as a midfielder at Crewe, attracted the interest of Leicester and went from there. But then, Robbie was always a bit of a one-off.

Football is a selfish game, though. It has to be about number one. After I became a fully-fledged pro, my priority was to avoid falling through the trap door. The boss sent me on loan in the 1993/94 season, and it was a window to a different existence.

Wigan were towards the bottom of the league ladder, near the foot of the old Division Three. The club reckoned that a couple of months there would strengthen me up.

It was an eye-opening experience. Back then, Wigan played out of Springfield Park, an old school terraced ground, in front of a couple of thousand spectators. The surface was good though, which couldn't be said for all of the grounds I'd visited.

My first game was at Doncaster's Belle Vue. One of our centre halves was poleaxed and ruptured his cruciate in the first 10 minutes. The tackles were flying in, and I was beginning to wonder if this was a death wish. But it went alright after that. They stuck me up front to utilise my pace, and I scored four goals in eight games, including a couple in a mad win over Chester that was scoreless after 30 minutes and finished 6-3.

I trained with them every day. One of the other lads picked me up from Manchester every morning. It was a no-frills exercise. We travelled on the day of away games rather than going down the night before, so you might be sitting on a bus for five hours, breaking the journey to stop for beans on toast.

Kenny Swain, the manager, looked after me and I realised the benefits of the exercise. Still, I was relieved when the gaffer turned down a request from Wigan to keep me for a third month.

The first team were well on their way to a second successive title. Roy Keane was a significant addition to the dressing room, bringing a bite to both games and training sessions. The Fledglings were mostly confined to the reserves in 1993-94, and provided the core of the team that won the Pontins League.

That summer, the club sent myself, Becks, Gaz, and his younger brother Phil – who the youth coaches were very excited about – off to the US to do some coaching at a kids camp in Santa Barbara around the World Cup. After a few days work, the rest of the trip was a holiday in scorching heat. We joined 93,000 others in the Rose Bowl for the fateful encounter between USA and Colombia. The latter's Andres Escobar, who scored an own goal, was shot dead upon his return home. Again, perspective was close at hand.

You never know what's coming next in life. I knew that Mum and Dad had been having issues in their marriage; I spoke to my sisters on the phone all the time, and they informed me there were problems. Being away from home meant that I missed out on it. Still, it was a shock when they told me they were splitting up. It's a normal thing, it happens – as I would find out later down the line – but it takes a while to get used to it. And it did upset me, although it was much harder for Angela and Heather who saw it develop before their eyes.

There was no big drama; they just grew apart. Mum had become a born-again Christian. Her faith was very important to her; she stopped drinking alcohol and devoted time to the church. Dad was a different type of personality. He liked a drink and a bet. So, they divorced. Mum met a lovely man named Ivor, who I grew very fond of, and Dad eventually settled down with his new partner, Marlene, who I've also warmed to. The important thing was that I remained close to both of them. I suppose it was another stage of growing up.

Things were moving fast in Manchester so I didn't have too much time to dwell on it. When I returned from the US, I moved house. The club wanted the new apprentices to lodge beside the Cliff, so I left Brenda's and relocated to a different digs in Irlams o' th' Height – we called it The Heights – which was around 10 minutes drive away. Colin Murdock moved in as well, which was handy because he owned a car.

Viv, my new landlady, was great. It was a more adult environment. We'd sit and have dinner with her and her partner and just chat away in the evenings. She realised we were young men now, and gave us an extra bit of independence. Within reason, we could do what we wanted. For example, there was no problem if we wanted to bring girls back. That was never an option in Brenda's, although it wasn't like I was overcome with offers. You needed a bigger first-team profile for that.

I had started to drink a wee bit, if not excessively. My first proper taste of alcohol was on Manchester United duty as a 15-year-old. I'd been flown in for a game with Colin, and Nicky Butt invited us out to Gorton after. I drank nine cans of Woodpecker cider and threw up all over the back of a cab. That experience scarred me for a while. I drank Bacardi and other stupid stuff until I started going out a bit more regularly, and developed a taste for beer.

The senior players had a good social life. Most Wednesdays and Saturdays, they'd be out and we had a good idea where to find them. Our ambition was always to track Lee Sharpe down. Good things happened if you hung around Sharpey for long enough. He loved a night out – too much as far as the gaffer was concerned – and women adored him. A huge three-storey club called Discotheque Royale was his playground.

We had a little Manchester United ID card that was enough to get us in for free, so I'd go in with the likes of Becks, Colin and John O'Kane. There was a bar out the back of Royales where you'd find a gang of the lads, with Sharpey at the centre of the banter. Giggsy would often be about too.

Women would flock around them, and if you hung about long enough you might get Sharpey's cast-offs. They wouldn't have any idea who I was, but probably thought, 'well, if he's with Sharpey, he must play as well.'

Our chances, on all fronts, improved at the beginning of the '94/95 campaign. We drew Port Vale in the League Cup in September, and the gaffer decided to throw us in en masse for the first leg. Gaz, Nicky, Becks, Scholesy, Simon Davies and myself all started the game, and John O'Kane came off the bench. After falling behind early, Scholesy scored twice to take a lead back to Manchester for the second leg a fortnight later which ended in a comfortable victory.

I was taken off with half an hour left, and was disappointed about that until the gaffer stopped me on the sideline and said that I'd be making my Premier League debut at Sheffield Wednesday that weekend.

He kept his word, and gave me the nod for Hillsborough. We lost 1-0, but I was happy with my contribution. Scholesy replaced me with 15 minutes to go. Incey approached me in the dressing room to ask if I'd taken a knock. "No", I said. "Why the fuck did you come off then?" he replied, shaking his head.

Two quickfire games with Newcastle later that month were the next step. First was a 2-0 League Cup loss on the Wednesday. The atmosphere was incredible; we all talked about it on the way home.

On Saturday, they came to our place in the league. Dad was over for the game with a supporters' club from Newtownards. My best pal, Jim, had also decided to come across. Neither had any idea I'd be involved. They were in luck.

We were a goal up when I was sent on for Giggsy midway through the second half. Shortly after, I cut inside from the left on a weaving run, threw a few shapes and smashed the ball home. Old Trafford erupted. I don't remember what the gaffer said after; I think the applause was still ringing in my ears.

That night, in Royales, I got the rock-star treatment. I didn't need an introduction from Sharpey. I took home a girl whose father I happened to know. He was a wheeler dealer guy from around the club. The phone rang the next morning, and I ran down to get it. The father, was on the other end. 'Uh oh', I thought.

"Is Chantelle there?"

"Yeah, yeah, she's here..."

"That's ok, just wanted to make sure she was alright."

And that was that. I guess a different set of rules applied once you made the breakthrough. Maybe I was son-in-law material.

From that night onwards, I was permanently in contention.

I was part of all the squads, with the exception of the Champions League games, where the manager was snookered by UEFA rules that limited him to five non-English players. Two of those had to be assimilated and the club initially thought I met that criteria until it transpired that you needed to be in the country permanently for five years. It cost me a couple of starts, and Becks capitalised. I was in illustrious company, and found myself sitting next to Schmeichel in the stands for the 4-0 thrashing to Barcelona at the Nou Camp. I'm often asked if I saw Alex Ferguson's hairdryer in full flight. He had a major blow-up with Incey in the dressing room afterwards, but I was already outside, itching to get home. By all accounts, it was an epic argument, although you'd expect some kind of row after a humiliation like that. More significantly, it was a night that made the boss realise what was required to succeed in Europe. In the short term, buying English was his priority.

Another positive of my progression was a full participation in Christmas party festivities. Unfortunately, it didn't go so well. I was in a group with Roy Keane that enjoyed a few drinks before rocking up to the Hacienda, a legendary Manchester hotspot. They thought we'd drunk too much and wouldn't let us in. It was all a bit chaotic. Mark Hughes had just been ejected from the premises for saying something to Incey that a bouncer had taken offence to, even though Incey was fine with it.

So, a gang of us were having words with the door staff when, out of nowhere, a fella hopped out of a car, barged into the middle of our group, and started throwing punches. Perhaps he recognised us, but it all happened so quickly that there was no time for introductions. People started weighing in from all sides and I received a ferocious dig that was my cue to leave. I escaped the riot to jump into a taxi.

Viv took one look at me when I arrived in the door and said I'd better go to hospital. Blood was leaking from a wound at the back of my head, and I required a couple of stitches which I tried to disguise at the Cliff. The gaffer knew we had a night out planned and usually heard if there was trouble. Miraculously, the details of our scrap never reached him.

I'd already fallen foul of him earlier in the season. When I was left out of the squad for a home game, I arranged a Friday night out with a few of the lads from Northern Ireland. We met at the Castlefield Hotel and I was carrying a couple of bottles of Budweiser through the lobby when I caught sight of the gaffer. He looked at me and said nothing. I hurried away.

On Monday morning, I was pulled into his office.

"A week's wages for telling the truth, two for lying," he said.

"They weren't my drinks."

"Ok, two weeks."

That incident was a minor blip, though, and long forgotten as we entered the festive period well in the title hunt, with Kenny Dalglish's Blackburn emerging as a strong rival. After sitting out a few matches, I came on at The Dell in a 2-2 draw with Southampton, and was reinstated to the starting line-up for the first game of 1995, the visit of Coventry to Old Trafford.

Scholesy and Cantona scored in a routine win, and I did reasonably well. The gaffer kept me on for the full 90, which was a good sign. If I had known what was coming, I might have taken a few pictures. There was nothing to suggest it was a pivotal moment in my career, but fate had other ideas. Why? Turns out, I had just played my last game for Manchester United.

7

Glory Nights

WHEN I was a young boy, the heart of Northern Irish football was the Spion Kop at Windsor Park. On international nights, the large old terrace behind the goal was a heaving mass of bodies, a wall of noise that was the backdrop to some unbeliev-able games. I used to stand there with my dad, in awe of the atmosphere.

It was a special time, with Billy Bingham leading a talented group of players to two World Cups. Big nations dreaded com-ing to Belfast. One evening stands out for me. September 12, 1984 – a qualifying match with Romania. Whiteside was in full flow. He grabbed the crucial goal, slipping the ball past their keeper right in front of the Kop. He ran towards us with his arms in the air. The noise was incredible. I imagined tasting that feeling.

Ten years later, my chance came around as the Bingham era ended and Bryan Hamilton took over. I can't say it was a surprise when I was given the nod to start a European Championship tie with Portugal because Alex Ferguson had actually told me two weeks earlier that I'd be making my debut in the game. He called Bryan to find out if I would play before giving me the all clear to go.

Knowing that far in advance probably gave me a little too much time to think about it. This was a big deal, and the build up was nerve-wracking. Portugal were a serious international team with stars like Luis Figo, Rui Costa and Paulo Sousa in their ranks. I was a raw youngster coming in from the periphery at Manchester United with a big reputation to live up to.

Then, as now, Northern Ireland had a small pool of players to choose from, lacking the depth to compose a squad entirely of Premier League performers. Managers had to look to the second division or maybe even further down the ladder. Although I had only made a limited number of first-team appearances, all the hype was about me because I was a Manchester United player. That old George Best comparison was thrown around again. Pressure. I fretted about what the other lads expected, thinking they might view me as some kind of big shot with ideas above my station. I had nothing to worry about. The senior figures immediately took me under their wing.

From my days in the under-age set-up, I had an idea what Northern Ireland teams were about. The dressing room was a communal environment, albeit with terms and conditions attached. You had to be able to cope with the banter and the slagging. And you had to be able to drink. That was the culture. Win or lose, we were on the booze. At that point in time, it was a mantra that applied to most teams in our part of the world. We just lived it better than most.

There were plenty of experienced figures knocking around at the time, really big characters. Guys like Alan McDonald, Jimmy Quinn, Gerry Taggart, Kevin Wilson, Nigel Worthington, Iain Dowie, Jim Magilton, even Steve Lomas who was only a year older than me but always had a bit of presence about him. It was a solid bunch and, while Bryan had big shoes to fill, he almost brought us to a major tournament in his first campaign.

My debut started with a near miss, a sign of things to come. We lost narrowly to the Portuguese. I did ok, nothing too spectacular. With so many friends and family there, it was a relief to get through it without any big mishaps. The reviews were generally positive.

A month later, we travelled to Vienna to take on a decent Austria side. That was my real initiation.

The key to those games was silencing the home crowd and, within three minutes, I turned down the volume at the Ernst Happel Stadium. Iain Dowie flicked a throw-in over his head at the edge of the box, right into my direction. I caught it on the volley, sweet as you like, and it flew into the top corner. One of my best ever goals. They equalised shortly after, but one of the lads I already knew in the camp, Phil Gray, put us back ahead before half-time and we held on for the win.

It was the prelude to an incredible night. All I remember is the lads in a bar in Vienna, up dancing on the tables and revelling in the moment. There's no better feeling in football than heading out after a hard-fought victory. Everyone was a part of it.

From that high we slumped to a shattering low a month later when the Republic of Ireland came to Belfast. Expectations were high in the wake of the Austria win, and this game meant everything to our fans.

The Republic were a good side who had just been to the World Cup. We came in full of confidence and got wiped off the park by our neighbours. 4-0. A humiliation. I missed my flight to Manchester the next morning. Not because I was out on the beer. I'd gone home to Bangor and slept in. I didn't want to get out of bed. One of the lads back in Manchester wondered if I'd thrown myself in a river.

We had until March, and the return in Dublin, to stew over that one. Bryan decided to have all the preparations in Dublin so we gathered there on the Saturday night ahead of a Wednesday encounter. By this time I was a more experienced player, with a higher profile and stronger stomach. After a few beverages in the hotel bar, we headed to the nightclub next door where a couple of lads decided to test my drinking resolution. Steve Morrow, then of Arsenal, was the ringleader. We worked away along the optics of the bar, going through all the spirits until we were necking Green Chartreuse, a 55 per cent strength recipe for disaster. I remained upright; Steve required assistance from the assistant manager, Gerry Armstrong, to get up the stairs. He was telling Gerry how they'd stitched me up. "Really", said Gerry, "then why is Keith still standing at the bar then?"

Those exertions didn't hinder the outcome. We were under the cosh for long periods at Lansdowne Road, and trailed to a Niall Quinn goal. But we had a serious resilience on our travels, and I managed to stick in a cross that Dowie converted to take away a draw.

Next up was a jaunt to Latvia, where the same toughness was evident. We were short of a few bodies and Barry Hunter and

Kevin Horlock, from Wrexham and Swindon respectively, were thrown in for their debuts. Dowie got the only goal from the spot, and we celebrated in style. Kevin, who was excellent in the game, overdid it in the post-match party. He turned up for the flight the following morning still pissed and with a big yellow face. When we landed in London, they needed a wheelchair to escort him off the plane. The phrase, 'Wheelchair for Horlock' followed him around after that.

People are always shocked to hear of professional athletes behaving in such a way, but, in those days, it was common-place. We felt fit enough to run off the excesses, and it really did help team bonding. If you're in a group where there is a tense atmosphere, the prospect of a few days away together is a nightmare. But we always had better results on our travels, and that was a testament to the spirit in the camp. We enjoyed each other's company.

The summer tours were the prime example. My first was to Canada, in the summer of 1995. That was a trip where discipline went out of the window. I was looking forward to my first, proper tour as a senior professional. The lads had been to the United States the previous summer and told me all the stories. Football-wise, we were heading to Edmonton for a three-team tournament with Canada and Chile. But it's fair to say that we weren't too focused on the games when we met at Heathrow.

Bryan was fighting a losing battle from the start. Myself, Phil Gray and George O'Boyle had gone for a few beers in the terminal and nearly missed the flight. On the plane, the drink was openly flowing. When we got to the other end, Bryan sent us out training straight away. He knew the majority were half-pissed and ran the hell out of us. It really kicked off a couple of nights later after we got thrashed by Canada. We were awful. The extreme humidity offered some sort of excuse but really, we shouldn't have been losing badly to a team like that. We reacted the only way we knew by embarking on a spectacular bender. I was on the local beer, Labatt Ice, and it went straight to my head. I was hopelessly drunk when we got back to the hotel, walking around the lobby vainly looking for a bathroom when I spotted Phil Gray standing at the reception desk talking to someone. For reasons unknown, I started pissing on Phil's leg.

There was a commotion over it, but I was ignorant to it. My focus was on extending the night so I went upstairs to persuade my room-mate, Gerry McMahon, to find a second wind and head out into town for another look. It was a huge hotel, with over 20 floors, and we were near the top. As we were going down in the lift, it stopped at the 19th floor and Bryan walked in. Someone had called him after my behaviour in the foyer.

"Where are you going?" he asked.

"I'm going out."

"No, you're not."

I said nothing. When the doors opened at the ground floor, I made a break for it and sprinted across the lobby. Bryan shouted at Gerry Armstrong, telling him to follow me. I burst out onto the street with a Northern Ireland legend in pursuit, a member of the 1982 World Cup side that I had watched as an excitable seven-year-old back in Islandmagee.

I knew he didn't have the pace to catch me. I kept running. And running. The problem was that I barely had a Plan A, let alone a Plan B. Three quarters of a mile later, I was on my own in a nondescript street with absolutely no idea where I was. I stopped to a walk, and allowed Gerry to catch up. He convinced me to go back to the hotel and sleep it off.

Bryan called a big meeting with the group the next morning which concluded with him turning to me and announcing that I wouldn't be having any more alcohol for the rest of the trip. Some chance. That night we were invited to an Irish bar and, on the coach there, the boys were putting beer in teacups for me. After we showed our faces there and made our way back towards the hotel, Bryan said that nobody was allowed out that night. Again, wishful thinking. It's not that we didn't respect him. But after a long season, we just wanted to kick back. There was nothing at stake on this trip.

As soon as the coach pulled up, everyone hopped out and marched to a small bar across the road. The Chile game two days later was the last thing on our minds. Bryan left it for a while and then arrived in, called over Alan McDonald, as the skipper, and said it was time to get the lads back. Big Mac ignored him, went to the bar, and ordered a round of drinks.

The manager went for a different approach. He came over to my table and ordered me to set an example by going home first. I accused him of picking on me because I was the youngest, and left for a bar down the street with Phil and George. The night finished up in a club where we walked in to find a gang of the others dancing on stage. When we belatedly got back to the hotel, the fire alarm was set off. The next morning, we found ourselves in the same meeting room for another dressing down from Bryan. Unsurprisingly, we lost to Chile. I was in the doghouse and only brought on for the last eight minutes.

Naturally I was read the riot act. It was a kick up the backside and resulted in me knuckling down for a really good pre-season, and the start to the club campaign which earned me the highest praise. So, I was flabbergasted when I came to Belfast in September for the qualifier with Latvia and found myself on the bench.

I couldn't help but wonder if it was punishment for Canada, but kept my silence. My room-mate, Gerry, was chosen instead. He was a good player, but only a reserve with Spurs at the time whereas I was a Premier League regular. I came on in the second half when we were 2-1 down, and couldn't turn it around. A stupid defeat and it cost us.

We went to Portugal next, where I was back in favour, and goalie Alan Fettis produced the performance of his career. Michael Hughes managed to score a deflected free-kick which was good enough for a point, to preserve our unbeaten away record. We were always better as the underdog.

Wins in Liechtenstein and at home to Austria – the latter, a thrilling 5-3 success – ultimately counted for nothing. We finished joint second with the Republic, but with an inferior goal difference. They went on to lose a play-off to Holland. All we could think about was the Latvia game, and ponder what could have been.

I loved those early years with Northern Ireland. I was always amazed by the attitude of people in England to my homeland. Other lads in club dressing rooms believed that I came from a war zone, like Afghanistan or somewhere like that. It was strange to encounter people with those perceptions.

I'd be lying if I said that political discussion was a hot topic in our dressing room. Once you moved away, it was easy to become detached from it. I knew terrible things had gone on, and was heartened by historic moves towards peace in the mid-nineties. But in a dressing room with people from both sides of the community, we didn't get bogged down in the serious detail. What we shared in common was the experience of how our country was stereotyped in England. It made us tighter.

Our group was a working example of Protestant and Catholic lads mixing together happily.

Religion was part of the banter. The louder Protestant lads, like Alan McDonald, Phil Gray and Tommy Wright, would be taking on the vocal Catholics, fellas like Gerry Taggart, Jim Magilton, Steve Morrow and Michael Hughes.

We used to stay in the Chimney Corner Hotel, 10 minutes outside the city, and on our way to training we'd go through some fierce Unionist and Nationalist strongholds. Our bus would pass the Shankill Road, a predominantly Protestant area decorated with Union Jack flags and loyalist murals, and the Catholics would pipe up about what a shithole it was. We'd then move along and pass the Divis Flats at the bottom of the Falls Road, a Catholic area, which had the Republic of Ireland flags and republican murals, and the Protestants would hit back with their own insults.

It was all good natured. There were no cliques based on religion. Some of the boys came from areas that were heavily involved in the conflict. Phil Gray's family hailed from the Shankill, while Jim Magilton came from the Andersonstown area, the opposite side of the tracks. And they were able to mix just fine, no problem at all. Football was the glue.

There were few boundaries in our camp. On away trips, our fans could freely roam around the team hotel gathering autographs or having a chat. With such a small travelling support, it made no sense to isolate ourselves. It was the same with the press. To be honest, after matches, we'd come back to the hotel and have a few drinks with them to start off the night. There was only a small number of them and we knew they weren't going to screw us over. That sort of interaction would sound crazy to an English player, but they wouldn't relate to our tight-knit environment.

A relaxed approach suited our circumstances. Given our size relative to other nations, the odds were stacked against us, and the players, media and fans were all in it together. I loved pulling on the shirt because of that togetherness and was determined to be there for my country, through good times and bad.

My second campaign was a struggle. We paid for our missed opportunity in the Euro qualifiers, and landed a group with Germany, Portugal, and an emerging Ukrainian side. As low seeds, it was always the risk. Our home form killed us. Ukraine won in Belfast and another new nation, Armenia, took away a point. We never got going after that and finished fifth, miles off the pace.

The IFA decided not to renew Bryan's contract, believing that we had underachieved. He felt like he'd been stabbed in the back. I'd had a few disagreements with Bryan, but he was a good person, and was a source of support for me long after he left the job.

History has judged his tenure kindly. Unfortunately, after his departure, a troubled period for Northern Irish football was looming over the horizon.

8

£7m Man

WHEN I travelled to Sheffield for an FA Cup tie on January 9, 1995, I was expecting it to be just another game in my football education. Instead, it was a night that would change my life forever.

There was a bug going around the camp and, after doing alright against Coventry, I was disappointed when the team was named at the hotel and I wasn't even on the bench. But I'd been that soldier before so I got on with the normal routine, went to the ground, and was standing in my suit in the away dressing room while the lads were getting changed when the gaffer pulled me aside and said he wanted to have a word.

We went into the toilets at Bramall Lane, and he cut to the chase.

"I've put this bid in for an English striker with Newcastle, and the only way the deal will go through is if you go there. Do you want to think about it?"

I just about managed to mutter a yes.

"There's no pressure. Just have a think and we'll talk about it after the game."

I knew straight away that Andy Cole was the player involved. We had an idea the gaffer was looking for a striker and it was always likely to be an Englishman because of the UEFA criteria on foreign players. I just didn't expect that I would somehow be involved. I walked out of the toilet and said nothing to the lads as they went out to take on Sheffield United. My head was spinning.

I had no agent at the time, nobody on speed dial who handled this sort of thing. So, I was locked in my own world. I sat next to Ben Thornley during the game and hardly paid attention to events on the field. With all sorts of thoughts racing around my mind, I started picking Squeaky's brain without telling him what was happening.

Ben had actually been sitting next to me on the bench when Newcastle came to Old Trafford, and we had remarked on the noise from their fans. I casually brought up the subject again. "So what do you think about Newcastle?" I said. "Would that be a good club to play for?" He was very positive, wondering aloud what it must be like to experience that kind of atmosphere every week. I agreed with his sentiments and, before the game was over, told him that it wasn't a hypothetical discussion for me. This was the real thing. And, in a short space of time, I had already come around to the conclusion that I was going for it. That was my gut instinct.

Although I had three years left on my contract, the fact that

Newcastle United wanted me now was decisive. Kevin Keegan wouldn't be looking for me unless he was going to put me in his team, and regular Premier League football in a passionate place carried a serious appeal. My life's mission had been to establish myself at Manchester United, but now my head was turned by a new Plan A.

I went down to the dressing room where the word was out. Steve Bruce, a Geordie, came straight over and said it would be a fantastic move. Brian McClair said the same thing. They were already preaching to the converted.

From there, it all happened very quickly. A private car arrived to take the gaffer and I to a hotel in Sheffield where a contingent from Newcastle were waiting.

This was new territory. I'd never entered these kind of negotiations before, and the gaffer must have sensed what I was thinking. "Look," he said, "if you're happy enough, I'll sort out the deal here and make sure it's a good one for you."

He told me to ring my mum who thought it was bad news when the phone rang close to midnight. The gaffer asked to speak to her and explained the situation, promising that he would do his best for me. She trusted him, and gave her consent. My manager was now my agent.

We then headed for a private meeting room where Keegan, the Newcastle chief executive Freddie Fletcher, and board member Freddy Shepherd were sitting around a table.

This was a serious deal for both parties. Cole was the form player in the Premier League, and it was obviously important for the gaffer that the negotiations went well.

But he was looking out for me too. I copped on to that pretty early in discussions. We were talking money and I was sitting

there, as a £250 a week player, unsure how much I could reasonably look for.

The gaffer was two steps ahead. "Keith's on £600 a week
at the moment so he'll be looking for an increase on that," he
announced. I put on my best poker face and rolled with it, wondering if this was normal. In those days, I was an innocent lad
about the ways of football.

But while I was trying to look cool about my fictional wage,
the Newcastle lads didn't seem too unhappy. They were happy
to double it and put me on a similar contract to Lee Clark,
a local lad who was making a big impression. As they talked
figures, the gaffer took out a pen and paper and started doing
the sums and working on the multiples, scribbling away while I
made small talk. It was a bit surreal.

Keegan was selling the club to me, although he was hardly
going to talk about his other transfer targets with a rival manager sitting there. He spoke about wanting to build a team to
challenge, and how he felt I could make a serious contribution.
After an hour or so of easy chat, I shook hands on a deal worth
£1,200 a week, with a £175,000 signing-on fee to be paid in
instalments across my four-year contract.

My temporary agent had served me well. He asked if I was
happy on the trip back to Manchester and, beyond saying yes
to that, there was little to say. There was no dramatic goodbye,
but I couldn't say a bad word about how he handled it. He
looked after me. I was in a lift at York races many years later
when the doors opened and Sir Alex and his wife walked in,
and my natural instinct was to sharpen up because he was the
boss, even though we hadn't worked together in years. That was
his influence, his presence. Maybe a different character would

have spent that last car journey through the night searching for answers about why they were being let go but I understood his reasons for doing the deal. My mind was already focused on the future.

I had an idea that a hectic few days lay ahead, yet it was only the following afternoon, when the news broke, that the scale of the transfer really hit home. It was a British transfer record deal, valued at £7 million, with Newcastle receiving £6 million and my £1 million valuation making up the rest. Keegan had refused to do business until my presence in the switch was guaranteed.

The rest of that week was a whirlwind. I went to the Cliff, grabbed my football boots, said my goodbyes and then a car arrived to bring me to Newcastle. Just like that. After spending so long at the club, it ended abruptly. That's how it goes in football. You may live and work beside people every day and then, out of the blue, you are shaking hands and wishing them well on their next journey.

Up in Newcastle, Keegan was firefighting, so I posed with his assistant, Terry McDermott for the publicity photos. I was whisked away to stay in Freddie Fletcher's house to throw any press off the scent. Some Newcastle fans were so furious at Cole's departure that they gathered at the ground to protest. Keegan went out to the steps of the Jackie Milburn Stand to address them, and plead for patience.

I admired his approach. Few managers would have done the same.

On the Thursday, I reported at Newcastle's Maiden Castle training ground in Durham to be introduced to my new team-mates and stretch the legs. I wouldn't be involved in that weekend's game as, by freakish coincidence, Manchester United were visiting St James' Park. Part of the deal was that neither myself or Andy would be involved. So, after my driver took me down to Viv's to pick up the rest of my possessions, I was given permission to fly to Belfast and appear on the main late-night talk show in Northern Ireland which was presented by a guy called Gerry Kelly.

Four days after heading to Sheffield as a low-profile Manchester United player, I was sitting in a green room with Michael Flatley from Riverdance and the actress, Dame Thora Hird. I have little recollection of what I said. My mother was invited on stage and asked if she was a calming influence in my life. She said my feet were firmly on the ground already. That balance was about to receive a stern test.

The following morning, I checked into the Gosforth Park Hotel, my home for the next five months. Shay Trainor, a Northern Irish guy who I'd befriended in Manchester, came up with a few of his pals and we decided to head out and see what a Saturday night in Newcastle had to offer.

We didn't know where the hot spots were, so headed in blind, down to the Quayside where we dropped in and out of a few bars. Suddenly, I was the centre of attention, on a different level to anything I had tasted in Manchester with people queueing up for photos or looking for me to sign this and that. Eventually, we wound up in Tuxedo Royale, a nightclub on a boat, with an attractive entourage. Some of the girls came back to the hotel's late bar. I didn't kick a ball, but I had no problem scoring on my first weekend in Newcastle.

I woke to an unexpected headache on the Sunday morning.

The back page of the Sunday Mirror claimed that Ferguson had got rid of me because he couldn't control my behaviour off the pitch. There was nothing to back it up. I turned up at the ground for the game, fearing some kind of backlash, and Keegan was sitting there, laughing, waving the paper at me. "What's all this then?" he said, with a smile. He could see right through it.

[Shay knew solicitors in Manchester who got on the case, and Ferguson offered to come forward as a witness. A year later, I received my first libel settlement, a sum of £17,500.]

Sitting on the bench that afternoon was a strange experience. I was rooting against Manchester United for the first time in my life. I'd been invited into the away dressing room before the game to have a chat with the lads, but when Paul Kitson scored for Newcastle in a 1-1 draw, I was off my feet celebrating. That's how soon it changes.

I made my debut the following Saturday at Hillsborough – Sheffield was a landmark location for me that season – as a substitute. That went well enough to secure a start for the visit of Wimbledon. The club flew my family over for the game, and I hit the ground running, skinning their full-back Alan Kimble in the first minute. Instantly, the home crowd were on my side.

A couple of weeks later, I was on the scoresheet twice, when Manchester City came to town for an FA Cup tie. I had the measure of my marker, David Brightwell, and collected the man of the match award in front of the Sky cameras. From getting a game here and there at Manchester United, I was now in the thick of the action, and loving every second.

Off the field, my pace of life had also changed completely. I was a young, carefree, single man with plenty of cash, few commitments and the luxury of staying in a beautiful hotel with all expenses paid. I made the most of my time in Room 131. The social life was fantastic. Younger lads like Lee Clark, Robbie Elliott, Steve Watson and Steve Howey all knew the town inside out and I slipped into the groove pretty easily, working hard and partying hard.

I was generally out three times a week. After a while, I fell into a routine. Fixtures permitting, Wednesdays and Saturdays would centre around the bars on the Quayside. Sunday was the Bigg Market, a legendary area packed with pubs and revellers, where we would start at one end, crawl down a familiar route and finish up in a place called Masters.

A lot of weekends followed the same path as the first one, with a new friend or two coming back to the residents' bar. I had to be careful who I invited, though, as I had become such a part of the furniture at the hotel that I actually started seeing a girl who worked on reception. If she was working a late shift at night and then up early for the morning, she'd sneak up to my room. But I had to be careful about bringing other girls back. I soon learned what a goldfish bowl the city was, and got used to reported sightings of myself in places I had never been.

That was a warning of things to come but at that point I was too young to care. I was busy enjoying all the perks. With the Premiership expanding into a league of global interest, TV money was making clubs richer, and players were beginning to really enjoy the benefits. It was a good time to be coming of age.

I turned 20 the day I scored against City, and also passed my driving test in the same week. The club had put me on a crash course when I signed, and a month later I was a proud licence holder. Immediately after receiving the good news, I was whisked to a garage to pick up a car from Rover, who were sponsors at the time. Every six months, we got an upgrade. Boot companies were equally generous and started sending me whatever new stock they had with the intention of getting my endorsement. It was just a matter of shopping around. I chose Adidas Predators and the PFA sent Brian Marwood, the ex-Arsenal winger who is now on the executive staff at Manchester City, to do the negotiations. I signed for £12,000 a year plus bonuses for goals, international caps and other add-ons.

The cheques kept dropping in, and I was on a high. There was slight disappointment around the club when we finished the season in sixth spot, considering they had challenged for top spot in the first half of the campaign. However, Keegan had major plans for the summer with a view to a launching a real challenge the following season, and I was confident of being a big part of that.

Football-wise, nothing fazed me. In the space of five months, I had come a long way. There was just one thing I didn't quite have under control.

9

A New Thrill

GAMBLING meant nothing to me until I moved to Manchester. It was something that other people did.

Sure, my Dad liked a punt now and again, but I paid no heed. We didn't have a family bet on the Grand National or go to the races or anything like that.

My addiction started innocently, just a few short weeks after I moved across the water. It was another lazy afternoon in the digs and Colin McKee announced that he was going to the bookies, the Ladbrokes at the end of our road. With nothing else better to do, I tagged along. What harm?

It was my first time in a betting shop. I remember the experience vividly.

Colin opens the door to an alien world. Instantly, I'm struck by the hum of activity, the maze of screens. Some showing horse races. Others displaying odds. Another for the greyhound racing.

The walls are covered in newspapers that are packed with colours, and names, and words that appear to be make sense to everyone but me. I follow the lead of people who look like they know what they are doing, and stare at the form, trying to compute the lingo. Horses with bolded abbreviations after their name. Jockeys with numbers in brackets next to them. They all stand for something. I just don't know what.

Every couple of minutes, a scramble begins for pens and dockets, followed by a rush to the counter as a faceless man announces over an intercom that a race is about to start. Another faceless man commentates.

As the race unfolds, the men stand watching, cigarettes hanging from the corner of their mouths, talking to nobody in particular. Most curse their bad luck, condemn a jockey, throw crumpled dockets aside and march to a different corner of the shop. To examine another race, to unravel another code.

I follow Colin's lead and start small. There is no other way. We are apprentice footballers earning just £46 a week, after all. I join the procession, study the form, read the newspaper verdict and draw my own conclusion.

I take the slip of paper, scribble down a £1 win bet and walk to the counter. I join the group of eyes trained on the screen, and mutter under my breath as another horse is called the winner.

I lose money, but don't care. The thrill is worth it. I bet on the next race. £2 win this time. I feel a rush of adrenaline when it comes into shot, and the commentator calls its name.

It's going well, but another horse is going better. Foiled again, but it doesn't matter. I was close, and I want that rush of excitement again. There's another race, another chance.

This time I'll get it right.

The next day, I returned on my own. And the day after, and the day after that, until the days that stand out are the ones where I didn't go.

My only break from the routine was the location. At the other end of the street there was another bookies, a Mickey Dines shop. I alternated between the two, and devoured information about horse racing form, quickly learning the slang and what the abbreviations stood for. CD beside a horse that had won over the same course and distance. BL next to a horse that wears blinkers. That kind of thing. In particular, I focused on the trainers and the jockeys and developed my own favourites.

As apprentices, we were training twice most days, finishing up around 4pm. For me, that meant a sprint to the bookies to catch as many races as possible. When the evenings were longer, the racing might go on until 9pm some nights. Winter was tougher; at best, I might be able to get an hour in. Eight or nine races perhaps. I always looked forward to the changing of the seasons.

Occasionally, I had company. Colin would still come in, but wouldn't stay as long. Darren Ferguson and Russell Beardsmore popped in the odd day too.

But, in time, I became pally with the regulars. After I made my Manchester United debut, they knew who I was, but nobody passed that much comment. We were part of a different club.

At the Cliff, my gambling habit was common knowledge, but

nobody expressed any concern. Instead, it gave me a handy little earner.

On Wednesdays, when the football coupons for the weekend were printed, I always used to stick a few in my pocket and bring them into training. For no particular reason at first, just to study them, maybe chat to a few of the other lads about the games.

The coaching staff liked a punt, and had established syndicates who would do the coupons every weekend. Eric Harrison ran one. Jim Ryan, Brian Kidd and Pop Robson went in together. The physios too. My habit saved them the hassle of going into the shop themselves.

We had a half day every Friday, but I would wait around while the staff sat upstairs, mulling over the possibilities. Eventually, someone would call me and hand over the completed coupons and the money. Then, it was my responsibility. I'd go to the bookies, place the bets, and collect any winnings ahead of the Monday morning, although sometimes if I looked at the selections and reckoned they had no chance, I'd pocket the money and pray they didn't come up. A risky strategy, but I was never caught out.

I'd never have dreamt of doing that with one person's coupon though. When Alex Ferguson got involved, and employed me as a runner, I felt extra pressure. He would generally stake £50 on his coupon, more than my week's wages, and I always had a special interest in his selections. If he came up trumps, I would deliver the prize to his office, and receive a healthy tip. I remember dropping almost £400 into him one Monday morning, and walking out with a crisp £50 note in my pocket.

The other syndicates were good to me as well. I could expect anything from £30 to £40 when they won – enough to keep me going in the bookies for another few days.

I should stress that my own strike rate was poor. It wasn't uncommon for me to get paid on Thursday, and find myself skint by Friday evening. After that, it would be a case of scraping enough money around for a couple of placepots.

A placepot is when you pick a horse in a number of selected races over the course of a day and, if they all finish in the first two, three or four depending on the size of field or type of race, you collect a portion of the overall dividend. It was the ideal bet to keep your interest going through a day if you were short of cash.

For a larger stake, it's possible to pick a couple of horses in each race and increase the chances, but I rarely had that luxury in my Manchester United days. Some Mondays or Tuesdays, I could be down to my last £1 or £2. In the 'A' team, we received a £6 bonus for every win. In my mind, £6 meant six placepots. That was my currency.

I did have the occasional lucky afternoon in Manchester. A few times I managed to walk out of a shop with a couple of hundred quid in my pocket. The problem was that I would give it all back in the next couple of days.

As much as I became aware of horses and jockeys, I really didn't have a rational approach. Professional gamblers might only have one bet on a given day, something they would channel all their energies and funds into. That approach didn't appeal to me. I liked to have a bet on every race. Before one race was over, I was already glancing at my options for the next. On really busy afternoons, with races going off every couple of minutes, my pockets would be stuffed with live dockets. My bedroom floor used to be covered with the losing ones.

The seeds of an addiction were sown but I was oblivious. I earned small money, so I didn't have anything to lose. When I moved onto my £250 a week contract at Manchester United, I was able to add an extra zero to my minimum bet. But I was a modest punter compared to the majority of the regulars. My flippant attitude to betting was my trademark. Frittering money away without a care in the world. If I was rich, I would have been dangerous.

Then, Newcastle happened. I was rich.

Suddenly, there were no boundaries. No fear of scraping around for loose change when Monday and Tuesday came around. I was on £1,200 a week and had also collected a six figure signing-on fee. Jackpot.

One of my first priorities in Newcastle was to find a bookies close to my hotel. Sure enough, I found a Ladbrokes two minutes drive away on Gosforth High Street. They did well out of me.

I made £100 my standard bet, and turned over cash with abandon. I could win £500 with the click of a finger, and lose it just as quickly.

As a first-team regular, I had more time to play with. Double sessions were rare. So I'd be in the hotel by 1pm, with a free afternoon ahead. The older fellas were married with kids and had other responsibilities; the younger local lads that were my drinking buddies in the evening generally had mates or girlfriends to hang out with.

Gambling was my hobby, and my new club were also cool

with that. Kevin Keegan and Terry McDermott were both interested in horses and often shared information. Terry was particularly well connected.

The only person who didn't know was Mum. I was still ringing home most days, chatting about what I was up to. But I neglected to mention my visits to the turf accountants. I knew she wouldn't approve, and didn't want a lecture. I was my own man, doing my own thing.

The hotel was right next to Newcastle racecourse, and when there was a meeting on I did go in, but days at the races didn't excite me in the way that a bookies did. I found it restrictive. I do remember going into the track one afternoon with the girl from reception, taking the time to just concentrate on the six races at Newcastle, and coming out with full pockets. I preferred Ladbrokes, though. The regularity of a race going off every couple of minutes rather than having to wait half an hour for another chance.

Just like in Manchester, I became acquainted with the regulars. As a first-team player, my presence probably turned a few more heads, but I was so focused on betting on everything and anything that the attention brushed off me. When they came up for a chat, I diverted the small talk to the horses, especially as the other players at the club weren't that big into nags. Alan Neilson, who left for Southampton six months after my arrival, was fond of a bet although he didn't want his wife to know. He was probably the only one aware of the extent to which my gambling was escalating.

Leaving the hotel was the catalyst which brought things to another level. I was in no rush to depart Room 131, but it was inevitable. In May, 1995, as the season drew to a close, I bought a four-bedroom house. I didn't stray too far; just five minutes drive away, so I was able to stay punting in Ladbrokes. Shay Trainor came up from Manchester to do the paperwork. He was 15 years older than me, a confident talker and therefore the right man to complete the deal. I paid £140,000 to become a homeowner for the first time, and Shay was my first tenant. He was an area manager in a double glazing company and was appointed to the Newcastle branch of that firm. It suited us both perfectly.

How did the house have an adverse effect on my betting? Simple. One afternoon in Ladbrokes, a chap I recognised as a serious gambler casually asked me why I bothered with the hassle of coming into the shop when I could do my betting over the phone.

I was so naive that I had no idea you could gamble that way, and was fascinated by the prospect. He recommended a local bookie, named Mickey Arnott, and said that I should open an account with him.

His argument made sense. So, I took the number, called Mickey and set the wheels in motion. Then, I moved my betting operation to the living room. I might pop into the bookies now and again for a change of scenery, but I did my serious punting from the couch. It was so easy.

No longer was I concerned about rushing to the counter, getting stuck in queues, finding myself in discussions from which I couldn't escape, or fiddling around in my pocket for a lost docket. With Shay out at work during the day, I resided in a blissful kind of solitary confinement.

Crucially, I didn't need to worry about cash. There's nothing worse than the moment in a bookies when you realise there's no money left in the wallet, meaning a trip to the bank and a loss of valuable punting time.

At home, it was a different story. I had a tab, and was betting with invisible money from the comfort of my own armchair. I laughed at how it had taken me so long to find this stress-free existence. All I had to do was dial a number, enquire about the odds, and put on as much I wanted.

What could possibly go wrong?

(10)

Black Friday

ON Sunday, October 29, 1995, I should have been the happiest man in the world.

I was on top of my game, top of the league, and received the ultimate compliment from two of the people I respected most in football.

We were on the way back from a clash with Spurs at White Hart Lane, a game that finished 1-1, making it our first draw from 11 starts that season. Aside from a loss at Southampton, we had won the rest with a swagger. Newcastle United were the talk of the country.

Kevin Keegan liked to have a glass of wine and wander down towards the back of the bus on our journeys home. On this occasion, he sat next to Peter Beardsley, and addressed him while pointing a finger in my direction.

"That lad there could just be the best player in the country at this time," he said.

"I wouldn't disagree," Pedro replied.

I'll never forget those words because of the timing.

To everyone else, I was a rising star with everything going for me. And I was overjoyed by the praise from the boss and a top senior pro.

But they didn't know the full picture. I was keeping a secret from everybody on that bus. One that would eventually catch up with me.

The truth was that I had produced a man of the match display at White Hart Lane after a destructive 48 hours of gambling that had plunged me into serious debt.

I had blown £62,000. Effectively, a year's wages. The vast majority of the losses had been incurred on Friday, October 27, 1995. A date etched forever in my memory as Black Friday. The day where I completely lost the plot.

Before telling the story of Black Friday, I need to place it in the context of my life at that point. I had grown into one of Mickey Arnott's most prized customers. We had established a strong bookmaker-client relationship. Every day, I was on the phone to Mickey, or the couple of staff he had working the phones in his small office. Then, at fortnightly periods, he would visit my house to settle our balance and reset the tab to zero.

If you had asked me before I met him to draw a picture of what a bookmaker looked like, I'm pretty sure that my sketch would have resembled Mickey. He was a small fella, with a bald head and a moustache. A big Newcastle fan.

Sometimes, when he knocked on my door, Mickey had cash to drop off. My favourite bet was a £500 punt on four horses over the course of the afternoon. I'd split them up into four £100 trebles and a £100 accumulator. If one of those came off, Mickey might have £6,000 or £7,000 for me. They were the rare good days. Generally, though, I was the one paying up. Still, before Black Friday, I'd never lost more than £10,000 in one day.

That week could easily have worked out very differently. Two days before Black Friday, I nearly won over £40,000 on betting on a football match. Not just any football match. It was a game that I was very much a part of; a League Cup tie away to Stoke.

I'd rarely bet on games in which I was involved. I'd won a few quid on the third-last game of the previous season, backing myself to score first against Tottenham. Alan Neilson owed me £30 for some tickets so I told him to stick it on me at 8/1. Seven minutes into the game, an accurate diving header made it a winning docket.

By and large, I tried to stay away from punting on Newcastle matches. That was complicated territory, although I wasn't aware of any rules forbidding it – aside from the obvious, which was backing us to lose, something I never would have even contemplated. I'd allow myself the odd first goalscorer bet now and again, but that was about it.

The genesis of my Stoke bet was an afternoon earlier in the week when, in search of a bit of cash in hand, I went to the bookies. Once more, I was influenced by a discussion with a betting shop regular. I really shouldn't have listened to those guys.

He pointed out that, under Keegan, we commonly won games 2-0, 2-1, 3-0 or 3-1. Betting on those outcomes were profitable for him. I filed the advice away in my head.

My world: I've loved the game from the moment I first kicked a ball. That's why I've kept playing as long as I could

Early promise: I managed to win plenty of cups when I was growing up, including this Player of the Year trophy from 1987-88

My hero: I was captivated by Norman Whiteside, who became the youngest player to appear in a World Cup in 1982. It was a great day when he made a school visit

FOOTBALLER VISITS SCHOOL

Northern Ireland and Manchester United footballer Norman Whiteside paid a visit to Bangor this morning and took time out to visit the pupils of Connor House.

Specfoto:

Going far: I enjoyed a successful trip to Aberdeen with Northern Ireland Under-13s in 1988. We won five games and drew one. I'm on the front row, second from the right

Fergie Fledglings: That was the name the press gave us when they realised we were a talented group of youngsters. I'm front row, third from right. You may have heard of some other players in this United youth team line-up – Gary Neville, David Beckham, Paul Scholes and Nicky Butt among others

The class of '92: Strolling on the Old Trafford pitch in our club suits showing off some silverware. Gary Neville is leading the way, holding the FA Youth Cup. It was the start of something special

Stepping up: Rising through the ranks (above) and graduating to the first team against Sheffield Wednesday (right)

Wembley thrill: Celebrating a 2-0 victory over Blackburn Rovers in the Charity Shield of 1994, below

Proud moment: Making my debut for Northern Ireland against Portugal in September 1994. I often came back with some good stories to tell after being away on international duty

A new Toon: Now a Newcastle player, relaxing at the training ground, preparing to take on my old team at Old Trafford. I soon got used to the idea of life in Tyneside

Golden feet: Boot deals were just one of the financial perks I enjoyed when I started to make a name for myself in the game

Keegan's army: I loved the passion of the Newcastle fans. Here I am celebrating at QPR in October, 1995 where I scored twice in a 3-2 win. Our games were usually entertaining affairs

Shear madness: A light-hearted moment in training. I lost the plot when I squared up to Alan Shearer on a night out in Dublin. We both laughed about it afterwards

On a wing and a mare: My gambling problems didn't stop me turning in some of the best performances of my career

Head boy: I scored the only goal to give us a 1-0 win at Leeds in May, 1996. After the game, Keegan let rip with his famous rant at Fergie. It didn't work – and the title dream was soon over

Magical memories: Lining up at St James' Park before playing Barcelona in September, 1997. This would become one of the best nights of my footballing life – a 3-2 win I would never forget

Final fling: All suited for the FA Cup final against Arsenal in 1998 but it wasn't to be – we lost 2-0

Do you know how much you cost me? Darren Peacock defied the odds to score against Stoke and deny me a big payout!

Out in the cold: Being put through my paces with team-mate David Ginola. I should have opened up to Terry McDermott when he asked about my gambling debts

We travelled to Stoke on the morning of the game and checked into a hotel for the afternoon to get a few hours sleep. I roomed with David Ginola and while he conked out, I sat up in the bed, with the Racing Post opened in front of me, glued to the hotel phone. I'd call Mickey to place a bet, and then dial one of the commentary lines to listen. The first three horses in my daily £500 punt came up. The fourth narrowly lost out in a photo finish. Close. Nevertheless, I was up a couple of grand, and remembered the words of the betting shop sage.

Pedro hadn't scored for a few games, so I stuck £500 on him to score first at 6/1. I then placed four £500 doubles, with Pedro to score first paired with final scorelines of 2-0, 2-1, 3-0, and 3-1.

I told nobody about my investment, although I must have raised eyebrows with an afternoon phone bill of £198. I had to borrow cash from Les Ferdinand to settle it.

Stoke were near the top of Division One, and there was a big crowd in the old Victoria Ground that night. The atmosphere was tense. A fabricated rumour went around that Newcastle fans had stabbed a little girl, and a section of home fans went on the rampage in the streets outside. We heard afterwards that the atmosphere around the ground was poisonous.

On the pitch, it was plain sailing. We took an early lead, courtesy of none other than Peter Beardsley, who must have wondered why I was so excited. Everything was going to plan. Pedro got another and, early in the second half, I set up Big Les for a third.

We were cruising, and I was running around the pitch calculating my winnings. When our defence switched off, and their main striker, Paul Peschisolido, raced through on goal, I quickly calculated that the odds for 3-1 were better, and willed him to score but he tried a lob and failed miserably.

Still, I was well on course for a win of around £50,000 as the game entered the final five minutes. Then, a remarkable thing happened. Darren Peacock ventured forward. Darren averaged a goal a season in his four years at Newcastle. When a loose ball fell in Darren's direction, I reckoned it was a good thing. Wrong. 4-0. The other lads raced to celebrate a collector's item. I couldn't bring myself to join in. I was up £3,000 from the first scorer bet, but it was scant consolation for what could have been.

I sat in silence on the way home with one thought dominating my mind. Should I have told the lads after the third goal? We were a close bunch, and comfortably into the next round. I really believe that if I'd asked, they would have taken the foot off the pedal. But to ask would be to confess, and to draw attention, and that was the last thing I wanted to do.

I brooded over my near miss on the Thursday, and dabbled in a few bets without getting too stuck in. By the Friday, however, I was back to myself and in the usual routine. Training, showered, changed, fed, and in situ on the couch, with the Racing Post in tow, by 2pm.

It was an unremarkable day's racing. A moderate flat card at Newmarket, and jumps racing at Bangor and Wetherby. My first bet, in the 2.05 at Newmarket, was £1,000 on a horse called Quandary from the all-conquering Henry Cecil stable. He won like a favourite should, but there was no time to dwell on it.

I picked up the phone to Mickey's office and had a punt on the 2.10 at Wetherby. No joy. The 2.20 at Bangor. Loser. Then it was time for Newmarket again, and the sequence continued. I suffered a bout of seconditis. When the odds were favourable, I appreciated a good each-way bet. But on this afternoon, I was betting on the nose, and chasing losses. I upped the stakes to £4,000 a race and got one up. Then stuck another £4,000 on the next and lost it. From then, it was £4,000 on everything.

I wasn't keeping record of how I was doing – that was the danger of betting with invisible money – but I knew I was having a nightmare when the television informed me that we had reached the last race of the day, the 4.40 at Bangor, a National Hunt flat race for horses with little or no racecourse experience. In other words, a shot in the dark unless you were in the know.

Just two and a half hours after a relatively sensible bet on a good thing at Newmarket, I was sticking £4,000 on a 12/1 shot called Dream Ride who was making his debut. He was from a good yard, but I had no evidence to suggest he was anything better than his odds suggested. It was just a hunch. I wasn't in the know.

Dream Ride finished 10th, some 40 lengths behind the winner. In vain, I had a few blind stabs on the greyhounds until they finished up for the day and there was nothing left to have a bet on. I called Mickey.

"What's the damage?"

"You lost £47,000 today."

"Oh..."

I pretended it wasn't a problem, and put down the phone. But I knew it was a problem. I didn't have £47,000. Not even close.

But I don't think I really appreciated the scale of it.

My instinctive ability to block out negative thoughts kicked in. Did I cry? No. Did I throw stuff around the house in anger?

No. I had my own way of dealing with things, which was to say nothing and try and forget about it. Put up the shutters. Delay and deny. Maybe it would have been different if I had physically handed over that amount of money but, at that stage, it was just a ledger entry in Mickey's office.

I lay in bed that night restless, but only because I was thinking about how to win some of my money back the next day.

We were travelling to London at lunchtime so I was up and about early, studying the form. I called the hotline to Mickey's again, and laid down a variety of bets on the horses and football. There was no mention of the day before. My bets were accepted, no questions asked. I can understand why they were so happy to take them. I lost another £15,000.

On Sunday, a degree of realisation briefly set in. With no racing in England, I took a break from the betting and concentrated on the game. I reset my mind when I crossed the white line, and gave the Spurs defence a few problems that afternoon. It was only after I got home from London that I really began to appreciate my own difficulties.

I called a halt to the phone betting, although I continued to have plenty of discussions with Mickey. It followed a pattern. He would ask where his money was. I would try to fob him off. When I scraped together a few quid, I'd send it his way, but it was a ticking timebomb. "I'll get you the money," I'd say to Mickey, "I've got money coming." He was under the impression that a famous Premier League footballer automatically had thousands in the bank. Not so.

I should have known that, in Newcastle, everybody eventually knows everybody's business. Around a month later, Terry

McDermott cornered me and said he'd heard that I owed somebody a lot of money. I denied it. Pride prevented me from telling
the truth. But I didn't have a solution. Instead, I went cash betting in the bookies again. I needed my fix and was hoping for a
miracle that might somehow wipe the debt.

Terry approached me at training again, and repeated the
same question. My answer was the same. "No way, Terry... not
me."

Over the winter, I was able to sort Mickey out with a few
grand here and there, while promising I was good for the rest.
The lie was less and less convincing. Towards the middle of
January, I heard murmurs that The Sun knew the full story,
and the whisper was confirmed when a reporter called to my
house to ask about Black Friday and said they were running a
piece the following day. I refused to comment, but had the door
open long enough for a photographer to pop out of nowhere
and take a picture.

There were a few calls I had to make. I knew the press would
be after Mum so I rang to prepare her for the storm. I said that
I'd lost some money gambling, and that the papers were going
to reveal the details. I heard a long sigh from the other end of
the phone.

"How much?" she asked.

"A lot."

"Thousands?"

"Yeah..."

"£10,000?"

"More..."

A pause.

"£20,000?"

"More..."

"£30,000?"

"No... £47,000."

"Ack... son..."

My hunch was right though. The press started knocking on her door. And, when she didn't answer, they started ringing where she worked – an old folk's home. Classy.

Then, I rang the gaffer. He told me to drive to his house straight away. I'll never forget how understanding he was about it. He let me stay and have some food while he rang Mickey and got it sorted.

My saving grace was that I was due a new contract because of my form, a £5,500 a week deal that would rise by £500 every season. The five-fold pay increase eased the burden. Keegan spoke to the club's hierarchy and organised an advance on the signing-on fee. It was that straightforward. The one thing the gaffer was really annoyed about was that I hadn't owned up to Terry. I could easily have avoided all the publicity; the club had the clout to sort it out. Now, it was too late.

The next morning, the story was splashed over the front page of The Sun, and all hell broke loose. A steady stream of journalists set up camp outside, and I had to run out to the car and reverse out the driveway quickly, ignoring their cries for a reaction. They followed me, but I knew the roads around fairly well so I managed to pull a few manoeuvres and throw them off the scent.

When I showed my face at Maiden Castle, the welcome was less sympathetic. The lads were pissing themselves. There was no arm around the shoulder; the unforgiving rules of the dressing room applied and, to be absolutely honest, I was glad of the banter. They seemed to be more amused by the fact that I'd backed a horse called Dream Ride.

The club never ordered me to stop gambling. There was no mention of going to Gamblers Anonymous or anything like that. I wouldn't have admitted weakness anyway. I was blissfully in denial and didn't really believe I had a problem. The gaffer said they wanted to treat me like an adult, so they left me be and that suited just perfectly.

I did stop punting though. Not because I wanted to; the reason was that I had nowhere to go. While the Black Friday story was fresh in people's memories, turning up in a betting shop was a no-no. The newspapers would have been all over it.

Lying low was the only option. I did a few interviews, insisting that I had learned from my experience and was ready to put it behind me. But, I was going through the motions, drawing on my media training and saying all the right things.

The yearning for a bet lingered. Long, boring afternoons spent playing Super Mario could only amuse me for so long.

11

Pipped At The Post

MY gambling meltdown was merely a subplot in one of the most dramatic Premier League title races of the modern era.

The 1995/96 season should have been Newcastle's year. Our collapse was the story that dominated the headlines. In horse racing parlance, we led early, idled in front, and got nabbed on the run-in by Manchester United.

The only surprise is that I didn't have us backed.

Man U had started the season slowly, lulling everybody else into a false sense of security. Alex Ferguson had dispensed with Incey, Mark Hughes and Andrei Kanchelskis and placed his faith in the lads I had grown up alongside at the Cliff.

The Fledglings had matured, and a serious transition was underway. Butty and Gaz Neville were given even more opportunities, while Scholesy and Phil Neville were thrust into league action on a regular basis. Meanwhile, the departure of Kanchelskis to Everton a month before the new season left a vacancy on the right wing. Becks stepped into the breach. But he wasn't the only option Ferguson had considered in the summer of 1995.

Six months after letting me go, he tried to buy me back.

It all came about during my early pre-season after the messing about in Canada. In unfortunate circumstances, I had some company. Jim, my loyal friend from home, was in Sandhurst training to join the army when a problem with his eyesight emerged. He was discharged, and understandably felt down in the dumps. Jim had always wanted to be in the army. I tried to lift his spirits, and invited him to Newcastle for a week. Every morning, I trained. Every night, we drank.

In the afternoons, we lounged around the house – I'd be having a few bets, of course – and this 0161 number kept flashing up on the phone. I didn't recognise it so, as usual, I let it ring out. They never left a message. Then, one day, the phone flicked straight to answering machine, and I heard a distinctive unmistakeable Glaswegian voice.

"Keith, it's Alex Ferguson..."

I leapt across the room to grab the handset, and got there just in time. True to form, he got to the point quickly. He explained that Kanchelskis was on the way out, and that he had been chatting with his staff about possible replacements. Brian Kidd had mentioned my name. He'd never thought about it until then.

"Are you interested in coming back?"

"Of course I would be..."

"Right, leave it with me..."

What else was I going to say? It was an instinctive response. I was never going to refuse Alex Ferguson and, ultimately, Manchester United were the biggest club in the world. My last contact with Newcastle had been a dressing down after some high jinks on international duty, so I just thought, 'fuck it, why not'.

The conversation was short. Jim was as shocked as I was, and we had plenty to chew over that night. But it never went any further. I waited for the phone to ring, but Ferguson never called again.

I spoke to Gaz Neville a lot – when my Manchester United-supporting mates wanted tickets he was the go-to guy – and he spoke to Peter Beardsley about it on England duty. Beardsley and Keegan were very, very close and Peter told Gaz that Ferguson had lodged a £4 million bid that was dismissed outright. I understood why. Considering I was a potential deal-breaker on the Cole transfer, Newcastle were hardly going to let Manchester United have both players. The club said nothing to me about it.

I was fine with that. Flattered, but not disappointed. I liked where I was and, as we burst out of the stalls and opened a clear advantage, the grass was greener in the North-East.

The gaffer wanted us to express ourselves, and assembled a talented team with a simple enough mission statement. Ginola had joined from PSG for £2.5 million and slotted in on the left, with myself on the right, and Rob Lee rampaging through the middle to provide support for Peter Beardsley and Les Ferdinand, who we'd signed for £6 million from QPR. The formula worked. While the cavalier approach left our defence exposed, we had so much firepower that management believed results would go our way if we played to those strengths.

We didn't go overboard on tactics and training was fun. Mostly five-a-sides. Team-talks were short. If we'd won the week before, Keegan kept it to no more than a couple of minutes. He preferred to go around one-to-one and give individual pep talks. That kind of man-management was his strong point. Big Les always said that the gaffer had this special way of making you feel like the best player in the world, and I related to that.

Until Christmas, we were practically unstoppable. Certain games stand out for me. We murdered Manchester City at St James' Park in September; it could have finished 30-1 instead of 3-1. Chelsea were the next visitors, in front of the Sky cameras, and I was man of the match in a 2-0 success, even though a former World Footballer of the Year, Ruud Gullit, was on the same park.

By January, we had opened up a 12-point lead. Losing at Old Trafford on December 27 didn't check our momentum. Instead, that setback was followed up with five successive wins.

The game in Manchester halted my progress though. I suffered a ruptured abdomen, a really unusual injury that left me on the sidelines for five weeks, just as the Black Friday story was about to break. The good vibes in the dressing room were a welcome distraction from my own troubles.

As a group, we revelled in the euphoria our exploits had created around Newcastle. We went out together every couple of weeks, and attendance was compulsory. The bonding sessions always began with a meal in a classy place called Unos, who reserved a private area, and we moved on from there. Peter Beardsley didn't drink, and I respected his patience. The sober guy was often left to pick up the pieces. One of the nights, I was sitting in Unos next to our Czech keeper, Pavel Srnicek, and he dared me to down a carafe of red wine. I rarely shirked that kind of challenge, and knocked it back in the space of three minutes. No hassle.

It was only when I went out into the cool air that the after-effects of the macho behaviour hit me. I ran up the street towards our next destination, oblivious to an open manhole in my path. Straight in. After that sudden jolt, the cut on the back of my neck was the least of my worries. The minute I got into the bar, I was spewing red wine all over the place. Pedro went to fetch his car and pulled up outside to take me home. Inevitably, I sprayed another shower of red wine all over the back seat of his Rover. He wouldn't take any money the next day for clean-ing it. That was Pedro all over. Always generous, always the first to the bar to buy a drink, even when he wasn't having one.

Often, the last stop on the nights out was my place, the bach-elor pad. For the lads who were living with wives and partners, it was a popular haunt. There was always a few women around the place. When I was injured, there was one particularly rau-cous night where a good crew landed back. Big Les was there, Warren Barton, Lee Clark, Steve Watson, Robbie Elliott and some of their mates. Ginola usually drank Amaretto but, for some reason, he ended up lying backwards on the front lawn with just a can of beer in his raised hand. My next door neigh-bour lodged a complaint and the gaffer called everyone into a meeting where he blamed the senior players for turning my place into a doss house. I escaped the rap.

In February, a superstar rocked in to join the party. Keegan believed we needed strengthening for the title run-in, and paid

£6.5 million to sign the Colombian striker Faustino Asprilla from Parma. 'Tino' had charisma, and arrived in the middle of a snowstorm with a fur jacket and a confident strut. David Batty was also recruited from Blackburn to add a bit of steel to our midfield.

We had a settled dressing room, and both lads fitted in to the banter just fine. Tino was a social animal, a real character. He had remedial English so his interpreter, Nick, was always by his side, be that in the dressing room or the nights on the town.

Nick was on a bigger wage than our left-back, Robbie Elliott. We'd see him on Tino's shoulder in a club, trying to help him with whatever girl had taken his fancy. Tino generally had enough English to get by in that situation though. He'd strike up a discussion and just say to the girl 'You come home with me, yes?' and, often, it worked.

Accommodating Tino on the pitch was a little bit more difficult. He was a flamboyant player, with gangly legs, quick feet, and a wonderful ability to make the game look easy. Naturally, the gaffer was keen to utilise his talents, especially after his debut as a sub at Middlesbrough when he turned a one-goal deficit into victory.

Big Les and Beardsley had forged a profitable partnership, but if Tino was to start a game then something had to give. So, Keegan put Tino and Big Les together and switched Beardsley to the right wing which was bad news for me. I was short of 100 per cent fitness after coming back from my lay-off ahead of schedule, so I could sort of understand the decision, although I also think it was easier for the gaffer to drop the young lad.

After Middlesbrough, we hit a rocky patch. People have asked me if there were visible signs that it was coming, but nothing was dramatically different at training. Maybe we were feeling the pressure of being on top for so long. All the same, it wasn't as though people were walking around with panicked looks on their faces. The spirits remained high.

On the pitch, however, something was missing. We had lost our fluency. The little things that were going our way early in the season were starting to go against us. Mistakes crept in, and we started to make things complicated. It was a slippery slope.

We won just one of our next six games, and lost our unbeaten home record to Manchester United. Schmeichel was inspired, Cantona nabbed a goal, and they grinded out the win. They were more streetwise in those situations.

The real sickener was at Liverpool, an iconic Premier League game that people in Newcastle would rather forget. I was an unused substitute, and spent those 90 minutes behind the gaffer on a bench that went through the full range of emotions. Tino put us 3-2 up shortly before the hour mark, but we lacked the solidity to shut the game out. Stan Collymore struck twice, with the injury-time winner striking a hammer blow. The gaffer stood up afterwards and said he was proud of any team that could score three goals at Anfield, yet the reality was that our vulnerabilities had been exposed.

My exclusion became a talking point with the press and in sections of the dressing room. Rob Lee told me he was going to see the manager about it. We trailed to QPR at St James' in the next game and the fans chanted my name. I was brought on and made an impact as Beardsley, who was moved infield, scored twice to claim the three points. Despite that, I was on the bench for the trip to Blackburn, although I was on the park as we suffered another late collapse to turn a win into a defeat. A

Geordie, Graham Fenton, grabbed the two late goals that really handed Manchester United control of their destiny.

The gaffer found that loss tough to take and began to show the strain. He cancelled one of our nights out, and broke from the norm by making our team-talks longer. Still, we were within touching distance as we headed into the final week of the season. A fixture backlog meant we had three games, and wins against Leeds and Nottingham Forest would have put us level on points going into the final day.

I was recalled for Elland Road and nabbed the only goal, but the only thing people remember about that night is the gaffer's post-match interview. He was seriously wound up. Alex Ferguson had hinted that Leeds and Forest might roll over for us because Leeds hated Manchester United and we had agreed to visit Forest for Stuart Pearce's testimonial. After a tough game with a Leeds side that were definitely trying, Keegan went on Sky and let rip at Ferguson with his infamous, 'I'd love it if we beat them, I'd just love it' rant. We only heard about it on the bus home when one of the lads got a call from his wife. A bunch of us went out in our tracksuits to Julies nightclub when we made it to Newcastle, and it was the talk of the place.

People say that Keegan's rant was evidence of him cracking, but the fact is that we were in control against Forest on the Thursday when Batty was unlucky to slip in possession with 15 minutes to go. Ian Woan capitalised to fire home a screamer for a 1-1 draw. That was game over in the title race. Manchester United were two points ahead with a superior goal difference that was ironically helped by a 5-0 win over Forest a week earlier. A point at Middlesbrough on the Sunday would do for them.

Only in the event of an unlikely defeat would our clash with

Tottenham become relevant. Man U won comfortably. We struggled to raise a beat and drew. The damage had been done at Anfield and Ewood Park.

We trudged down the tunnel in low spirits. The fans wanted us out for a lap of honour, but Keegan, normally so positive, was reluctant. He never seemed to lose hope that we could turn it around, but now it was over, the realisation was setting in.

After a bit of encouragement, he agreed to go back out, and the supporters greeted us like champions. Around town that night, the well-wishers were all saying the same thing, stressing that the club was only three years back in the top flight and would benefit from this harsh experience.

That optimism was misguided.

(12)

Breaking Point

SOMETIMES, I wondered if trouble was attracted to me like a magnet.

I'm not looking for pity. I've never claimed to be an angel. But there were times when events that were completely outside my control caused real problems. Take Sunday, October 20, 1996, for example, the night which led to my first proper brush with the law.

The context is important. The incident occurred a few hours after we had swept Manchester United off the park, a 5-0 drubbing that was particularly sweet after the pain of the previous season. I say 'we' when, in fact, I had nothing to do with that victory.

It was a game I had anticipated starting. The gaffer had taken us to St James' the day before to work on set pieces, and he always gave the team away in those sessions. There was no announcement, but the players knew the score from their role in proceedings. It was clear that I was in, and Ginola was out. There was a huge gang over from home for the game, including my Dad and Jim, and I was delighted to give them the good news on the Saturday night.

I reported for duty the next morning and my mate Paul Ferris, our Northern Irish physio, pulled me aside. He tipped me off that Ginola had marched into Keegan's office after training and threatened to leave unless he was put back in the side. Paul reckoned it had worked. The gaffer named his team and, sure enough, Ginola was in at my expense. I stormed out of the dressing room, kicking the door on the way. Keegan followed me into his office and we had a blazing row. He denied the story, but I wasn't buying his response and told him that I wasn't in the right frame of mind to even sit on the bench. This was no ordinary game, and I was embarrassed after telling all the lads I'd be in.

The gaffer convinced me to stay, but I was still seething at kick-off. You know what happened then. Ginola was outstanding and produced a goal of the season contender as we tore my old club apart. It was hard to argue with that.

I went into Masters afterwards to catch up with my lot and, naturally, town was hopping. As I sipped on a drink, I was approached by a fan I recognised. His name was Terry Mann, a hefty guy in his 30s who looked older. The local players knew him to talk to and while I'd heard rumours that he was associated with a hooligan element, he seemed normal the few times we had met. I expected a hardcore Newcastle fan to be in heaven after a win like that but, as he drew closer, it was obvious that he was bladdered and had something else on his mind.

"You don't want to play for us anymore," he said, jabbing a finger at me. "You want to be back at fucking Manchester United."

I was a bit shocked. A few weeks before, I'd delivered one of my best ever performances in an epic 4-3 win over Aston Villa so I didn't understand how anybody could think I wasn't committed; especially if they knew how angry I'd been earlier in the day. The tirade continued. It was a waste of time listening and Frances, my girlfriend, grabbed my hand to take me away.

As I turned, Mann swung a fist in my direction. Like a natural winger, I dropped the shoulder to dodge and instinctively went to hit him back in self defence. Otherwise, he was coming back for another go. I connected with a right hand punch under his eye which had extra impact as I grazed him with a ring I was wearing – a 21st birthday present from my mother.

Blood poured down his face as the bouncers swarmed in to eject him from the premises. The staff in Masters always looked out for the footballers. He didn't go quietly and one of our group went to the front door to see what was happening. Mann was taking a few steps back, charging at the bouncers, getting nowhere and then trying the same again. I thought it was safe to go and order a round when I heard screaming and shouting and turned to see that Mann was no more than five yards away from me, jogging on the spot, with the doormen slowly dragging him back out. Then, we learned that a posse of his mates had gathered with intent outside. It was time to leave.

One of the bouncers, Gary, ushered Jim, myself and my Dad to a side door, and we sprinted up the road to hop into a waiting taxi. Frances and the others followed. I was pretty shaken. My relationship with the Newcastle fans had been rock solid until then. This was totally out of nothing, and yet it was inevitable there would be repercussions. And headlines of course. It was a simple story to write. Pissed-up Keith Gillespie punches a fan in a bar, a tale which suited my bad-boy reputation.

On Tuesday, I was called into the gaffer's office. The news was worse than I thought. He said that Mann had been to the police, and reported that I'd hit him over the head with a bottle. Utter bullshit. The advice was to hire a solicitor and immediately go to the police to give a statement as the alternative was the cops knocking on my door which wouldn't have looked good. When I went to the station, I had to be formally placed under arrest because a complaint had been filed, although I was then allowed to leave straight away to await further developments.

Fortunately, the bar had clear CCTV footage of the incident which backed up my story, and the investigation was dropped. Still, when you're in the public eye, it is the arrest that people remember, not the subsequent exoneration. Maybe I shouldn't have struck Mann, but the alternative was getting assaulted in a public place. Standing up to a thug who would later be convicted as a hooligan only succeeded in adding weight to the rap sheet against me. I struggled to make sense of it.

For the club, the destruction of Manchester United was hailed as evidence that we were ready for the next step. Instead, it was a false dawn. Our form tailed off dramatically, with just one win from the next nine games. We had fine individual players that just weren't clicking.

The new star of the show was Alan Shearer, a world record

breaking £15 million capture. It was the feel-good story of pre-season, a local boy coming home to provide the missing link. We were on a lengthy tour of Asia when the deal was completed, and watched the footage of Shearer being greeted like a God on Tyneside. There was a little bit of a stir over his demand for the famous number 9 shirt because it belonged to Big Les who had performed brilliantly the previous season. He was unhappy to be moved to number 10 and, as a knock-on effect, Lee Clark, a lifelong Newcastle fan, was switched to 21. It may sound stupid, but footballers can get attached to shirt numbers.

The players generally took to Alan, who was a good character to have around the place as he demanded high standards from everyone. But it quickly became apparent that himself and Ginola would find it hard to work together. Alan was intolerant of the quirks that the rest of us were already accustomed to. Ginola was a lazy type of player, more concerned with throwing his arms in the air in disgust rather than trying to get the ball back when he lost it. There was less of that behaviour in the English game at the time and it grated with the others. Shearer couldn't handle it. They'd argue on the pitch and in training. The mutual dislike never boiled over into anything physical; it just simmered, and that was a problem because they were two important elements of the team. I know there are plenty of examples of players who don't get along clicking on the pitch, but when a team is struggling it can become an issue. It certainly did in our case.

Still, despite our disastrous run into Christmas, a 7-1 filleting of Spurs demonstrated that we retained the ability to turn it on. We followed that up with a comfortable win over Leeds and a draw away to Charlton in the FA Cup. Considering how strong we were at home, there was nothing wrong with that result. Certainly, no reason to believe that something major was coming down the tracks.

Two days later, I pulled into the car park at the training ground where the first person I saw was our press officer, Graham Courtney. He greeted me with news that I could scarcely believe. The gaffer had resigned. Kevin Keegan was no more.

I didn't see it coming. I'm not sure if any of the players did. Terry McDermott said that a load was lifted from the gaffer's shoulders when he made the decision, so he was obviously feeling the burden of a stressful year. We read afterwards about disagreements with the board and other stories. But whatever was going on behind the scenes or in his own head, he never displayed any weakness to the players. From our point of view, it was midway through the season and we weren't a million miles off the pace. This was completely unexpected.

It was my first experience of losing a manager. In later years, I was in dressing rooms where the banter was back to normal within 24 hours, and certain players were secretly delighted. With Keegan, there was genuine sorrow. For a couple of days, everyone went about their business silently. Our veteran coach, Arthur Cox, tried to lift the spirits. Himself and Terry were put in charge for our next league game at Aston Villa. Arthur had plenty of knowledge, but also had this ability to make people laugh when he didn't mean to with his range of old school phrases and mannerisms. He lightened the mood in the team-talk ahead of the Villa game and we should have won after scoring a couple of early goals. They came back to claim a point. Old defensive habits died hard.

The club moved fast to find a replacement. With the fans still grieving for Keegan, they needed a big name and delivered one when they appointed Kenny Dalglish, with Terry staying on as his assistant. When I was a young Manchester United fan, I despised Dalglish because of his central role in Liverpool's dominance of the '80s. My adult perception was different. I liked his interview manner, the dour sense of humour that was his trademark when it came to dealing with the press. Shearer and Batty had won a league title under his stewardship at Blackburn, and spoke highly about his managerial style.

He probably endeared himself further to Shearer by quickly freezing Ginola out of his plans. Although he came in and gave the usual speech that a new man gives, which basically involves promising a clean slate for everybody, he made a statement of intent by dropping Ginola for his first game in charge – against Southampton at the Dell. I remember looking over to the bench and seeing Ginola sitting there wearing a pair of trainers instead of boots, which was odd but not out of character.

Sympathy was in short supply. It was awkward for me because we roomed together on away trips and I probably knew him better than most. He was a decent bloke but the frequent strops didn't do him any favours. Within two months, he handed in a transfer request.

After a rocky start, which included an FA Cup defeat at St James' to Nottingham Forest – bloody Ian Woan again – we found some form under Dalglish although we did manage to lose another 4-3 at Anfield. This time, I was part of the drama and scored on the way to coming back from three goals down, only for Robbie Fowler to pop up with a final-minute winner. We had the last laugh on Liverpool that season though.

They were pushing Manchester United at the time, but their challenge went off the rails and we went unbeaten for the last 10 games to nab second spot and a place in the Champions League qualifiers.

Even though the man who brought me to Newcastle had departed, I ended up being involved in 32 Premier League games that season. I was confident that my future was safe under Dalglish so I sold the party house in Gosforth and splashed out £250,000 on a new property in a village called Whickham. My Northern Irish buddy Phil Gray, who was playing for nearby Sunderland, had introduced me to a guy named Ian Elliott who became my first agent, and he helped with the purchase.

Ian lived near Whickham and we socialised together quite a bit. One afternoon, we were chatting about things to do when you live outside town, and Ian casually asked if I had an internet betting account. I didn't know such a thing existed. Remember, it was 1997.

In the year since the fallout from Black Friday, I had resisted the temptation to visit a bookies in case I was caught. Phone betting had proved my undoing the last time. The internet seemed like the perfect solution so I signed up, registered my credit card details, and got back in the game.

I started off betting more conservatively than before and with less frequency. The missus had moved in with me and only worked a couple of days a week so I knew I couldn't get away with sitting in front of the horses every single afternoon. Maybe a few hours here and there. I convinced myself that I was in control. This time it was going to be different.

(13)

Blackout

I OPEN my eyes to a world of confusion. No idea where I am. No idea how I got here.

There are faces looking at me that I don't recognise. Mouths that are saying nothing. All that's audible to my ears is a humming noise, a whirring. And a gentle beep, that sounds like an alarm clock dying a slow death. Maybe it's in my head. A dream.

I close my eyes. Time passes. How do you measure sleep when you have no idea where it started?

Eyes open again. This time, it's a little clearer. I see people in white coats. I hear Irish voices. But it's like I'm trapped in that Talking Heads song. The one where the lyrics are mostly questions.

'You may ask yourself, well, how did I get here?'

Slowly, my memory is decoding. Little things make sense.

The Irish voices? I'm in Dublin, with my Newcastle team-mates, for a bonding exercise. That's why Steve Howey is standing there too. Wait. Why is Steve Howey in this strange place with the humming and the beeping and the people with white coats? In a hospital.

'You may ask yourself, my God, what have I done?'

Seriously. What have I done? I'm not sure I want to know but Steve tells me the story. I sigh, and decide all I want to do is sleep. And the kind people in the hospital want to keep me here for the night. The only problem is they insist on waking me up every two hours. I ask why.

"We have to be careful sir," explained the doctor. "With head injuries, you can never be too sure."

I'm scared, and don't feel like sleeping for a while.

After September 17, 1997, sweet dreams were an anti-climax for me. I had already lived a real one. If I could bottle the feeling I experienced that night, then I'd never have to worry about money again. Send me to a desert island and tell me I can only bring a video of one football game, and I wouldn't even have to think about the answer. Newcastle 3 Barcelona 2. That Wednesday night in St James' Park, I tasted perfection.

A nervous qualifying round win over Croatia Zagreb had booked the club's place in the Champions League proper for the first time in its history, and the fact that Barcelona were coming to town made it very real. Home games were always special, but there was just something extra in the air in the hours before the game. It seemed like everyone had come to the ground that little bit earlier. Even the warm-up had an atmosphere.

Barca's team was a who's who of the European game. Luis Figo, Rivaldo, Sonny Anderson, Luis Enrique, Miguel Angel Nadal, Michael Reiziger, Ivan De La Pena. Christophe Dugarry on the bench. A serious array of talent.

I knew the names but didn't watch much Spanish football in those days. There wasn't the same level of coverage or interest there is now. And, the strange thing is, despite watching Euro 96, I really didn't know much about Sergi, the Spanish international left-back that I would be duelling with. Maybe knowing nothing about him removed the fear factor. Ignorance was bliss.

We took the lead early when Tino took a tumble in the area and slotted away a penalty. The ground erupted. I wanted a piece of the action, and Steve Watson gave me the opportunity by sending a quick free-kick in my direction. Sergi approached, and I took a couple of touches to get the ball under control. We were just outside the box, and he was trying to block my path into the area so I acted on instinct, dropped the shoulder and burst into a sprint on his outside that caught him by surprise. The extra yard was all I needed to nick the ball ahead and whip it into the box. Tino, as ever, had made an intelligent run into space and produced a gigantic leap to dispatch a header into the back of the net.

After that, I demanded the ball. Wingers know when they have the measure of an opponent. The actions of the full-back always give it away. I'd been told that Sergi liked to get forward, but he stopped crossing the halfway line when they had the ball and concentrated on sticking tight to me instead. He was petrified.

Early in the second half, Philippe Albert broke down a Barca attack. They were stretched and Rob Lee slipped it out towards me. I was still in our half, and Sergi bore down on me instantly. But there was room on his outside again so I clipped the ball in that direction and skipped away. *See you later, mate*. All I could see ahead was open space.

So, I ran, and ran, and ran as the crowd roared with encouragement. I glanced into the area where Tino was sneaking into a gap between two Barca defenders. After a 30yard dash at full tilt, with an angry Spanish man behind, executing a cross was a big ask, probably one of the most difficult skills in football. I fell to the ground as I curled the ball in Tino's direction, and watched as he sprung off an invisible trampoline to meet it perfectly. 3-0. What a rush.

They pulled a couple of goals back, with Luis Enrique chesting one in, and then Figo capitalising on a rare error from my new neighbour and pal, Shay Given. But this was our night. The final whistle saved the memory.

It was a Wednesday like no other, especially when I didn't end up in town to celebrate. With a game at West Ham on Saturday, the club had checked us into the Gosforth Park before the game so they could keep an eye on us afterwards. I wouldn't have lasted a minute in town anyway. The weight of the occasion had drained all the energy from my body.

Mum was over, and I was sitting with her afterwards when Shearer walked in.

He looked at me as though he was thinking of something to say, and just shook his head with a grin that basically said 'Where did that come from?'

I wish I knew the answer.

Unfortunately, the Barcelona game was an exception to the rule in '97/98. A chink of light in a season of darkness. Dalglish rang the changes in pre-season and it backfired. Ginola was sold to Tottenham. Big Les was going the same way. On the day he was putting pen to paper, Shearer tore his ankle ligaments badly in a pre-season friendly at Goodison Park and was ruled out for up to seven months. The club tried to stop the Ferdinand sale, but Big Les was unhappy about the original willingness to let him go and pushed through his transfer.

We missed Shearer desperately, and his absence was a major factor in our struggles.

The Champions League experience peaked on that glorious opening night. We actually finished above Barcelona and still went out – Dynamo Kiev and PSV Eindhoven proved stronger over the six games. The gaffer was so short of forward options for the home game with PSV that I started up there. They won 2-0 and that was it for us really. I was suspended for the Nou Camp trip which turned out to be a bit of a let down for the boys with the stadium just a quarter full.

Goals were the problem. The highly rated young Dane, Jon Dahl Tomasson, was brought in from Heerenveen in Holland, but he missed a sitter in the first game and that set the tone for his year. He went on to have a great career with his country and with some top clubs, but Newcastle was the wrong place at the wrong time.

Aside from his magic against Barca, Tino was struggling with injury, and the club decided to get some of their money back by selling him to Parma in January. It was a quieter town when he left. He always had a few Colombian mates over and, on one of his last nights, I remember ending up back in his house, with some fella just hammering away on this set of bongo drums. It was never boring when Tino was around but, with Shearer on the comeback trail, Dalglish reckoned we could survive without him.

The gaffer was heavily criticised for his dealings in the transfer market. He brought in Ian Rush, John Barnes and Stuart Pearce, a veteran trio that failed to excite the fans. Barnes and Pearce played quite a few games, but were past their prime. Rushy, who I enjoyed a bet with every Saturday, was unable to help the striking situation.

Their experience might have complemented the squad if the gaffer's foreign signings had worked out. Our new Italian defender, Alessandro Pistone, looked like a world beater in his first game at Everton. The problem was that he spent too much time on the treatment table with nothing more serious than a broken fingernail. His standing in the dressing room was reflected in a later Christmas raffle when Shay had to buy him a present and handed over a sheep's heart because the boys reckoned he didn't have one.

Temuri Ketsbaia had plenty of heart, but struggled to control his passion. He scored the goal against Croatia Zagreb that booked our passage into the Champions League proper and that made him popular in the dressing room as every man collected a £20,000 bonus. Temuri was unpredictable, though, and always seemed to be angry about something. Like a volcano that might erupt at any minute. He is remembered for going nuts after scoring a winner at St James' against Bolton. Temuri was furious that he was coming off the bench in most games, and celebrated by throwing his shirt into the crowd, kicking the advertising hoardings like a man possessed, and then tossing his boots away. He was crying violently and so out of control that when the game restarted and the ball came in his direction, he just belted it into the far stand. The gaffer lost the plot with him after.

Even in victory, there was chaos, and we soon followed that up with an eight-game winless run in the league. The return of Shearer wasn't enough to get our campaign back on track. From the high of a top-two finish, we slumped to a finishing position of 13th. The only thing that kept our season alive was a run in the FA Cup.

For all the troubles on the pitch, we retained a healthy social life and, at the end of February, the jaunt to Dublin was organised. The road to the confusion of the hospital bed started in the Teesside Airport bar.

We'd drawn at Everton on the Saturday and travelled the next morning. The gaffer had sanctioned the trip but decided against attending, so Terry was in charge.

I recall how the day kicked off, but need the help of others to piece together the rest.

We were staying in a decent hotel close to Dublin city centre, and went straight from there to Cafe En Seine, an upmarket bar, for an early drink. I was in giddy form, and started flicking bottle tops in the direction of other players. Shearer was struck by a couple and getting wound up, which I found enjoyable, so I made him my target and tension brewed.

It came to a head when I clumsily knocked some cutlery off the table. "Fucking pick it up," Shearer snapped. But the lounge girl was already over clearing up the mess. I thought he was talking to me like a small boy, and shouted back. Red mist descended. We had a bit of a row and, for some reason, I asked him if he wanted to take it outside. Madness.

Cafe En Seine is a long, narrow bar so it was quite a walk to the front door. There was no discussion en route. I was mulling over my next move. We emerged to a busy street, where Sunday afternoon shoppers were going about their business. It didn't deter me from the battleplan. I took a swing at Shearer but I was punch-drunk and inaccurate. He responded with a blow that sent me flying backwards against a plant pot. I cracked my head and entered the blackout zone.

The next thing I remember is the view from the hospital bed. Thankfully, a night of spot checks convinced the medics there was no potential for long-term damage.

So I was discharged, and returned to the hotel to find that all the lads were out at a function. The peace and quiet of my hotel room was disturbed by a knock on the door. An unfamiliar journalist was standing there. "Is it true you had a fight with Shearer?" he asked. I slammed the door in his face.

A few minutes later, there was another knock. This time, it was Shearer and Rob Lee. Peace was restored before they had even come inside. We ended up laughing about it, although we knew a media storm was inevitable. Which was fair enough really. What else do you expect when the England captain knocks out a team-mate in broad daylight?

Tales of my wild boy reputation were filling newspapers again. It didn't help that I'd been involved in another incident in a hotel in Whickham a few weeks previously, another case of some arsehole having a go, words being exchanged, a scuffle ensuing, and the aggressor pressing charges by claiming that I'd attacked him. It came to nothing, but the damage was done.

One newspaper wrote that I'd been told by the club to curb my drinking or else I was out the door. No such discussion took place, and no fines were handed out after Dublin either. Perhaps I was fortunate that Shearer was the other player involved. They couldn't have punished me without punishing him and he was so important that I'm sure they wanted to avoid going down that road.

The stuff in the press pissed me off. Others got off lightly. Take the second night of the Irish trip. Stuart Pearce was the most senior player of a group that tossed a traffic cone through the windscreen of an innocent motorist's car. Pearce handed over the money to pay for the damage there and then, and somehow managed to come out of the incident smelling of roses. They said he had taken control of the situation quickly.

Pearce loved his image, the whole 'Psycho' nickname that portrayed him as a real tough guy. I thought it was nonsense. He never intimidated me when he was a Nottingham Forest player, and I thought a lot of the fist pumping stuff was for show. My view didn't change when he became a team-mate.

One incident springs to mind. We had moved training ground to Chester-le-Street and the fans were allowed to come in and watch open sessions. A big crowd showed up one day, so 'Psycho' was out, desperate to show everyone that he cared. He started bollocking me in a training game, and flipping at the slightest of errors. "Move about, you Irish fucker," he barked. I'd had enough of the posturing and decided to react in full voice. "Stop trying to give it to people to look like a fucking big man!" He looked surprised and backed off. Funnily enough, he barely said a cross word to me afterwards.

The up and down nature of that season was summed up by

the fact that we managed to make the FA Cup final despite our awful finish in the league table. My own rollercoaster year was rounded off by missing the bloody game.

I'd missed the quarter-final win over Barnsley because of the head wound from Dublin, but Dalglish called me in for the semi with Sheffield United at Old Trafford where Shearer came up trumps on a fun afternoon. My friends and family were thrilled and booked trips for the big day. Arsenal, the champions elect, would be our opponents.

Disaster struck in a meaningless league match at Tottenham. The awkward thing about White Hart Lane was that the pitch slopes down to a path that goes around the playing area. If you were near the endline, there was always a chance of a nasty fall. I came off the bench and was chasing a nothing ball when Colin Calderwood needlessly shoved me over. My left foot landed on the edge of the slope and it turned as I slid down. I was in agony, and my first thought was Wembley.

There was a boost when nothing showed up on the x-ray machine and, considering it was three weeks until the game, the doctors reckoned I would be fine. But the pain remained. It was still there when we travelled to London on the Wednesday of cup final week, and I failed a fitness test after just two minutes when I attempted a block tackle. Any kind of contact was painful. The physios were mystified. I was devastated.

Darren Peacock was in the same boat, and we were like the invisible men for the rest of the build-up. It was hard to be around the hotel.

We pottered around the dressing room beforehand wishing everyone luck, but I struggled to put a brave face on it. The game made it worse.

A defender, Warren Barton, was moved to the right wing because we were so stretched. Arsenal won 2-0.

I sat high in the stands having a few beers with Darren, and wondered if I would get another chance to play in this arena. That old Talking Heads song from Dublin came back into my head. The title is sadly appropriate – 'Once In A Lifetime'. My only shot at a Wembley cup final had passed me by.

(14)

Matter Of Trust

IT took me too long to figure out there are very few people you can trust in football.

Perhaps that came from spending the early days with clubs who were competing at the top end of the table. Ferguson and Keegan both had the power to hand out long contracts, and life for the talented younger players was relatively stress-free. It probably gave me an idealistic view of the game.

The illusion was shattered when I reported back for pre-season at Newcastle in the summer of 1998. There was a significant difference in my situation compared to before. I had just one year remaining on my contract and, instantly, the vibe towards me was different.

The club offered a four-year contract on just over £7,500 a week. Good money, but there was a number of first teamers on more than £10,000 and I didn't want to be earning less than the lads around me. Ian was negotiating on my behalf but the Newcastle hierarchy refused to budge.

I sensed there was something going on. The Bosman ruling had changed the landscape of football transfers because the new law stated that I could just stay for the season and leave on a free at the end of it. Newcastle had to make an attractive offer to stop that scenario developing. The alternative was cashing in.

Towards the end of July, Ian rang to say that Middlesbrough had made an offer of £3.5 million and it had been accepted. Boro were managed by Bryan Robson and were offering £10,000. The combination of a good wage and the chance to work with a man I idolised sounded attractive. I spoke to Robbo and liked what I was hearing. In fact, negotiations went so well that Boro released a statement saying that the deal was done pending the completion of a medical. Ironically, Newcastle were in Middlesbrough for a pre-season tournament and Dalglish was asked about the move. I hadn't spoken to the gaffer, and he indicated to the press that he was in the dark about developments, which I found strange.

There was one catch. I was still feeling the problem that kept me out of Wembley. It wasn't excruciating, but I was conscious it was there as the Boro medical staff examined me. The next day, Robbo rang with shattering news. The MRI scan from my medical had revealed that I had broken my talus bone in my ankle, which transmits the body weight to the foot. I was furious that it took the work of another club to reveal the cause of my ongoing pain. It was an unusual injury, and a costly one. Robbo was apologetic. "I'm sorry Keith, but we can't risk signing an injured player for that amount of money."

I called Dalglish to tell him the bad news. "That's not bad news to me," he said, "you're still in my plans." That gave me a certain piece of mind, but the calm was disturbed two days later when the back page of the Newcastle Evening Chronicle splashed with the revelation that my career was in doubt. Nobody had thought about telling me, and I was straight on the phone to the medical staff. They seemed confused by the story, and called me down to the club to allay any fears. A meeting was organised with a specialist who said that while it was a complicated bone to break, the healing process would be relatively straightforward for a healthy 23-year-old.

I was suspicious as none of this information tallied with the Chronicle story. Soon, it all made sense. With the Middlesbrough deal collapsing my contract situation was an issue again, and Freddie Fletcher and Freddy Shepherd contacted Ian with drastically revised terms. They had reduced the offer to a one-year deal, citing the Chronicle story as evidence that I should be grateful for the guaranteed wage, given the question marks over my future. Ian spoke to a contact at the Chronicle who tipped him off that the info for the story had come from Fletcher. I was raging. Not only was it an attempt to trick me into signing a bum deal; it was also a story that would scare away prospective buyers.

I wanted Fletcher to know I was onto him and didn't have to wait too long. He arrived in the car park with Shepherd as I was getting treated in the physio room so I made my way towards the entrance so they'd have to walk past. I greeted Shepherd, and then Fletcher held out his hand. "Fuck off," I said. He said nothing in response and must have known why I was angry because Shepherd, who was now club chairman, called me in for a meeting to apologise on Fletcher's behalf. The coward couldn't face doing it himself.

That episode hastened my departure from the club. I was fine with Dalglish, but he was no longer making the decisions. The writing was on the wall when players were effectively being sold behind his back. Two games into the season, he was gone.

The board had another big name in mind, and Ruud Gullit rolled in the door, the man I was privileged to share a pitch with two years previously. It was an exciting appointment. A Dutch legend preaching a message of sexy football was just what the Newcastle crowd missing the excitement of the Keegan years wanted to hear.

I was still on the recovery trail when Liverpool thrashed us 4-1 in his first match in charge but, by coincidence, I bumped into him in a restaurant in town that night. He asked me into the corridor for a word, and spoke about his plans for a 4-4-2 formation with two out and out wingers. It sounded promising, but it was bullshit. When I was fit again, the bench beckoned, and Gullit suddenly wasn't in the mood to talk any more. His team weren't exactly playing sexy football either.

He was the classic case of a manager living off the reputation of his playing days. It was difficult to warm to Ruud because of his arrogance. On a good day, he would strut around the place like he was responsible, yet when the team got into trouble he seemed unable to react. There was no shouting or roaring. He just didn't have the ability to grasp why players would make the kind of mistakes that he never did in his pomp. Without that understanding, he was a terrible motivator. He rarely spoke to us individually and, when he did, it seemed as though he was looking through you. Keegan made you want to play for him. Gullit struggled to inspire anybody, and seemed happier alienating people, even if it was a key player like Shearer, which ultimately cost him his job.

His number two, Steve Clarke, was a dour character. The longest conversation I had with Steve was in December when he called to say that a bid from Blackburn was accepted. I'd played a bit in the previous month despite persistent speculation about my future with the contract running out. I was linked with Everton as part of the deal which brought Duncan Ferguson to the club, but nothing came of that and I actually put in the cross for one of his debut goals against Wimbledon. I broke my toe in a 2-2 draw at Middlesbrough at the beginning of December, and that was the end of my Newcastle career.

Blackburn's interest was unsurprising. Brian Kidd had taken over as manager, and Gaz Neville rang to say they would be making an approach. Newcastle were happy with a fee of £2.3 million, and I was satisfied with a four-and-a-half-year deal worth £11,000 a week in the first year – rising to £14,000 in my final 12 months. A signing on fee of £850,000 broken into five instalments was an additional sweetener.

Moving was a no-brainer. Newcastle will always be close to my heart, but the messing around with the contract taught me a lesson about loyalty. I had to be selfish and look after number one.

My learning curve didn't stop there. I say that I had to look after number one, but footballers rarely do the actual minding. Agents do. Ian handled my tax, insurance and all the other bills. He also became the first person to steer me towards some investments. I liked Ian's company, and thought we were mates.

Agents make their money from transfers. My arrangement with Ian was that he would get two per cent of the value of my contract, which was roughly £75,000 when the various elements of the Blackburn deal were calculated. I would have paid it too until I studied the first payslip from my new employers. It detailed transactions arising from my move and one line jumped off the page. 'Fee paid to agent: £100,000.' I was liable for the tax on the figure, because the statement implied they had paid the £100,000 on my behalf.

I waited to see if Ian would mention it. But he said nothing, and billed me separately for his £75,000. I couldn't be sure about what had happened, but it didn't look good. I was staggered, especially as the move had nothing to do with his legwork. It was me who notified him of their interest after the chat with Gaz. All Ian did was drive down and iron out the terms. For his troubles, he had appeared to collect £100,000 from the club, and now he wanted another £75,000 from me.

I deliberated over my next move. I felt that I couldn't trust him any longer, but I had to decide how to go about it. A confrontation didn't appeal to me so, instead, I rang to say that I would be coming to Whickham to collect any documentation in my name, making the excuse that I wanted all my papers in Lancashire in case something cropped up at short notice. A week later, I made the trip, kept the small talk to a minimum, got what I needed, and never spoke to him again.

It turned out to be a lucky break, for otherwise I might never have encountered Phil Munnelly. I was looking for a replacement agent and Darren Peacock – who had moved from

Newcastle to Blackburn six months earlier – recommended Phil, a London-based businessman with an Irish family background. He had fallen into the game by accident. Phil owned a construction company and was a sponsor at QPR. A couple of the players got to know him and asked if he could help with their contracts. It spiralled from there, and he ended up with over 20 lads from various clubs on his books. Darren was one of the first on board, and promised I could trust Phil. He set up a meeting and we hit it off on the right note.

One of the first things he managed to do was clear up Ian's mess. For a while, it looked as though I'd be landed with a £40,000 tax bill for the £100,000 fee, but Phil took control of the situation. Ian had been making threats about the £75,000 when I started blanking his calls so Phil did his homework, went to Newcastle, and made it clear he wouldn't be receiving another penny. Ian backed off and turned his attention to other clients, including Stewart Downing. In 2012 Ian was prosecuted for the way he handled Downing's financial affairs. I just wish I had met Phil earlier.

Of course, in hindsight, everyone would make better decisions. Brian Kidd thought leaving a comfortable job at Manchester United to be the main man at Blackburn was the correct call. Wrong.

Kiddo inherited a tough situation. The club were in the relegation zone when he took over from Roy Hodgson, and the owner Jack Walker had committed money to buying our way out of trouble. Matt Jansen, Ashley Ward, Jason McAteer and Lee Carsley were also brought into an already crowded dressing room. Kiddo collected the Manager of the Month award for December following a decent start, but it only delivered false hope.

Kiddo struggled to cope with the definition of his role. At Manchester United, he was always first onto the training ground, laying out cones and making meticulous plans for the day's session. As a manager, he tried to do all of that as well as the time consuming responsibilities of recruiting players, bartering with agents, and all the press duties. Other managers knew when to step back and let the coaches do their work, but Kiddo was more comfortable in a tracksuit than a suit. He brought Brian McClair with him as assistant, and the lads dubbed him 'BBC' standing for Bibs, Balls & Cones because carrying them around was the height of his responsibility. Kiddo wanted to do too much.

Still, I maintain the biggest problem he encountered was a lack of fight in the dressing room. We had the quality to be competitive higher up the table, but didn't have the application. Some members of Dalglish's '94/95 title-winning side were still around the place. There were contrasting attitudes. Jason Wilcox had a real passion for the club and cared about our position in the table. If every senior player had his attitude, then I don't think we'd have been in a relegation battle.

Chris Sutton was the top dog, though, a player with the ability to turn our fortunes around. But he spent most of the season injured and when he came back, his attitude towards Kiddo was poor. Sutton was an odd fish. He seemed decent one-to-one, but in a group he was an annoying show-off, picking on people who he wouldn't say a word to otherwise. Everyone should have been fighting for their lives, but Sutton knew he was going to be in the Premier League the next season whatever happened and didn't contribute enough. Young Kevin Davies was struggling under the weight of a big price tag and was taken out of the firing line; Kiddo needed Sutton at his best to give us an outlet up front. He didn't get it.

I have to admit that I could have done better too. My form was inconsistent. We were all making mistakes, stupid errors in games we should have won. With six games left and survival possible, we led 3-1 at Southampton and conceded twice to end up with just a point. We could only manage one draw from our next three games, which meant we had to win our penultimate game of the season or else it was relegation time. And the task was made harder by the identity of the visitors. With Kiddo's history, it just had to be Manchester United.

It was an awkward one for Kiddo, with United a couple of weeks away from completing a historic treble through that comeback against Bayern Munich at the Nou Camp. Later that summer Fergie released his first autobiography, in which he was very harsh on Kiddo, saying that he was too complex and insecure to manage a top club. I believe there was some tension between them towards the end of their time together, but I couldn't understand why Fergie was so nasty in the book. Maybe he was sour that Kiddo upped and left, because he'd been an important part of their success and remained popular with the players.

United were cagey that night, and below their best, but we still couldn't break them down. It finished scoreless, and our fate was sealed. There was an air of disbelief in the dressing room, and some were more upset than others. Sutton, who would join Chelsea for £10 million, wasn't too fussed. Jack Walker was in tears.

That season was an education, a reminder of how rare senti-ment is in football. I was hurt when I was booed on my return to St James' in the FA Cup. Maybe if the fans had known the full story about Fletcher it would have been different, although in Newcastle they are so fanatical about the club that it's almost like a cult. They couldn't understand why someone would ever want to leave.

I had realised, however, that everything isn't always black and white.

(15)

Temptation

I WAS always shy when it came to approaching girls, so football was the right profession for me. It's a world where you don't have to work very hard to succeed. The girls come to you.

Newcastle really opened my eyes. Picking up girls was easy. The formula was simple. Head for the usual spot in Julies night-club, relax, have a drink and wait for the offers to come. It was common knowledge that the players always went there and our corner always attracted attention. Geordie girls have a reputation for being quite up front and straightforward, so there was no bullshit.

They'd come up, strike a discussion and, in no time, you've pulled them. The tactical types might start off by looking for you to sign something for a family member, or pose for a photo, and it would go from there. Others were more direct. After a few minutes chatting, I knew they'd be coming home with me.

I don't know how many girls there were, although I'm not saying I pulled every night.

There were times when I just wanted to chill, and I've always had this thing about staying until closing time anyway, paranoid that I might miss something good. But the option was always there, a perk of the job. It was perfectly normal to have girls throwing themselves at you. That's not a boast. It just goes with the territory.

Monday mornings in training were always the same. A time to compare stories.

"Out the weekend?

"Yeah."

"Doing a bit?

"Yeah – had a girl back."

Simple as that. And the dressing room code made sure that certain tales always stayed in-house. The lads rarely brought their other halves to Julies, and it was a bit like what goes on tour, stays on tour in there. I got up to things that I shouldn't have. Temptation was hard to resist.

It is true that footballers who stay faithful are a rare breed. Personally, I can't say that I've encountered many. I heard a story recently about a player who had never cheated until he slipped up on a trip to Asia. He was so overcome with guilt that he told his missus and she smacked him across the head with a saucepan. There was no sympathy for him when the other lads at his club enquired about his substantial bruise. "Why did you bloody tell her?" She might have told the other wives and that would make them curious about what the others were up to. Nobody was going to put an arm around his shoulder and ask what this meant for his relationship.

I'm not trying to defend anyone's actions here, and I'm certainly not looking for sympathy. Footballers have a reputation for a reason. But I don't think anybody can be too high and mighty about what they would or wouldn't do unless they have been repeatedly put in a situation where attractive girls are offering themselves up to you. Serious willpower was needed to stay onside, and I didn't have that strength.

It's remarkable what you can get away with.

I remember playing with a guy who was so hooked on prostitutes that his missus got wind of it and they agreed he would go and see a sex therapist. The 'expert' reckoned that he was just addicted to paying for it, and recommended that he started financially rewarding his wife for sexual favours. Strange advice, but they went with it. A month later, the player rang his agent. "I'm bloody broke," he said. And so he went back to the prostitutes.

It's a different world, and there's always enough people around to make allowances for your behaviour. The boundaries are pushed out. I can't say I did anything too extreme, but I wound up in a few strange scenarios. Like getting padlocked in a student flat by a crazed girl who simply wouldn't let me leave until she got what she wanted. Or sneaking into an upstairs bedroom with the daughter of a Manchester United legend while her Dad was out at a wedding. A pal of mine claims I brought two girls back to a hotel room while he pretended to be asleep in the double bed next to us. Drink was involved, and his recollection of the story is entirely different to mine; I think I'd remember a threesome. But I do recall the girls being up for coming back. Some women wanted footballers so much that they didn't care about the consequences.

The stand-out example came in my final months in New-castle. I'd gone for a drink with Ian when it looked as though the Middlesbrough move was on track. He buggered off and I wound up talking to a couple of girls who happened to also live in Whickham. We shared a cab home and dropped the first girl off. Her friend, who seemed a good bit older, immediately invited me back to hers, and it was obvious what was on the agenda. We headed straight for the bedroom and were getting down to business when I thought I'd heard the front door open downstairs.

"What's that?" I said. A look of panic crossed her face.

"It's my boyfriend!"

Her boyfriend? She'd never mentioned him. I made a break for the nearest door and entered a room where the presence of empty bunkbeds suggested that children also lived in this house. I climbed onto the top bunk and pretended to be asleep, conscious that a pair of large feet appeared to be stomping up the stairs. The door opened. There he was. A Geordie, comfortably taller than six foot, marched in.

Think on the spot time. I did a pretty poor job of pretending that he'd just woken me up, rubbing my eyes and producing a fake groan as he turned the light on. The brightness alerted me to the walls, which were covered with Newcastle United posters, and the centrepiece was a team shot with my mug right in the middle. The man of the house squinted and produced a facial expression that combined anger and amazement.

"Fucking 'ell, it's fucking Keith Gillespie," he said, in a thick North-East accent. "Have you been shagging wor lass?"

I jumped down to the floor and pleaded innocence. "No,

no, of course we weren't, don't be stupid." But my flustered demeanour gave the game away. Hero worship was out of the question here. A signed jersey wasn't gonna make this any better. He swung a fist, I retaliated, and all of a sudden it was like a fight scene from a Steven Seagal movie. We ended up grappling on the floor, and rolling down the stairs in a ball, raining punches at each other, while his bird screamed at us to stop. He'd obviously brought the kids home as well, as there were two little boys standing there watching too, just to make the situation that little bit worse. They were probably wondering why Daddy was fighting with the man from the poster. The saving grace was that he'd left the front door open. I wrestled free and ran for freedom.

Garry Flitcroft, my captain at Blackburn, loved that story. I scored a goal at Ewood Park once and he leapt on me in the celebrations screaming "have you been shagging wor lass?" in my ear. I always enjoyed Garry's company, but he learned the hard way about getting involved with the wrong girl. He slept with a bird who, he said, started blackmailing him, saying she'd go to the press unless he gave her money towards a boob job.

Garry was married with a kid, and he was totally freaked when this woman sent a parcel to his mother's house with evidence of their affair. He said another girl was looking for a few quid to stop her from going to the papers as well. It was an awful time for Flitty, and the shit hit the fan in 2002 when he found out that he was going to be exposed in one of the Sunday papers.

We had an away game at Leicester and got wind that a crowd of photographers were waiting to catch him coming off the team bus. The lads decided to do something because, deep down, we knew it could have been any of us in this situation. So we all agreed to put our tracksuit tops over our heads so they wouldn't be able to figure out which one was him, a ploy that worked a treat. As it happened, the Queen Mother was unwell at the time, and one of the boys remarked that the only way Flitty would escape the front page was if she died. He was bloody right as well. She passed away, and his infidelity was relegated in prominence.

Still, the entire episode had a major effect on his family. Flitty was convinced that his father, who suffered from depression and tragically committed suicide years later, never fully got over the negative attention that followed the revelations. The poor man stopped attending his games, unable to cope with some of the abuse that his son was getting. Flitty thought it was fishy how the tabloids had tracked down the women, and ended up giving evidence in the Leveson inquiry. Something didn't add up at the time. There's a dark side to the glamour, as I would later learn.

I never got stung by a kiss and tell. Being honest, I don't think I was high profile enough when I was up to it regularly. The girls in Newcastle didn't seem to be motivated by that anyway. They were happy to just get hold of a footballer; I'd see old conquests on other nights out, and there was never any hassle. Just a knowing nod. Maybe it was different for the lads down south, where the girls might have had different motivations. London is a different scene, full of girls who are intent on becoming famous through whatever means. They target footballers, and the high profile lads now have to be so careful. With camera phones and social media, it's hard to get away with anything. Even an innocent photo can be spun into an incriminating story. It used to be easier to get away with messing around, although I don't think it's going to stop anybody. Boys will be boys. When it's on a plate, there will always be takers.

With the lifestyle I led, getting married was a crazy idea, but that's exactly what I did on June 14, 1999, on the Caribbean island of St Lucia, in front of an attendance that consisted of my fiancee's best mate and her boyfriend, a pair of photographers from OK magazine, and two random couples from Manchester who I'd met on the beach a few days earlier. That was it. No family. Why? It saved me the hassle of public speaking. The prospect of it terrified me. My wife-to-be, Frances Reay, felt the same way, a rare example of us totally agreeing on something. From the moment we met, ours was a fiery relationship. An ominous sign of things to come.

I first set eyes on her at a joint engagement party for Steve Watson and Lee Clark in the Gosforth Park Hotel in February, 1996, just after the fall-out from Black Friday.

I instantly spotted the small, attractive, blonde girl across the bar, and made it my business to wander close enough so we'd have to start a discussion. She was 18, a local girl, and worked with Lee's missus, Lorraine, in a clothes shop in town called Life. I'd just turned 21, and had never really had a serious girl-friend before.

We clicked, she gave me her number, I called the next day, a date was arranged, and it quickly escalated from there.

A year later, we were engaged, even though we'd already broken up a few times and reunited. It was usually over nothing, immature stuff, arguing for the sake of it. Her parents were separated and she'd lived with her father before coming to live with me for a while when things got serious. We rowed even more then. I'd disappear out with the lads and wouldn't come home – she'd lose the plot, and return to her Dad's. But Frances loved her nights in Newcastle, and drink has a habit of bringing people back together. It was a small town when you knew where to go, and on the Sunday night crawl we always seemed to bump into each other at the last stop. If I was at home, I might receive a call asking if I could pick her up, and all would be forgiven.

And when things were good, they were very good.

She wasn't stupid. Frances spent a lot of time around footballers, and knew their habits. Heck, I might be out with her, and girls would still come up and try their luck, so her eyes were open to what was going on. But we were in love, a fiery kind of love, and believed that marriage was the natural step to security. It was a decision rather than a spur of the moment thing. I didn't get down on bended knee. We talked about it in the house one evening, and decided it was the way forward. I know Alex Ferguson encouraged his lads to get married early, but there was nobody at Newcastle advising me to settle down. This was our call.

I went out to splash £5,000 on an engagement ring, and we made it official, even though it was stop-start right up until we left Newcastle and moved to Blackburn in December, 1998. The wedding was set for the following summer, and we were determined to do it our way. A Caribbean holiday sounded good, but the real paradise for me was avoiding the traditional big day with the pressure to speak and entertain.

My family was down the list of concerns. There was no tension over Mum and Dad's divorce because they remained on speaking terms. In fact, by complete coincidence, Dad was remarrying 10 days later, and my sister Angela was getting married a week after that. But I didn't use the wedding congestion as an excuse for inviting nobody. I'm sure they would have liked to be there, especially Mum, but I was in my own, selfish zone. This suited me, and that was all that mattered. All Frances wanted was her mate Michelle to be there, and she brought her boyfriend along, a Welsh lad called Johnno who was good company. The one thing we did want to get for our families was good photos, and that's how the OK magazine deal came about. Phil spoke to them, and they were given exclusive access in return for giving us the pictures to keep. We didn't receive a penny.

Our beachside hotel, Sandals, offered the whole wedding package. When you walked down the steps from the main building, you turned left for the sunbeds, and right for the marriage area. Local laws said we had to be in the country six days before the service, and we saw other couples enjoy their special moment as we lay enjoying the sun. I was recognised by two boys from Manchester, big United fans, and we told them to bring their girlfriends along for our turn. They joined Michelle and Johnno in the seats as I stood at a makeshift altar, waiting for Frances to make her grand entrance down the stairs. I'd be lying if I said it was a dream ceremony. The lady Reverend kept telling me to look at Frances as I repeated the vows, but the sea breeze made it almost impossible to hear. I needed to train my eyes on the Reverend to lip read what she was saying, so it wound up being a bit of a struggle. Fitting really, given how the marriage turned out. Half an hour later, we were pronounced man and wife. I rang Mum to let her know it was done, and then moved to the beach for the photographs. Then, we went for a low-key meal and that was it.

Our honeymoon was already underway. Part of the package was another week in the Caribbean before heading for home. It was a peaceful time, a stress-free seven days for a 24-year-old lad and a 21-year-old girl who had promised to spend the rest of their lives together. We really believed it too.

It was the calm before the storm.

16

A Winner

GRAEME Souness walks into the canteen wearing just a towel around his waist and a pair of smart, black suit shoes. He puffs his bare chest out and sits down to tuck into lunch. We knew our new manager was a vain man, but this is taking it to the extreme.

I turn to one of the lads. "If he had the time to put on his shoes, why didn't he just put the suit on?" There is no answer. Souness was frequently a mystery to us.

He arrived in March 2000. Our promotion ambitions had long since disappeared, even though we had the most expensive squad in the division. We were sixth from bottom with just three wins to our name when Kiddo was sacked in November. Jack Walker made the decision and then came into the dressing room to tear us to pieces, pointing out a nice man like Kiddo deserved better. It was a strange thing for the owner to say considering he'd just booted him out after only a year in charge, but I did feel guilty. Although I was injured for the start of the season, I wasn't offering much to the team. Just two years after the Barcelona dream, I was playing at places like Stockport and Crewe, and struggling for motivation.

Tony Parkes stepped in temporarily, a nice man better suited to being an assistant manager. It was his fifth time as caretaker, and the lads knew he wouldn't be getting the role full-time, so he didn't command much respect. Tony didn't have the personality to give anyone a bollocking or stamp his authority. Players need that kick up the arse, to be afraid of underperforming. But the club were basically writing the season off as a bad debt by keeping Tony in charge for almost four months. There was a casual attitude around the place.

Then Souness rolled in, another Liverpool great that I had bad memories of from childhood. It was difficult to forget his success at Liverpool because he never stopped talking about it. We all respected his record but there's only so many times you can hear the story of how he won the European Cup.

The only positive thing about hearing one of those stories is that at least it meant he was talking to you. That wasn't always the case. My four-and-a-half-year stint at Blackburn is the longest I spent at any club in my career, which surprises people given that I'm generally associated with Manchester United or Newcastle.

The confusion probably stems from the fact that I was exiled for a large chunk of my time there. Weeks and months passed without much happening. I trained during the week with no game on Saturday to aim towards. So, I didn't look forward to training very much. During Souness' first year in charge, I may as well not have been there.

At first, my exclusion seemed logical. The gaffer said that with promotion a lost cause, he wanted to have a look at younger lads or those coming towards the end of their contracts. His tune had changed by the summer, a time of change at the club after Jack Walker passed away with lung cancer. Graeme brought in some of his own players and said that I simply wasn't in his plans. Sunderland talked about making a bid, but nothing came to pass, so I continued with a club where I wasn't wanted and accepted rejection instead of questioning it. Seeking out a meeting with the manager was rarely my style, and Souness didn't seem the most approachable person anyway. He blanked me every time we passed in the corridor. So, I adapted to the role of invisible man and reserve-team footballer.

Souness did put me on the bench for the opening game of the season, but I soon got used to the situation where I was included in a squad and then didn't even get a place on the bench. In October 2000, we stayed over in London between away games with Fulham and Wimbledon. The boys were struggling and the gaffer was under serious scrutiny. Myself, Egil Ostenstad, Jason McAteer and Marlon Broomes were confined to the stands at Fulham so we found a lounge in Craven Cottage and went on the piss. I finally knew how Neil Webb felt at Middlesbrough all those years earlier. By the end of the game – which Fulham won – I'd drunk nine bottles of beer and three Red Bulls. We kept on sinking the drinks, not realising the rest of the lads were waiting for us on the bus. Souness said nothing when we showed up looking worse for wear.

Remarkably, when we got back to base at Richmond, he gave

us permission to hit the town. I ended up in the hotel residents' bar at 7.30am with our assistant manager Phil Boersma, a Scouser who enjoyed his drink and could usually hold it quite well. This was an exception, and I had to carry Boey up to his room where he bounced off the wardrobe and the wall before falling face down on his duvet. There was no sign of him when I made it up for training at 9.30am. The masseur had gone in to wake him, but all Boey could do was sit up in bed before falling straight back down again. In his absence, Souness had to step in and bark the orders. We could see he was in a temper on the bus afterwards, and suddenly our whereabouts at Craven Cottage were top of the agenda. He came charging down to ask the Fulham Four where we'd watched the game and how many drinks we had taken. Jason, Egil, and Marlon all said they'd had one drink. I tried to make my story more credible and failed. "Five," I replied. "One before, three at half-time, and one afterwards."

I don't really know why I thought that saying I had crammed three drinks into 15 minutes sounded any better. Souness wasn't happy either way. "If you need that much drink at that time of the day, you need help," he shouted.

His mood improved when he selected a side to win at Wimbledon, the first of six victories in a row. It was a turning point for his team, but not for me. As a punishment for London, I was banished. Phil had a contact at Wigan and arranged for me to go there on loan. They had changed as a club, with a new stadium and a well-known manager in Bruce Rioch suggesting they had ambitions. But I was only passing through really, and didn't make that much of an impact, although apparently the Christmas party was good. I don't remember much of it.

It was a boozy time in my life, and relations with Frances were deteriorating. I hit the bottle hard when I returned to Blackburn to continue my exile. There were two young Northern Irish lads in the reserves, Gary Hamilton and Steven Hawe, and I preferred drinking with them than going home to the missus. Sometimes, I didn't arrive home at all.

I took up smoking as well. Just like that. Another impulsive decision. It had never interested me until Gary handed me one on a night out, and for some reason, it developed from a social habit into a regular part of life. Anything to relieve the boredom.

Souness called me into his office on a Sunday morning in January. He liked to bring everyone for a warm down the day after the game, even if you weren't involved. It was a bit of a pain although we'd then get the Monday off. I was hungover after a typical Saturday night with the boys when he surprisingly acknowledged my presence and asked for a chat. He wanted to throw me into the side for the FA Cup tie at Derby.

"I'm giving you another chance," he said.

"I can't play, boss, I'm cup-tied. I played for Wigan in the second round."

"Oh..."

Luckily, this wasn't a one-time only offer. Something had changed. He never really told me why I was back in fashion again, especially with the team doing so well, but I didn't seek explanation and just got on with being a footballer again. I was brought on as a sub at Nottingham Forest and then started my first league game of the season at Watford on February 20. We came away with a win, and I was part of a side that was on the way back to the Premier League. The decisive three points came against fellow promotion contenders Birmingham in March. I made the first for Marcus Bent before Damien Duff added the clincher with a brilliant solo run. Souness was delighted afterwards, saying I'd set the tone with a crunching tackle on their left-back, Martin Grainger.

He was a nicer man to be around when we secured promotion and the pressure was off. Sure, the arrogance remained, and he never lost the fondness for striding topless around the training ground, but I actually grew to quite like him. I began to understand his personality a little bit more when we returned to the top flight.

I was in favour and satisfied with my contribution. I even scored against Manchester United in a cracking 2-2 draw, and hit the target again in a 3-3 at Arsenal. My reward was to be dropped for the visit of Leicester. I was shocked, but said nothing. The gaffer approached me. "Why did you not come and knock on my door and ask why you weren't playing?" I said I wasn't the confrontational type. He wanted me to show more desire. It was a test. I had failed it during the exile.

Souness had other opinions about my development as a player. Once he wasn't talking about his own glory days at Liverpool, he was insightful. He thought I had become too defensive for a wide player since I left Newcastle, and believed I was spending more time covering our full-backs instead of getting forward and giving their defenders problems. It was a fair criticism. He liked it when I was brave. That's what he asked of his players.

My abiding memory is a League Cup quarter-final against Arsenal at Ewood Park in December. For some reason, I always had the edge on their Dutch left-back, Giovanni van Bronckhorst, and this game was no exception. The gaffer was out of his technical area, roaring at me to get at him. So the next time I got a chance, I poked the ball ahead and burst down the wing. I felt van Bronckhorst's presence over my left shoulder, but I was also aware of someone over my right shoulder. Souness. He got so caught up in the moment that he was sprinting down the touchline shouting encouragement. The other boys thought it was hilarious.

At the end of December, Souness made a significant move in the transfer market. Almost seven years after we moved in opposite directions, I became team-mates with Andy Cole. He had won a lot of trophies at Manchester United, but had dropped down the pecking order since the arrival of Ruud van Nistelrooy. Andy arrived at Blackburn in time to help us win some silverware.

The Worthington Cup was the highlight of 2001/02 for the club. We thrashed Arsenal 4-0 on the night that I tormented van Bronckhorst, with Matt Jansen scoring a hat-trick. Matt was a terrific prospect who was destined for the top until a motorbike accident in Rome left him with injury problems that he never recovered from. He was brilliant that season, and Andy was signed to form an exciting partnership. It also strengthened the ex-United contingent in the dressing room. Even though he was almost 40, Mark Hughes had stayed on after being recruited to help us get promotion. Sparky could still cut it at the highest level in a new midfield role, and offered valuable leadership.

Although we were inconsistent in the league, it all came together when it mattered in a knockout format. We overcame Sheffield Wednesday in the semis to set up a decider with Spurs.

As Wembley was being rebuilt, we prepared for a trip to Cardiff's Millennium Stadium although there was no guarantee I would get to sample the atmosphere. Craig Hignett had been used at right midfield against Wednesday and was a key factor in the victory, and Souness had a big decision to make. Boey, who was always a big fan, approached me with good news on the Tuesday before the game and said, "I've got you a start next Sunday." For this final, my friends and family wouldn't be making a wasted trip.

With the roof closed because of the lashing rain, there was a terrific atmosphere in the stadium. It was Blackburn's first cup final in 42 years, and Spurs were the hot favourites. Souness had us well prepared though, with Sparky a key presence in the centre of the park. Matty was a handful up top, and put us ahead after my deflected shot fell into his direction. Christian Ziege levelled for Spurs before half-time, but we responded with Andy showing he still had the magic touch by striking the winner. Craig replaced me with 15 minutes left so I watched injury time from the sidelines, and invaded the pitch with the rest of the staff when we heard the sweet sound of the referee's whistle. I felt like I was on top of the world. A year after my return from the wilderness, I finally had a senior medal for the mantelpiece.

I grew to cherish it even more in the darker times that lay ahead.

17

Cashing In

I'M sitting in a room, surrounded by footballers, listening to a presentation that I don't quite understand.

We're in London, some time in 2001. A Scottish agent is addressing a group that includes internationals and Premier League stars.

The purpose of the gathering is a business proposal, and there's a lot of talk about investment schemes and loans and tax and details that I'm not really taking in. But my ears prick up when he tells us something that I do want to hear, the details of a plan that will give us a lot of money in a short space of time. And I like the sound of that.

I'd made the journey from Blackburn with Darren Peacock, who seemed more clued up on the whole thing. Tony Grew, a well known figure within football, knew about the idea.

Tony worked in association with the PFA on pensions and other matters, and he was my financial advisor at that time.

While I was reckless with my gambling, I wasn't totally ridiculous when I was earning the big bucks at Blackburn. Tony sat me down and convinced me to invest a portion of my monthly take-home in bonds and a few other things. Good advice. In fact, he tried hard to increase my contributions so it would limit my betting but, considering I was betting on credit, there wasn't much he could do to totally curb my behaviour.

Tony had become aware of a scheme that was growing popular in football circles. Essentially, it was buying into film syndicates. These syndicates provided the capital for production companies to make movies and TV series – although there were layers of legal people and financial institutions that acted as the conduit between A and B, all of which were charging major commission for their input.

That was about as much as I knew, but Darren and his wife, Simone, had done some research and seemed to think it could be lucrative. The purpose of the trip was to learn about the finer points. Phil was invited too, but he seemed to think there was nothing in it for him because he wasn't generating enough income to get involved.

And that was the kicker, here. I gathered that the people who were behind the financing of these film syndicates wanted footballers because we raked in high income. And, in return for committing to the scheme, we could immediately get some cash back – in the form of tax relief.

So, this is what led me to the meeting. The agent wasn't running the project, but he understood it. There was a Scottish company behind it, a legal firm called Scotts. Some of what was said registered. Essentially, the fact we commanded a huge salary meant we could be returned tax by creating trading losses in film investments. With my permission, a loan would be registered in my name from Sovereign Finance [a subsidiary of Alliance & Leicester – now Santander Bank UK]. I'd never see the money, but it would appear in my personal accounts. In my case, the loan was just over £1.3 million.

How would I pay it back? Well, apparently, an income stream from this syndicate would pop up in my account from 2006 – for the following 10 years – although I'd never see that money either. A different bank had a charge on that income as security for my original loan. There was a bit of interest involved and some commission but that was to be expected. I didn't have to worry about any of the paperwork.

The bottom line for me was that the £1.3 million I invested became a trading loss and as such qualified me for tax relief set against my income of the previous two years. I totted the sums in my head. £500,000. Half a million quid! Yes!

Now, there were people talking about investing that money properly, doing the right thing with it because five years down the line, we'd start to get taxed on this income stream that was paying off the loan. Blah, blah, blah. On our wages, there was nothing we couldn't afford and, besides, there was also a possible dividend if the movies we financed turned out to be successful.

But that was all long-term talk. This was half a million quid, in my account, once I joined up.

I could spend 50k on that new kitchen Frances had been going on about, divert some of the cash for Tony to invest and then use the balance to top up the betting kitty.

Other lads I spoke to were thinking in similar terms. We hardly gave the small print a second thought. There was only one question dominating the minds of everyone in that room.

'Where do I sign?'

The road to bankruptcy started here.

(18)

Beyond A Joke

ATHENS, October 2003. A visiting Northern Ireland fan sprints onto the pitch before a European Championship qualifier and blasts a plastic football into the back of the net. The travelling support go crazy. They always had the best sense of humour.

We knew what the gag was. The national football team of Northern Ireland had failed to score a goal in 12 games, a run that stretched back a period of 20 months. The invader wanted to inspire us, but he failed. Greece scored the only goal to qualify for Euro 2004, a competition they would go on to win. Our performance that night was respectable in its own right, but the statistics across the whole campaign made for miserable reading.

Two years without a win. Bottom of the group with a big fat

zero in the 'goals for' column. Add in friendly failures for a grand total of 1,242 impotent minutes. Or 20 hours, if you like.

We had also lost a key player, Neil Lennon, who retired from international football because of sectarian death threats, an episode which just about summed up a time that was far removed from the happiness of my early days in the green jersey.

Bryan Hamilton was replaced in 1998 by Lawrie McMenemy, a 62-year-old Geordie who had enjoyed great success at Southampton in the late '70s and early '80s and later served as assistant to Graham Taylor in his disastrous spell as England manager. He was a shock appointment.

Joe Jordan came in as assistant and a local legend, Pat Jennings, was drafted in as goalkeeping coach. With our dressing room being run by an Englishman, a Scotsman and an Irishman, people wondered what the punchline was going to be. The team ended up being the joke.

I didn't get to know Lawrie too well. He seemed a nice man but would mostly spend his time ambling around the training pitch chatting on a mobile phone while Jordan did most of the work. Lawrie was from a different generation, and it really showed on his first trip away with the group. We had won a couple of friendly games in Belfast, before an end of season trip to Spain that I missed with my talus bone injury. After a 4-1 defeat, the lads embarked on a customary night out in Santander and were still in good spirits when they boarded the plane the following morning.

Gerry Taggart, who had scored our goal on the night, was always at the heart of the banter. Just after the food was served, Taggs pressed his call button and the air hostess came to his seat. "Is this supposed to be in this sandwich?" he asked. She looked down and Taggs had taken out his cock and placed it between two slices of bread. There was uproar but Lawrie didn't see the funny side, words were exchanged and he never picked Taggs again.

We missed him. Lawrie's first competitive game was away to Turkey, which was always a horrible place to visit. The changing rooms in Istanbul were downstairs and you'd have to wait for the riot police to surround the entrance before you could walk up or walk down or else you'd be pelted with objects. George O'Boyle was struck by a coin after the warm-up and was really dazed. I was in the firing line too, but immune to any pain as I'd taken a couple of Voltarol anti-inflammatory tablets for my first game in five months. Turkey ran out comfortable 3-0 winners, and our night got worse when we returned to find that our dressing room had been raided. They even took a pair of my underpants.

Taggs was such a mad-man that he probably would have revelled in that atmosphere. We just lacked a bit of steel in that campaign, the same toughness that had allowed us to pick up good results on our travels under Bryan. Lawrie wasn't a motivator and rarely showed any anger. I don't think he really had faith that we could be competitive. Home and away draws with Moldova put us out of the Euro 2000 race early. Germany and Turkey both knocked three past us at Windsor.

There's no fun getting beaten out of sight. I really have no idea how the boys who play for the likes of San Marino cope with going out trying to avoid a hammering in every match. It must be depressing. The only funny memory of that campaign is Barry Hunter with his trousers down, bunny-hopping through a bar in Dortmund with his cock tucked between his legs while confused locals looked on. I'm not sure if they knew that the bunch of lads in Northern Ireland tracksuits that were rolling around with laughter beside the pool table would actually be playing Germany a couple of days later. We lost 4-0 there, and then 4-1 to Finland in Lawrie's swansong. I'm glad to say I was absent for that game. It was an appropriate finish to a depressing chapter.

I have always believed that a national team should be managed by someone from that country so I was delighted when Sammy McIlroy landed the job. He was a hero of the '82 and '86 World Cups and understood the surroundings and expectations.

Sammy had the respect of the dressing room and made a positive start. He recalled Taggs and blooded young David Healy from Manchester United, a striker who scored twice on his debut in Luxembourg. We clicked on and off the pitch. Our mutual love of cards and gambling made us obvious mates.

We collected four points from the opening pair of World Cup 2002 qualifiers and should have taken a lot more in a campaign where luck abandoned us, especially when we battered a very good Czech Republic team at Windsor but somehow lost 1-0. They were hoofing the ball away at the end and hanging on for dear life. When we found our shooting boots and scored three in Bulgaria, the locals scored four.

Suspension ruled me out of the return with the Czechs. They won 3-1, although the game is remembered for very different reasons. I was bringing my car back from Belfast to Stranraer on the ferry when I flicked on the radio and heard that five of the lads had ended up in cells. They'd gone to a nightclub in Prague and weren't too happy with the bill. A row kicked off, a plant pot was thrown, and Glenn Ferguson, a real old school forward from the Irish League, kicked one of the bouncers. The reward for all concerned was a night in custody. My selfish, gut reaction was relief. I hung around with Healy, Glenn, and Michael Hughes who were all involved, and I definitely wouldn't have missed a night out with them. They were part of the group known as the Prague Five, but the gag in the dressing room was that it should have been the Prague Six.

There was a predictable public outcry, but Sammy knew that banning the nights out after games would have a negative response so he didn't get carried away in-house. We drew away to Denmark – who were top of the group – and he allowed us to celebrate. I had a few too many and was so smashed in Heathrow the following day that Sammy dragged me into the toilets to deliver a warning. He said the press had noticed my state and that it would become an issue if I didn't produce the goods against Iceland on the Wednesday. The little pep talk worked. I set up three goals, and the campaign finished on a positive note. We looked forward to the Euro 2004 qualifiers with optimism.

Cyprus came to Belfast for our final warm-up game in August 2002. Sammy confirmed at the start of the week that Neil Lennon would be taking the captain's armband.

Neil was popular in the group, although he had taken stick from some supporters at Windsor since his move to Celtic. With so many Northern Ireland fans having Rangers loyalties, he was never going to be their favourite person but it descended into something far more sinister than that.

We had our usual nap in the hotel before the game. I popped

down to reception after and knew from the looks on people's faces that something was up. Neil was gone. Death threats had been phoned through via the BBC and, after consulting with police, he would be taking no part in the game. He was so shaken up by the incident that he had quit Northern Ireland completely. Sammy called a meeting to explain the situation and, while we chose to go ahead with the game, I really don't think anyone was in the mood. It finished 0-0. Fitting, because there were no winners that day.

I've already outlined the dressing room attitude to matters of religion. There were plenty of harmless insults for the sake of banter but the bottom line was that nobody cared what side of the community the person sat next to them was from. What happened to Neil was completely wrong, especially at a time when the country seemed to be moving on. Catholics had worn the jersey during the height of the Troubles. Anton Rogan represented Northern Ireland as a Celtic player in darker days, and didn't receive half as much abuse as Neil did. So it was hard to stomach. He was a good man to have on your side, and I don't know how anyone who considered themselves a genuine Northern Ireland fan could have been happier without him.

I always enjoyed Neil's company and I've met him since but it's not something I've ever brought up in discussion. I try to steer clear of the political chat. But we understood his decision. Some idiots had also painted sick graffiti on a wall near his home and, when other members of his family were feeling threatened, then you had to respect the path he chose.

On a selfish level, we were short of top players and certainly couldn't afford to lose one of them. From there, we began the embarrassing journey to Greece. The strain was visible on

Sammy as the negative results stacked up. There were some good draws in there – holding Spain at Windsor stands out – but our inability to score became a saga and it reached the stage where the players weren't thinking about winning games. We just wanted to get a bloody goal.

Healy was still maturing and beyond that Sammy's striking options were so limited that he even had to use me up front in the Greek game. As much as we were always realistic about what was possible with a small group of players, going through an entire group without scoring was unacceptable. Sammy was in tears in the dressing room in Athens, and decided to pack it in for a job at Stockport.

I still remember Greece fondly, though, for one very simple reason. It was the occasion of my 50th cap and Sammy marked the occasion by awarding me the captaincy.

The other boys chipped together and presented me with some crystal on the night before the game. I was humbled by the gesture and decided that, whatever happened, I would keep hold of the jersey from that night. Some players always hold onto their shirts, but I always gave mine away. This was an exception, and I've got it framed in my house.

It's a proud memory from a grim time.

(19)

Rover And Out

WITHIN a year, I knew my marriage to Frances was doomed. In all honesty, the writing was probably on the wall inside a couple of weeks.

Even though I had a ring on my finger, the lifestyle remained the same. I wasn't ready to settle down and become the faithful husband who clocked in at home every night.

The absenteeism might have been less of an issue in Newcastle, where Frances had her own family and friends. But she didn't have those distractions in Blackburn, and found it difficult to make pals. Instead, she relied on me, spending her days waiting for her husband. I'd come back from training and want to relax when she was desperate to escape the house and go somewhere. And when evening came, I preferred to spend time with the boys.

She did become friendly with Darren's wife, Simone, and the four of us would often go for a meal together. Yet when I went out on a lads night with Darren and didn't return, Frances would ring Simone in the early hours to enquire about my whereabouts. When she heard Darren was home already, trouble beckoned. I'd eventually surface, either late that night or the following morning, and plunge headlong into another row.

I remember coming in with Gary Hamilton on a Sunday morning after a boozy Saturday night, getting changed to the sound of Frances' screams, and then heading straight out again. After we got promoted, I left home on Wednesday, and didn't get back until Friday. I always had an excuse. I'd met a friend, ended up at a party, and couldn't escape. Darren tells one about a time I got talking to a bloke in a bar and went back to Morecambe to have a look at his Harley Davidson. A great story, apart from the fact that I've never been to Morecambe, and have no interest in motorbikes. But that tale made it back somehow.

There were plenty of stories spun. Generally, I'd end up in the doghouse, and we'd continue as strangers in our own home, sitting watching TV in different rooms and not talking for days.

It was more than just the disappearing acts. Frances wasn't happy with my gambling, and tried to restrict my outlay to a limit of £800 a month. Some chance. I'd gone through a period of cutting down to internet betting and casual flutters in a quiet local shop in Lancashire, but the boys at Blackburn liked the horses. I'd sit on the coach next to Garry Flitcroft and he would be looking through the Racing Post and calling in bets.

I hated listening to chat about races I didn't have a bet in. Gamblers delude themselves into thinking they'd have backed the winner if they'd been involved. So, I couldn't resist getting properly stuck into the phone betting again. It was a slicker operation now. I signed up with Ladbrokes and gave them my bank card details. Rather than a fella like Mickey Arnott coming over to settle any debts, it all just went on the bill.

At first, there was a £1,000 limit on my card, which I only learned about when a bet was refused. I immediately raised it to £10,000. Soon, I was betting with more frequency than anyone else on the bus. I really couldn't let a race pass without having an interest, and the others got a laugh from the rapport I developed with the staff at Ladbrokes. Regularly, I'd ring up and ask to put on a bet and the person at the other end already knew who it was from the caller ID and didn't bother with a security check because they had my details memorised. "Mr Gillespie. Account number QT 3561439, is it?", they'd ask. "Yes, that's the one." The boys were only hearing my side of the discussion and always let out a big cheer when that happened.

Frances wasn't amused by it though. Her plan to limit my gambling kitty failed miserably. I'd pretend to go along with it, and then the credit card bill would come through the post, thick with pages of deposits to betting accounts. I was staking thousands again, which was easier to do on a £14,000 a week salary. Whatever happened, there was still going to be money in the bank. But when Frances saw the statements, she would go out shopping and try to spend as much as possible on the American Express Platinum Card I'd given her. There was no limit on it. That was her revenge, I guess.

The marriage was going nowhere. The low point was a blazing row in a restaurant that concluded with Frances chucking her wedding ring across the table, and the staff on their hands and knees searching for it. We couldn't find a solution to our problems so I bought her an apartment back in the North East, in a place called Wilton, near Middlesbrough, and we separated, barely on speaking terms. The silence was better than the shouting.

There was nothing acrimonious about my departure from Blackburn. My relationship with the club had also run its course.

The contract was up at the end of the 2002/03 season and it was obvious I would be moving on. There was no attempt to instigate discussions and the only development that might have changed the situation was a new manager. But Souness was in the process of steering the club to sixth position in the league, so his position was rock solid. As much as I had learned to get on with the gaffer, it was clear he wanted to spend my substantial wage on somebody else.

I was happy to leave anyway after an incident in November, a row with the reserve-team coach, Alan Murray, that was a long time coming. Murray was a stocky bloke from the North-East who had managed Hartlepool and Darlington. He had worked with Souness at Southampton, and was initially brought in as chief scout before being promoted. Nobody could really see why. I didn't like him and he seemed very unpopular with the players.

I'm not sure how seriously he took his own position because he constantly rescheduled their training sessions so he could stand on the side of the pitch and watch the first team train. Maybe it was because he'd spent his career in the lower leagues, but he absolutely loved being around the dressing room. We didn't like having him there. He basically seemed to do whatever was necessary to curry favour with Souness.

Much to our dismay, the gaffer started to give him extra responsibility. We played Charlton in a live TV game and neither Souness or Boey were on the bus home afterwards due to other commitments. Murray was the most senior member of management on the bus. A week earlier, Souness had changed the rules with regard to reporting at the club the day after a game. If you didn't play more than half an hour, then you were in the next morning. I'd come on in the final few minutes, and sought clarity from Dean Saunders, who was another member of the coaching staff.

"Who's in tomorrow, Deano?"

He went to ask Alan and came back to say that myself and Corrado Grabbi – another late introduction – were expected in.

I wondered why Dwight Yorke, our first sub, was being given the day off when he should have been in under the new criteria. Yorkey was a high-profile summer recruit after Matty's accident in Italy left him on the sidelines.

The gaffer wanted to recreate his successful partnership with Andy Cole, but ended up falling out with both of them. Yorkey was a bit of an enigma. He always had something else going on, and there was no sign of him on the bus. I couldn't understand why he was being given special treatment.

"Tell Alan Murray he's a prick," I said to Deano. He laughed. "Go and tell him yourself."

I decided it was about time I did just that and left my card game to wander up to the front of the coach and give Murray a piece of my mind. "Why fucking put these new rules up if they're not going to be abided by?" He seemed flustered and started ranting and raving before saying I could have the day off as well. I was turning around to go back to my seat when he tried to have the last, sarcastic word. "Aye, you're a fucking good player."

He'd flicked a switch. I wasn't taking that from a jumped up nobody so I reached across to his window seat and pushed my head against his. Straight away, he jumped up and grabbed a hold of me. We had each other by the throats with no room to throw a punch. I was calling him a snake and a brown nose and all the other things I'd always wanted to say. Craig Short and Andy Cole tried to drag me away but I wasn't budging. Andy lost balance and his trainer came flying off, but they eventually managed to break us up. I went down the bus and Flitty asked what was going on. "Ah, it's that fucking prick up there," I said. "But it's alright, I got the day off." We all had a good laugh.

Flitty was a real joker and when I arrived in on Tuesday he had covered the training ground with boxing-themed posters advertising a rematch between myself and Alan. Even Souness had a laugh when he saw them, although he called me into his office for a meeting. He said that I should say sorry to Alan, but he wasn't aware of the smart comment that set it off, and admitted that was out of order. I made it clear there would be no apology and thought the case was closed.

On Thursday, I came in, trained as normal, and was back home when Phil rang to ask what the hell I'd done. The chief executive, John Williams, had called to say the club were suspending me for three weeks. I couldn't believe that nobody had the balls to say it to my face that morning. Straight away, I picked up the phone and rang my good pal Craig Short, who said he would speak to Flitty. I was pissed off and jumped on the first plane to Northern Ireland.

Craig rang the following day. Flitty had arranged a team meeting with Souness where the senior lads had spoken up on my behalf. Even Yorkey, who I liked on a personal level, supported my cause. On Sunday, a day after I had missed a league game at Fulham, the manager's secretary, Katherine, rang to say that my ban was over. Two days later, I was on the bench for a League Cup game at Rotherham. While I appreciated the show of player power, that was the start of the countdown to the summer.

I had started to spend a lot of my spare time in Northern Ireland. Kelly Maguire was the reason, a tall blonde girl who caught my eye in a trendy Belfast spot called The Apartment after an international match. We chatted for a bit without swapping numbers, but I knew she was a friend of Albert Kirk, a cameraman from UTV, so I asked him for her number and eventually plucked up the courage to make the call. It started from there. A few weeks later, I flew back for a weekend with her and, from then, I travelled back as much as was possible. We clicked. Kelly was a smart girl, with a degree in politics, and beautiful as well – she'd finished runner-up in Miss Northern Ireland.

Our relationship began to attract column inches at home, and that did make me slightly uncomfortable. Kelly was a manageress in the bar at the Odyssey Arena in Belfast, a big venue that played host to loads of high-profile concerts. There was a VIP area where a lot of the acts went afterwards, Westlife and groups like that, and I'd go there to see Kelly. There were showbiz journalists around who spotted me, and I suddenly found my love-life splashed across the celebrity pages.

With Kelly's beauty queen background, the local papers tried to make a story of it and she gave a couple of interviews which, looking back now, is a sign that she was as interested in my profile as she was in me. I hated that kind of attention but knew that if it was going to become serious, she'd have to come across to England to be with me. That would take us away from the spotlight.

I just needed to know where my next move would take me before she could move over properly. The departure from Blackburn was a poorly-kept secret, and fliers started coming through the letterbox from people asking if I was looking to sell my house, so that was sorted quickly. Down in the club, the goodbyes were low key. Tony Parkes had the decency to approach me in the gym, shake my hand and say thanks for my contribution. I heard nothing from Souness, and wasn't especially surprised either. I was no longer useful to him.

Phil was sure that finding another Premier League club would be no problem, and I was enjoying a break with Kelly when he called to say that Leicester were keen.

They had been promoted and were on an impressive recruitment drive with my old pals Les Ferdinand and Steve Howey already signed up. The manager Micky Adams was certain he wanted me and the club were willing to match my salary at Blackburn.

I didn't feel the need to fly to England to sort it out, and gave Phil the go-ahead to finalise the small print of my two-year contract with the director of football, Dave Bassett.

I signed officially on the first day of pre-season and with Craig

Hignett and John Curtis also joining from Blackburn, there were plenty of familiar faces in the dressing room.

I bought a new house in a quiet village called Queniborough and looked forward to a fresh challenge. Instead, it was the start of a season that would leave a disgusting stench.

(20)

Accused

'A WOMAN allegedly raped by Leicester City captain Paul Dickov claims fellow player Keith Gillespie pinned her to the wall during the attack... In a police statement, she said Northern Ireland international Gillespie also threatened to throw her from the window of her third floor hotel room, hit her in the face, and battered her on the shoulder. As Dickov carried out the alleged attack, a third man is said to have stood by applauding and egging him on. If the allegations are true, Dickov, and team-mates Gillespie, 29, and Frank Sinclair, 32 – who are all charged with rape – could be jailed for up to 12 years.'

– Daily Mirror,
March 8, 2004

La Manga. The slightest mention of that place darkens my mood. It's impossible to reflect on a life-changing experience without the old feelings of anger and injustice rushing back.

My mother still has all the newspaper cuttings and flicking through the lies is a reminder of the nightmare, a twisted chain of events which led to me being accused of a vile crime. I spent a week in a Spanish prison, presumed guilty of rape and powerless to prevent my name from being dragged through the mud while the real low-lifes lined their pockets. I was no stranger to bad publicity but this was a totally different ball game.

Oh, it was a great story alright. Premier League stars boozed up abroad, drunk on power and forcing themselves on women because that's just how we rolled. I can see why it made the news around the world. There was just one significant problem. It wasn't true. Not even remotely true.

The sad fact is that while it might only take one day to blacken someone's reputation, it can take a lifetime to remove the stigma. Some people will always associate me with an incident that I'm convinced was a set-up.

What happened? All I can do is tell my story.

It was just another mid-season trip. We were deep in relegation trouble, a dressing room packed with experience but short of inspiration and confidence. Micky thought it would recharge the batteries.

La Manga is a popular destination for football clubs. On paper, it offers the complete package. A five-star Hyatt Regency hotel, good facilities, attractive weather, a golf course, plus a bar and casino for unwinding. Leicester had run into a bit of trouble there a few years previously when Stan Collymore was part of a group that let off a fire extinguisher, but it wasn't an obstacle to going back. Being honest, I can't say I was looking forward to it very much. The way my season was going, I would have preferred a few days at home. After making an effort to sign me, Micky didn't play me very much. He preferred James Scowcroft on the right wing because he was good in the air and could get his head on diagonal long balls which probably says something about our style of play.

Micky didn't like gambling, and thought I spent too much time looking at the Racing Post instead of concentrating on football. It didn't help that his assistant, Alan Cork, was keen on the nags. Micky followed Corky a few times and found him grilling me for tips. I don't think that reputation helped my cause.

But Micky enjoyed stamping his authority. Although he was from Sheffield, he'd storm around with a Cockney accent. 'Fack this' and 'Facking that'. Annoying as that was, he did allow us to enjoy ourselves when the time allowed, and the itinerary for the Spanish trip was player-friendly. Training was scheduled for the evening, which meant no early starts and permission to have a couple before bed. So, there was no rush to the airport bar when we travelled on Sunday, February 29, as we were going straight to training when we landed. Then, we had the night to ourselves.

Inevitably, I was drawn to the lights of the casino where I parked myself at a blackjack table with our keeper, Ian Walker. The others split off to do their own thing, with the non-gamblers pitching up in a bar at the opposite end of the room. We heard laughter and were aware they had some girls in their company but there was nothing unusual about that. I was more interested in winning cash, and had no intention of moving until closing time when the staff cleared everyone out towards the lobby. The boys from the bar had brought the birds with them, three African girls who lived in Germany which explained their rapport with our recent arrival, the former Spurs midfielder Steffen Freund. They were dressed up for a night out and lapping up the attention.

With my usual roomie Craig Hignett out on loan, I was sharing with Frank Sinclair for the first time. Frank was a prolific ladies man and, unsurprisingly, doing a lot of talking with the girls. I was quite sober, so I left them to it and ducked off to the room. The card was faulty so reception sent a member of staff to make sure the new key was working. Then I rang Craig Short, because Blackburn were in Marbella, and we'd been texting during the night. By the time our chat finished, the main group had moved to the corridor. My door was open, and Ian Walker and Matty Elliott came in for a few beers – they were in the room opposite.

It was getting a bit rowdier outside, and we heard a few shouts. Paul Dickov, our Scottish striker, walked into the room, saying that one of the birds had attacked him and yanked a chain off his neck that was a present from his wife. He was pretty pissed off. The bird came in to continue the argument. Paul wasn't the tallest guy in the world, and she'd taunted him about that, saying he must have a small cock. It was silly stuff. She sat on Frank's bed, in no rush to go anywhere. I didn't know this girl, didn't know her name or anything about her. So she had overstayed her welcome. "Could you get out now?" I said. She refused to move. I went to lift her by the arm and she jumped up and grabbed my throat. I stood back, and threw my hands in the air. She sat down again. We kept asking her to go and five minutes later she finally left.

The next thing we heard was more screaming and shouting in the corridor. The birds were fighting between themselves, shouting so loudly across each other that it was hard to understand what language they were even speaking. All we knew was that they were annoying. Eventually the noise died down. Frank, who'd been missing for a while arrived back, and I dropped off to sleep, oblivious that I would have to tell the story of that tame night so many times.

Monday was business as usual. We lounged by the pool during the day, and trained in the evening. The majority went for a meal after, but all I was interested in was blackjack. Frank and a few others sneaked out to a nightclub after their food, and there was no sign of him when I went to bed.

Tuesday followed the same routine. The rest were out for grub in the evening. I was sat in the Piano Bar with Ian, waiting for the casino to open, when the gaffer marched through the foyer screaming into his phone. He spotted us and came charging over. "What do you know about rape?" he screamed.

We hadn't a clue what he was talking about. Micky said the Spanish police were looking for everyone's passports and called the other lads back from their restaurant for an urgent meeting. It was held in one of those big conference rooms with a pen and paper at every seat. Ian and I thought something had happened in the nightclub trip on the Monday night and started joking about by drawing up a list of suspects as we waited. Number one was Frank. Number two was Frank. Number three was Frank. You get the picture.

The gaffer was in no mood for messing when everyone had

turned up.

"What do any of you know about rape on Sunday night?" he announced. Now, we were really confused.

"Sunday?"

Steffen Freund put up his hand and admitted to shagging one of the Africans early in the night. They'd nipped back to his room for a quickie before returning to the bar. In the rest of our minds, that solved it. Steffen was fucked. We weren't thinking that he'd raped her – he said it had been consensual – but it cleared up where the allegation had come from. The mystery was over. It was his matter to sort out.

Micky ordered us to stay in the hotel area for the night, but Ian and I slipped out of sight for another blackjack session before finishing up with a drink back in his room where Matty had stayed in to eat. When Ian fell asleep, we squirted tomato sauce and mayonnaise on his hair. Matty knew he would get the same treatment if Ian stirred during the night so he came across to stay with myself and Frank. We woke in the morning to a knock from Ian who was standing in the corridor with his hair all over the shop. He went off for a shower and someone else rapped on the door. This time, it was a sombre looking Corky, who quickly wiped the smile away.

"Your face has been picked out of the passports. You've got to go to the police," he said. They also wanted Matt and Frank as well as Dickov, Scowcroft, Danny Coyne, Lilian Nalis, Nikos Dabizas and, of course, Steffen. It was a strange collection of players. Scowy hadn't bothered leaving his room, and we reckoned that Lilian, who had long hair, was chosen because he looked like Ian's dated passport photo from his Tottenham days. Considering I'd barely left Ian's side for three days, it made little sense that one would be picked out and not the other.

But we weren't too worried on the way to the station. We all thought it was about Steffen and, while Micky was a bit hyped, the rest of the staff seemed laid back. By coincidence, the chief executive Tim Davies was out in Spain to catch up on a few things, and he had quickly arranged a local solicitor to represent us. Her name was Ana Ruiperez, a woman in her 30s with long brown hair. Ana worked with her father, Luis, a leading lawyer from nearby Cartagena. She said we might be cautioned but it would only be a formality.

We were even more relaxed when Steffen was called in for his interview first and emerged within five minutes to say he was allowed to go.

Paul was in next while the rest of us sat in a reception area. When the door opened, we expected him to walk out free. Instead, he was led out handcuffed by a pair of police officers who marched him past. Suddenly, this was serious.

My turn. I was brought into a room where two male police officers and an interpreter were sitting behind a table. Ana was in the room too. I was asked to give my version of events. When I finished, they said I was being charged with an accusation of rape, and would be kept in custody. There was no time for discussion. I was ushered through reception, and down the stairs into a dimly-lit basement where my belt, phone and other possessions were taken away. The guards opened the door of a cell. A distraught looking Paul was slumped on a bed in the corner with his head in his hands.

Five minutes later Matty joined us and, one by one, the others followed. Lilian took the fourth bed in our cell. Scowy, Danny, Nikos and Frank were together next door. Nobody knew what the hell was going on. Frank had a confession to make. He'd ended up in the girls' room after the row had gone off in the corridor, and had received a blowjob from one of them while her mate was in the room. He'd said nothing until now because we all thought Steffen was the story. Frank's revelation didn't change that feeling.

After a while, Tim Davies came to visit with some sandwiches. He said the rest of the training camp had been cancelled and they had decided to get the other players out of there immediately. The news was hard to take. Steffen, who did have sex with one of the girls, was on the way back to his family, while we were stuck in this dungeon. He said the legal team were doing their best to make sense of the situation.

We were trying to do the same as the night dragged on. Some were quieter than others. Paul, a solid family man, was really downbeat. Lilian was pacing around in circles wearing these annoyingly squeaky pair of trainers and Matty lost the plot with him. But Matty was a funny lad who also helped to lighten the mood. "I'm not being funny," he said, "but Scowy has got locked up for not going out."

Proper sleep was out of the question. We had enough to occupy our minds before a local drunk was taken off the streets and thrown into a neighbouring cell where he spent the next few hours loudly abusing the guards. Just what we needed after the day we'd had. The wailing stopped and I nodded off.

There were no windows in the dungeon. We had to assume it was morning when the warden called us. It was time to go to the courthouse so we were handcuffed together in pairs. I was tied to Matt Elliott and emerged into the light and the madness of a media scrum which confirmed that the situation was already big news. The cops bundled us into a van and, when we reached the court buildings, directed us towards a cramped single cell downstairs. It was a warm day, and the wrong place for eight grown men who hadn't showered. The smell was horrible.

We were called in turns to have a longer chat with the police about the Sunday night.

I just went through my story again in more detail. I've no idea how Scowy managed to talk to them for half an hour considering he was in bed on the evening in question.

The legal team had good news for us. They'd discovered that the African birds had tried to check back into the hotel on the Monday knowing we were still there. And our crowd had also spoken to a taxi driver who said they were in good spirits when he'd taken them to the airport on the Tuesday when they filed the complaint to the police.

They didn't sound like the actions of rape victims, and we thought the info might have been enough to get us out but it wasn't that straightforward. The club were concerned that our side of the story didn't appear to be registering with the local authorities. Also, an inexperienced judge had been assigned to the case, which was another worry on top of the language barrier. Tim had called on the help of the Foreign Secretary, Jack Straw, and a local Leicester MP, Keith Vaz, as well as a Spanish-speaking solicitor in the UK.

They said we had to return to the station cells for another night, but it didn't seem as horrible a prospect with the knowledge of the girls' strange behaviour. There was confidence we would be released the following day. On the Friday morning,

Ana met us in the court building. "Your story is fine," she told me, from behind a glass screen which had enough room underneath for her to pass through a cigarette so we could smoke as we talked. "You'll be out of here today."

We waited for news. In the afternoon, they called us in to meet with Ana again. The minute I saw her, I had a bad feeling. Her expression had changed, and it looked as though she was about to cry as she delivered a fresh update.

The novice judge had stepped aside, and a more senior figure was coming in. That would take time, but some of the charges had either been dropped by the investigators, or not deemed serious enough to keep some people in the country. She cut to the chase. They had identified their main suspects for the most serious offences.

"Everyone is free to go except Paul, Frank, and Keith."

It felt like blood was being drained from my body.

My legs went, and Matty grabbed hold of me as I collapsed into tears. Paul and Frank broke down too. She said they would be transferring us to a prison.

There was no noise apart from the sound of gentle sobbing. Scowy piped up. "Are we free to go now then?" Matty flipped at him for being so insensitive. But the lads did have to go. We promised to see them soon.

After that, everything seemed to happen in fast-forward. Micky appeared, and asked if there was anything we wanted before they took us away. We all smoked so he sorted us out with a few. He then handed over his mobile and said we could each make a quick call.

I rang Kelly. She wasn't angry. The club had been in touch to assure her it was a stitch-up and she had spoken to Mum as well. We talked for less than a minute, but it was a reassuring chat. Paul and Frank took their turns as the driver of the prison van revved up his engine. Apparently, the police were doing us a favour by allowing this communication with the outside world.

When the last call ended, we climbed aboard and left through an underground exit to escape the media.

Next stop, Sangonera Prison.

(21)

Banged Up

'NORTHERN Ireland star Keith Gillespie was last night on suicide watch with two other team-mates in a grim Spanish jail. Paul Dickov, Frank Sinclair and Gillespie are also under threat of attack from fellow lags. They were yesterday moved on to the sex offenders wing at the tough Sangonera Prison for their own safety.'

– The People,
March 7, 2004

I expected prison to be hell. Wrong. While people at home were fed a load of bull, the three Premier League jailbirds found Sangonera to be strangely welcoming.

I'm not saying we were happy; we were worried and frustrated. But those feelings were caused by the circumstances that brought us there, and not by the people around us. The other inmates actually gave us strength. Prison guards didn't have to move us to a sex offenders wing. In fact, I'm not even sure there was one.

I never once felt suicidal and the suggestion really annoys me because it implies guilt, like we had something to run away from. Our situation was the opposite. We lived for the truth. Believing it would come out kept us going.

So, I felt safe in Sangonera. Prison didn't live up to the hype, and I was pretty damn happy about that.

All the worst case scenarios ran through my head on the way there, and I'm guessing it was the same for Paul and Frank on the silent journey through the night.

We reached the entrance and went through the checking-in process. Then, we were weighed, photographed and handed a bag of essentials. I stared at the contents. Toilet roll? Obviously. Toothpaste? Makes sense. Condoms? Not good. We agreed there would be no solo trips to the showers. Thankfully, after three days in the same clothes, they took us for a long overdue wash when we arrived.

It was after midnight when the guards led us to our cell. We nervously followed them up a flight of stairs onto the first floor, which had cells on four sides, all looking down on a courtyard below. Our cell was small, with a triple bunk bed.

I called the top one straight away. It was dark and quiet although we heard some whispers from Spanish voices. We didn't say much and instead tried to sleep but we were fighting a losing battle.

Morning introduced us to our neighbours, and also gave us a

better picture of the living quarters. Turned out the cell was luxury compared to the stale, dank police cells where we'd spent the previous couple of nights. Cleaner than we envisaged. We looked nervously at the other prisoners, noticing that when the guards turned their back, they passed handwritten messages from one cell to another using a piece of string. But the vibe wasn't threatening. Most of the other inmates had TV in their rooms and had obviously been watching the news because they knew who we were. And they seemed to be supportive as well. I'll never forget one guy across the way waving to get my attention. He didn't have any English, but I understood his message. 'Lay-chester, Lay-chester, Manana, Manana', he shouted, while acting out the charade of handcuffs being taken off. Tomorrow, tomorrow, we would be free.

If only it was that simple. We didn't know how long it would take, and fell into a routine that didn't change from day to day. Breakfast at 8am. Then, the computer room, for long games of Pacman. Lunch was followed by siesta time, but we played cards instead with a pack that one of the other prisoners gave to us. Dinner was at 5pm and then it was courtyard time for three hours. There was a gym, but we were in no mood for exercise. The club had put money in an account for us, so Frank would go off and fetch us a cup of tea and some smokes before we went back to the cells at 8pm. The lights went out at 11. That was the worst part.

The days were easy. We mixed with the locals, in spite of the language barrier. The long termers all had various jobs to do in the prison. One of the inmates ran the kitchen, and he looked out for us straight away, giving us a nod so we got in before the rush at mealtime. He was a big friendly guy in his 40s who used to be a bullfighter and had enough English to start a discussion and entertain us with stories about his old life. After a few days, we felt comfortable enough to ask what crime he had committed, a curiosity we shared about everyone in there. He said he was in for fraud but didn't really elaborate and we weren't going to push him on it either. Maybe they kept the murderers somewhere else.

There was only one flash of trouble, a young fella who took a dislike to us and spat through a window while we chatted with some of the others. Instead of reacting, we just ignored it. One of the senior prisoners mentioned it to the warden and we didn't see the culprit again.

I think the Spanish authorities were under orders to protect us after Leicester called the Foreign Office in. They didn't want a diplomatic incident.

I was the upbeat one of our group. We all helped each other at various times, but Paul and Frank would lie in their bunks in the early hours talking about all the things that could go wrong. "What if they don't believe us? What if we have to stay here?" I kept telling them to trust in the system. The more I thought about how ridiculous the girls' story was, the more I believed our innocence would be proven.

My visitors added to the confidence. Kelly had flown over and was allowed to visit once, where she reminded me that the people who were important knew the truth. I found out that Mum and my sister, Angela, were in the country as well, along with Phil and Kelly's sister, Nicola.

Beyond the obvious, there was little to say. We talked about her flight over, silly things like that, it didn't seem like the time for a heavy chat. I was back in the cell when the warden dropped in a letter that Mum had written to me.

'I want you to know that I am thinking of you and love you and am looking forward to seeing you. I am glad to know that you got the top bunk. Lots of people back home have texted me and phoned Ivor at home to say they are praying for you. Keep your chin up. We know you are innocent. Ivor, Heather, Davy, and your dad send their love. Love and prayers. Mum xxxooo.'

Angela sent in a short note too.

'Keith. We are all with you. We love you and we know you will be out soon. Can't wait to see you. Everybody back home is on your side and thinking of you. Love you, Angela, xxxx.'

Sleep came a little easier that night. I knew my family would believe in me, but it was nice to read those words, even if it made me a little teary. This was tough for them too. I had to put this right.

Ana, as our legal rep, was the other person permitted in to see us and, as the week developed, her news on the ongoing investigation improved. The women had waived their identity to sell the story to the News of the World, so other papers had started to dig into their background. The info was already out there about their attempts to check back into the hotel, and their high spirits in the taxi. Also, the Swedish guests in the room next to where we were supposed to have attacked them came out to say they heard nothing but laughter and shouting.

But more stuff came out when their names were revealed. Their solicitor was claiming they were all happily married.

Other tourists said they were escort girls who had propositioned them, and there was evidence they had all previously been involved in the sex trade. They wouldn't reveal who had paid for their £300 a night room in the hotel. All they said was that 'wealthy golfing friends' were putting them up. But there was no trace of those people. The story was full of holes.

There were two obstacles to our release. Bail had been set, a sum of almost £200,000 between the three of us. Leicester were refusing to pay it. They were getting hammered at home because they had a reputation as a family club and, while Tim was doing brilliant work on our behalf, the board thought we had enough money.

Phil sorted my share without any hesitation, and nearly ended up paying Paul's as well because his agent was reluctant to put up the cash and was making excuses. That dragged on until Steve Howey wired through the money from England. Paul's wife, Jan, had come in for his prison visit, and was really upset with the delay. I was glad to have Phil in my corner.

The other issue was getting Steffen over. He was the key to the case. The girl hadn't mentioned having sex with Steffen in her statement. She'd described him as a gentleman who sat and talked with her and nothing else. Steffen was afraid he would get arrested if he came over and told the truth, and knew his wife would probably chuck him out. But the club persuaded him to do the right thing. When the bail was paid, and Steffen was booked on a flight, a private hearing was arranged for the Thursday. We said goodbye to Sangonera after a six-night stay, not knowing if we would return.

It was strange when we arrived back at the court house. There was a lot going on, and not all of it made sense. They called me in for a police line-up. I glanced up and down the line and saw that the other blokes were different shapes and sizes and didn't look remotely similar. My face had been plastered over the newspapers and TV for the last week. Obviously, I was going to be picked out.

Paul and Frank didn't have to go through that process, but it confirmed that the girls were in the same building. One must have been behind a screen looking at the line-up. Knowing they were nearby wound me up. A guard was leading me down the corridor for a toilet break when I glanced through a small window into a diagonal room and saw them sitting there. Before I could react, he hurried me along. But the fuse was lit. "Those bastards are down there," I told the boys. I was angry now, and stood at the door with my eye pressed against the tiny peephole, knowing they would have to pass by at some point. When they did, around half an hour later, a week's worth of frustration came out. I pounded on the door calling them lying bastards and whatever else sprung to mind. The other boys found it funny. What had happened to the chilled out guy? We'd reversed roles.

Down the corridor, the hearing was going in our favour. Paul had already stated it was impossible that his DNA could be found on underwear the girls had handed in as part of the investigation, while Frank admitted to the blowjob but stressed it was all that happened. We were all happy to be tested to confirm the truth. Then, we heard that Steffen had been brought in to face the girls. He pointed out the one he'd shagged. Our solicitor told us that she tried to make a big scene, shouting "Why do you lie, Steffen? Why do you lie?" Apparently it wasn't a very convincing performance.

Bail was approved, and the only hold-up was the paperwork. In the early hours of the morning, they gave the green light for us to go. There was a car waiting outside, parked a bloody long walk from the door, with an army of reporters and cameras blocking the route. We pushed through and sped away to a villa that Tim had arranged, which had clean sheets, fresh food, and no bloody bunk beds.

The club had booked us on an easyJet flight home the following morning. We faced another media scrum at the airport, mostly from English voices. Spanish minds were elsewhere as, the previous morning, 191 people had died in a sickening terrorist attack in Madrid. Al-Qaeda were suspected of carrying out the bombings so, naturally, airport security was strict. Our presence was causing a distraction so they skipped us up the queue and made sure we boarded the plane as quickly as possible.

We flew to Luton, and left through a private entrance when we landed. Kelly, who was home already, drove back to Leicester. Almost the perfect getaway until we reached our cul-de-sac in Queniborough. We passed a motorbike with a TV logo on its side. He was just leaving the estate when he obviously spotted my face and tried a rapid U-turn but he couldn't manage it and toppled over.

Before he could recover, Kelly accelerated into the driveway. We bolted the door behind us, closed the blinds, and pulled the curtains. Shutting myself away from the world was the only option.

I had moved from one prison to another.

22

Innocent

'KEITH GILLESPIE yesterday accepted substantial undis-
closed libel damages for a newspaper claim that he took
part in a sexual assault. Mr Gillespie brought high court
proceedings after an article in the News of the World
detailed claims by three women against him and two other
Leicester City players.

'The women accused the three men of rape and attempted
rape, and alleged that one of them had threatened violent
recriminations if any of them spoke out. The advocate
David Price... said the claims reported in the newspaper
were "entirely untrue", and that Mr Gillespie did not sexually or physically assault, let alone rape, any of the three
women, nor did he try to do so. In March 2004, Mr Gillespie
was released on bail and the criminal proceedings against

him were dropped in May. The women's appeal was dis-
missed in December. Benjamin Beabey, for the newspaper,
offered News of the World's sincere apologies for the publi-
cation of the false and defamatory allegations.'

– Press Association,
July 7, 2005

£115,000. That was the compensation for being portrayed as a
rapist in mass circulation newspapers. £60,000 from the News
of the World, who paid the women for their story, and allowed
them to describe me as an animal that was capable of a violent
sexual attack. £40,000 from the Mirror, which suggested I held
one of the women down while Paul Dickov had his way with
her. And £15,000 from the Daily Star, who made up a phone-
call from myself to Kelly where I admitted to having consensual
sex with the women.

David Price Solicitors did Trojan work on my behalf. They
offered to work on a no-win, no-fee basis and when the DNA
test results came through two months after we got home, the
newspapers were in trouble. Traces of semen were found in
the underwear alright, but they didn't belong to myself, Paul
or Frank. All charges were dropped. The girls' appeal was just
taking the piss.

Still, I often wonder if £115,000 was enough. La Manga sold
newspapers. The scandal was front page news for over a week,
and the papers who paid damages still profited from the story.

Phil had information which added another dimension to the
case, arising from a call he'd received from a trusted contact in
The Sun. He believed that the News of the World had planted

the girls in the hotel to land the story, a theory that was ripe in football circles. Dave Bassett had also heard it on the grapevine. Crucially, Phil's source also warned us to be careful about what we said on our mobiles after we got back from La Manga. Seven years later, when the News International phone hacking revelations emerged, leading to the Leveson Inquiry that Garry Flitcroft wound up involved in, we truly realised the seriousness of that advice. It showed how low some elements of the media were willing to go in search of a story. When our libel settlements were reached, in the summer of 2005, they were relegated to the side columns. And so was I. For the first time in my career, I didn't have a club when pre-season kicked off. Phil tried to be sensitive and only revealed the full truth later down the line. Nobody wanted me. I was tainted by a crime I didn't commit.

The 2003/04 season was over for me post-La Manga. Micky wasn't playing me before, so he certainly wasn't going to involve me after. I followed Leicester's first game after the scandal through the updates on Soccer Saturday. Against all the odds, they went to Birmingham and won. I punched the air when the full-time whistle went, but wanted to punch the television that night when Ron Atkinson came on ITV and said the club should have sacked the three players who had been released from Sangonera Prison just 24 hours earlier. I didn't have much to smile about in the couple of months that followed La Manga, but when Big Ron lost his job after making racist comments about Marcel Desailly, I raised a glass.

The club was under pressure to show us the door, though. When the story broke, fans had turned up at the ground to burn shirts and hand back season tickets, and the board was shitting themselves that big sponsors like Alliance & Leicester and Walkers would pull out. But they stayed loyal, and common sense prevailed. Paul, a key player, was brought straight back into the side. They couldn't afford to continue without him.

In the immediate aftermath there was a well publicised internal investigation. We were all called before Tim Davies to explain what happened. But it smacked of an exercise to show they were taking a stand. The reality was that nobody had broken any rules. Micky had allowed us to have a drink. In the end, a few token fines were handed out to satisfy a few board members who knew fuck all about what happened on trips away.

The boys in the dressing room did what footballers do best, and slaughtered us. Until the case was struck off, the 'La Manga Eight' had to board a train to London on the last Thursday of the month, walk two minutes to sign a form to prove we were still in the country, and then go back to the station and make the return journey. We were the butt of a fair few jokes. It was a serious subject and that shouldn't happen but that's what dressing rooms can be like. The birds' German connections gave them an easy angle. A text went around about the eight of us being in the room asking the girls if we could shag them. They say "Nein", so we reply, "Oh, so we go and get one more?"

All you could do was laugh. Privately, most of the boys were supportive. Paul lived nearby and we had socialised together before all the drama, so we looked out for each other in the fallout. Frank was based in London, and looked out for himself. Phil advised me to play the PR game to speed up the process of clearing our names, and the ideal chance arose when the producers of Tonight with Trevor McDonald approached with a request to make a special programme about the case. Sir Trevor, the famous ITV news anchor, separately visited Paul and I for a lengthy sit-down. Then, we learned that Frank had gone on a solo run and poured his heart out to the BBC. The makers of the programme had lost the exclusive element, so the planned hour-long show was reduced to a tiny segment.

I left a number of messages on Frank's phone asking him why the fuck he was making himself look good while leaving myself and Paul out to dry, but he didn't respond. Maybe he felt under pressure to do something special because his missus only found out about his blowjob when it came out in the hearing, but I can't see how that could have caused him too many problems. Frank was always able to spin stories and usually seemed to get away with it. I've talked to Frank since, but the way in which he handled that has stuck with me. The profile of the ITV show would really have helped our cause. With that opportunity wasted, all we could do was wait for the formal exoneration.

Micky was never the same after Spain. All the attention around it wore him down. Wrongly, he seemed to feel responsible for what happened. It was made out that the drinking on the trip had undermined his authority when the reality was that he had sold it to us as a bonding exercise. Perhaps the club were telling him that shouldn't have been the case, but the theory that he'd lost control of the dressing room was miles off the mark. That said, he didn't win himself any friends in the post-mortem. In crisis mode, his temper was shorter than usual. One day, during the internal investigation, the club wanted to interview every-one and Peter Shirtliff, the reserves boss, spoke up and asked if the lads who were playing for him that night could go in first. The gaffer turned around in front of the group and screamed, 'I don't give a fuck about the reserves'. Shirty said nothing, but he was seething. Micky didn't seem to realise he was treating a popular member of staff with so little respect.

He blamed the fall-out from Spain for our inevitable relegation, which was a load of crap. The real reason was that we weren't very good. Silly mistakes throughout the season were our downfall. A team that leads Wolves 3-0 at half-time and loses 4-3 deserves what it gets and, for us, that was the drop. Micky stayed on and tried to build a promotion-winning squad, but I think he was still hurting from the season before and quit after two months back in the Championship.

It was already obvious we wouldn't be going back up. As ever, the 'big boys' that had just dropped a level were the scalp that everyone wanted. And it was in the smaller grounds that I learned that some fans would never allow me to forget the recent past. Millwall stands out. I remember collecting the ball to take a throw, and taking a few steps back, while the crowd just hissed the same word over and over again in unison. 'Rapist, rapist, rapist.' There's nothing you can do in that situation. If you react to a thug shouting abuse in your ear from two yards away, then you're the bad guy.

The funny thing is, I quite enjoyed that season.

Micky was replaced by Craig Levein, a Scot who I found to be a fair guy. He brought in stuff like Prozone analysis, which could drag on at times, but I actually found it to be quite beneficial in terms of understanding the game. My performances improved and while we finished well down the table, the fans, who had previously booed me off the pitch, voted me as their

Player of the Year. It was a goodbye present. My contract was up, and financial problems at the club meant that a slashing of the budget was necessary. Phil thought they wanted rid of me anyway because of my association with the Spain episode. Relegation had already cut my wage in half to £7,000 a week, and Craig made it clear that a new deal wouldn't even be close to that.

"I wouldn't want to embarrass you with the offer they have made," he said. We parted amicably.

It was a time of change. There was plenty of coming and going in my personal life as well. Kelly was a huge source of support during the La Manga fallout, but the spark that brought us together had disappeared. She was putting pressure on me to speed up the divorce with Frances, but there was no sense that we were growing any closer to a real commitment.

The longer we lived together, the clearer it became that we didn't have very much in common. Old habits died hard, and I was always looking for something else, or someone else. On a trip to London, I met her. I'd gone out for a drink with Phil and bumped into some lads he knew in the pub. Phil went off to a game at Stamford Bridge, and I stayed with my new friends. They took me along to a boxing match and, afterwards, a club, where I got talking to a small, beautiful blonde girl named Vikki Morley. She was a real southern girl, different to my previous conquests. We hit it off, swapped numbers, and kept in regular touch. Texting mostly, or a phone call when the opportunity allowed.

I always thought I was a good liar, that I could cover my tracks fairly well. But Kelly sensed a change. She went out to meet a friend one evening, and I took the chance to sit in the bedroom and call Vikki. Kelly must have expected me to do that because she'd hidden a dictaphone in the room and recorded the whole thing. She confronted me with the truth, and that was the end of the relationship. There was no point in trying to save it. Our moment had passed and, given her fondness for the limelight, it didn't surprise me that Kelly ended up going to the papers about it.

It didn't speed things up with Vikki, however. We lived a fair distance apart, and there's only so much texting and talking you can do without seeing each other face to face. I thought nothing was going to happen, so I knocked it on the head. Besides, there was another face on the scene. My wife. After putting it off for ages, I'd finally decided to make some progress on the divorce with Frances. We started to speak again and, surprisingly, the tone was quiet pleasant. The premise of our discussions was the logistics of the split, but it developed from that to personal chat, to familiar talk. She came down to Leicester to see me, lying to ourselves that it was to go through the formalities when there was clearly another motive. Discussion flowed, one thing led to another, and suddenly the plans to divorce were shelved. Six years after St Lucia, we were giving it another go.

I moved into the apartment in Wilton that I'd bought her as part of our separation and, for a month, it was great. I was comfortable in the area; my lifelong mate Jim and other pals lived nearby. 'Maybe this is fate,' I thought. But the old saying is true. You should never go back; to a football club or a woman. The tensions that led to the initial parting never disappear. They just lie under the surface, waiting to rear their head.

Eventually, history began to repeat itself. The rows, the shouting matches. We called it quits again, and this time it was for good.

My football life was as uncertain as the love life. I assumed there would be clubs lining up after the way in which I'd finished the season with Leicester. Wrong.

The only real offer came from Leeds, who invited me down for a trial where their manager, Kevin Blackwell, treated me like a twat. He claimed he wanted two players for every position and the only other right winger, Steve Stone, injured his Achilles just after I arrived. Blackwell didn't say a word to me after our first meeting, but he had plenty to say to everyone else. His personality grated. The end of my week approached and, on the Saturday, we played a practice match. All the other boys were asking if I was coming away with them on the Monday for a pre-season trip to Norway. I didn't have a clue so I went to knock on the manager's door to find out where I stood. "Look," he said, "I've had a word with the chairman and we don't have any money available to offer you anything."

I wondered when he was planning to tell me that my week had been a total waste of time. This was taking the piss. I wanted to tell him what a prick he was, but I kept my mouth shut, shied away from the confrontation, and walked back into unemployment, consoling myself by concluding that I wouldn't have fancied dealing with a guy like Blackwell every day anyway.

As the days and weeks passed, and a new season dawned, the positives were harder to find. Phil kept my spirits up. Only later did he admit how worried he was. Every avenue he tried led to a mention of La Manga. I'd coped with the stigma of the gambling and the punch-up headlines; this was far worse and piled on top of the old rap sheet. It cemented a perception –

Keith Gillespie means trouble. From the first time I'd kicked a ball, I was always in demand. Now, I was desperate for anyone to ring, so I'd have news when Mum or Dad called to ask about my next move.

I needed a favour and my old pal from Blackburn, Craig Short, delivered. He'd moved to Sheffield United because of a long standing association with their boss, Neil Warnock, and put in a good word that led to an invitation to come training. It was the final week of pre-season and after stretching the legs on Monday and Tuesday, a friendly with Scarborough on the Wednesday was the chance to shine. I quickly learned that training alone leaves you miles behind fitness-wise. Warnock was blunt afterwards. "You did nothing right for 45 minutes," he said, "but you put in 14 unbelievable crosses into the box after the break." He offered me a year's contract, and on the Saturday, I found myself coming off the bench to set up a goal in a live TV game. The opponents? Leicester. A sweet 4-1 win, given the circumstances. "Just the kind of delivery I'd expect from an international player," Warnock said afterwards on the box.

Nice to hear, but the terms of my contract had planted the feet on the ground. I'd have scoffed at a £2,500 a week deal a couple of months earlier, but I had no bargaining position and signed what Sheffield United put on the table.

This was La Manga's legacy. £115,000 in damages was considered a large payout in libel terms, yet it paled in comparison to the bigger picture. Within the space of two years, my annual salary had dropped by £598,000.

23

Ups And Downs

"TIME for Gilly"

My fellow substitutes at Sheffield United always reacted the same way when Neil Warnock turned around and told me to warm up. Like an announcer at a boxing match calling a prize fighter into the ring, they'd bellow 'Time for Gilllyyyyy'.

I always had an instinct when that moment would come during my first season in Sheffield. We'd be in front, looking to close out the three points, and the gaffer would bring me on. My football evolution was complete. I used to be a flying winger who was considered a risky proposition. But now I was the safe pair of hands, a thirty-something with a lot of mileage. "Look at Gilly," Warnock would say, as he talked an audience through a video of our previous match, "never gives the ball away."

Warnock was old school and, on the football pitch, I thrived under his influence. He was unique, a real individual whose mood and mind would flick in an instant. A ranter and raver, but never cruel. It was just a short temper. We never knew what would come out of his mouth. He might be on the training ground, talking us through a set piece in detail and then he'd go off on a tangent and inquire about someone's family. I remember Neil Shipperley, who had just moved to the club from London, asking around to see if anyone could recommend a babysitter. Mick Jones, one of the backroom staff, was recommending one of the girls from the club shop when the gaffer interrupted. "I'll do it," he said. He was 100 per cent serious as well, but his kind offer was politely refused.

That was typical of Warnock – he was hard to predict. Occasionally, he'd take a step back and leave the training to Stuart McCall. He might arrive 45 minutes into the session and stand at a distance with a brolly over his head. But he knew exactly what was going on. And I joined at the start of a special season. He'd been at the club for six years and steadily constructed a team that was good enough to win promotion. His only real flaw was an addiction to buying strikers. Loved them. We always had far too many.

I liked the way that Warnock dealt with players. He allowed lads to miss training if there was a good personal reason. Because I had a four-hour round trip, he used to give me an occasional day off to relax and I appreciated that.

Phil had an entirely different view of the man. I was thrilled when, after just a month at the club, Warnock beckoned me up the bus on the way home from a League Cup game in Shrewsbury and offered a contract on the spot, an increase to £3,000 a week and an extra year on my deal. Without hesitation, I agreed. Phil was furious. "They've mugged you into signing on the bloody cheap," he screamed.

But after the uncertainty of the summer, I was content and enjoying football again. Everything fell into place that season. Ourselves and Reading set the pace, with Blackwell's Leeds pushing us close after the New Year as the final straight approached. The gaffer sanctioned a trip to Cheltenham in March, the mecca for a horse racing fan like myself, and by chance we bumped into a gang of Leeds lads. Sam Ellis, Blackwell's assistant, was in my ear saying they should have signed me because they were having problems on the right side of midfield. Our squad strength shone through over the closing weeks, with Danny Webber clinching promotion with a winner at Cardiff, a game I watched at home due to injury. After contributing to over 30 games, I could reflect with satisfaction. Not bad for a free agent who nobody had wanted.

Two and a half years after La Manga, I was back in the Premier League, and desperate to prove I could still cut it. I came off the bench in the opener with Liverpool and laid down a marker. Warnock was happy and, gradually, I progressed from super sub to regular. He even gave me the armband for the trip to Newcastle in November, knowing the significance of the fixture. We took home the three points. A month later, I banged home an 88th-minute winner against Charlton, one of the best strikes of my career, to lift us clear of the relegation zone. It was always going to be a battle to stay up, but it seemed as though we had control of our destiny.

As my influence grew, so did Phil's anger at the contract I'd rashly signed a year earlier. Promotion had increased my wage to £3,500 a week, well below standard Premier League terms. Phil was constantly trying to speak to Neil or the chairman, Terry Robinson, to improve it, but he was getting nowhere. We wanted £10,000 a week, a figure which the club were baulking at. Relations soured. The gaffer rang Phil and said, "Keith is the sort of player who shouldn't earn a lot of money, he should earn it by bonuses. If you give him money, he'll spend it."

I thought that was a load of bollocks, paying a player below the market rate because of how he might use the cash. I know that I threw cash away flippantly, but I'd never known a club to show too much concern. It was a tough one. I didn't want to rock the boat because the football was going well, but Phil was adamant that I had to force the issue and his argument made sense. I had only six months left on my contract and the club didn't seem to be in any hurry.

"Tell them you're not fucking happy," he'd say. "They're trying to convince me you're as happy as a pig in shit."

By January, it had become apparent that slapping in a transfer request was the only way to go. We typed up a letter that I brought in my bag to a game at Reading. I was staying in London afterwards, so the plan was to get it to Robinson before the boys travelled home. My timing was poor. There was an edge between the teams after our promotion fight the previous season and Neil had a long-running feud with their assistant, Wally Downes. Things were already fraught on the sidelines when I came on in the 53rd minute. My first act was to challenge their winger Stephen Hunt, for a throw-in, and he pinched me on the hip as a greeting. I swung my arm back and caught him around his throat. He went down dramatically, and Mark Halsey flashed a red card.

I lost the plot and, after walking a few steps down the touch-line, I went back to have a proper go at Hunt, leading with my forearm. I was dragged away and marched down the tunnel into the dressing room, not realising that I had made history – the quickest-ever sending off for a sub at that level. I'd been on the pitch for 12 seconds. The throw wasn't even taken. Hunt had flicked the red mist switch and although I hadn't worked up a sweat, I needed a shower to cool down. When I came out, Warnock was standing there, scowling.

"Is that what your fucking agent told you to do?" he screamed. "Get fucking sent off!"

I flipped, grabbed one of my boots and hurled it at the wall. "It's got fuck-all to do with fucking agents."

That was the end of the row. The game was still going on so I had no idea what the gaffer was doing there. It turned out he'd gone to war with Downes after my dismissal, and Halsey had sent him off too.

We lost 3-1 and I pondered whether to hand in the letter. But it was now or never so I gave it to our goalie, Paddy Kenny, and asked him to pass it to Robinson on the coach home.

I was London-bound when he opened it, with the lads on the phone giving me a running commentary on his reaction. They thought it was hilarious. "Oh, he's not happy... he's straight on the phone."

The request was refused, and the tension between Robinson and Phil escalated. The club had learned that Phil's agent's licence had expired. He had missed the papers in the post, and needed to go through the formalities to renew it. Robinson went to the press with the story and said they would be postponing all talks until June. Phil was certain it was just an excuse to delay negotiations, and was convinced that Warnock was part of a plot. He brought in a lawyer who could represent me in discussions instead of him, but they still baulked at our demands.

Despite all of that, I maintained a good relationship with the gaffer. I respected that he kept me in the team during the contract dispute when others might have taken a different course. He didn't even hand out a fine for the sending-off. Perhaps they were trying to drive a wedge between myself and Phil, but that was never going to happen after all we'd been through.

Unfortunately, the Reading game was part of a sticky patch that dragged us right into the dogfight again. Warnock had assembled a capable squad, a grounded set of lads.

The only exception was Colin Kazim-Richards, a youngster who was a bit of an idiot. He would come into training wearing a t-shirt with a picture of himself on it. Paddy Kenny drew a little moustache on it one day when he was in the showers. He was a cocky little kid. Even when I scored that screamer against Charlton, he ran over to tell me what a fluke it was. Nobody was sad when he left for Turkey.

With a good spirit and solid work ethic, I reckoned we would pull through in the final weeks, particularly when our main rivals were an inconsistent West Ham side. They were struggling and their fate looked to be sealed when it emerged that their Argentine signings, Carlos Tevez and Javier Mascherano, were effectively owned by a third party, their agent's company, which represented a breach of Premier League rules. Mascherano had moved to Liverpool in January, but Tevez played on for West Ham, even though he had been signed illegally.

The vibe was that West Ham were in real trouble. They went before an independent hearing in April and were fined £5.5

million. But there was no points deduction. The verdict gave the Premier League the power to terminate Tevez's registration, yet they allowed him to play on. He scored seven goals in their final ten matches.

It wouldn't have mattered to Sheffield United if we'd taken a point from our final game of the season. Wigan, who were also part of the equation, were the visitors to Bramall Lane. They needed a victory to overtake us. Considering that West Ham also had to win away at Manchester United to send us down, we kicked off 'Survival Sunday' in a strong position. But it all went wrong. I had a terrible game. Wigan led 2-1 at the break, and word filtered through that Tevez had scored a goal at Old Trafford that would be enough to keep West Ham up. We dominated the second half and missed chance after chance. Danny Webber clipped one over their keeper and was following up for the rebound off the post but the ball took a weird ricochet in a different direction. That summed it up. Time ran out and we had that horrible, sinking feeling.

Warnock resigned, while the club promised to fight the injustice and got stuck into a messy legal battle. I was part of a group of players that filed for compensation, but that went nowhere. The club eventually settled out of court for a substantial sum in March 2009, a piece of news that meant nothing to me. By then, I was on a short-term deal with Bradford, a world away from the bright lights. The Wigan nightmare was the end of my Premier League career.

I was oblivious to that reality at the time. True to form, I didn't get bogged down in disappointment and, instead, looked on the bright side. Warnock's departure had a silver lining. Eight years after the move to Middlesbrough fell through, I finally got a chance to work under Bryan Robson, who was drafted in as the replacement. Robbo immediately showed a desire to sort me a new contract. And, even though we'd been relegated, I secured a deal that was close to Premier League level. £6,500 a week with a £3,000 appearance fee. The tension between Robinson and Phil was still there as we reached agreement. "I like you, but I don't like that fucker," Robinson said.

My luck was in, even when it came to the horses. I'd moved to Harrogate, a beautiful spa town, that was closer to Sheffield. So I was spending less time in the car and more on the gambling. One morning, I stopped in a bookies on the way to training and stuck £20 on a Lucky 15 – an accumulator bet involving four different horses. They all came in, at prices ranging from 9/4 to 15/2. The shop wrote me a cheque for £24,000. A few weeks later, I landed another for £6,500. I diverted the winnings into my William Hill account, fuelled by a thirst for more.

Robbo could have done with some of that fortune. It just didn't happen for him. Really, we had a formula that should have worked. Warnock had brought in Kiddo towards the end of his reign and he stuck around, so we had an iconic manager and a top coach, in addition to a squad with plenty of Premier League quality. But it ended up a bit like the Blackburn experience. Teams lifted their game against us and we crumbled under pressure, right from the opening day when we conceded a late equaliser to Colchester. Robbo was under pressure from there on.

Outwardly, he didn't show the strain. He didn't go around the place bollocking people or throwing teacups. But when he raised his voice, it meant something. And he was capable of constructive criticism. I wasn't giving him enough. I know he was disappointed with me, especially after pushing for the contract.

We lost 3-2 at Scunthorpe and he called me into his office.

"How many crosses did you get in?" he asked. I had no idea.

"You didn't get any in. What's happened to you?"

The words stung and in the next game, against Cardiff, I started well and delivered a few decent crosses. And then I pulled my hamstring. It was typical of Robbo's luck. He was getting the grief when his soft players were to blame. After Christmas, the murmurs about his future grew louder, to the extent that we were all talking about it. I think everybody knew what was coming. We did hint at promise, winning an FA Cup tie at Bolton, but then followed it up with another dismal show against Scunthorpe, a team we should have been beating 10 times out of 10. Fittingly enough, Robbo's final game was at promotion-chasing West Brom, where we fully deserved our point. On paper, the two teams were evenly matched. The problem for Robbo was that they were Premier League bound, and Sheffield United were 16th.

I remember looking at him on the sideline that night, a former West Brom player and manager, listening to the chants of 'you're getting sacked in the morning' from their fans, and thinking what a lonely place management must be. Here was a legend of the game, a decorated former England captain, being mocked by people who used to sing his name. The club tried to persuade Robbo to stay on in an ambassadorial role but he saw that offer for what it was, and they parted ways.

I was genuinely upset, and when I learned who the club had quickly drafted in as his replacement, I was even more upset.

Mum actually heard it on the news, and called with information that made my heart sink. They'd appointed Blackwell.

He had served as Warnock's assistant before setting off for Leeds, and the board obviously remembered him fondly. All I could think about was his lack of respect when I didn't have a club. I'd talked with a few people in football about him after that, and the stories weren't very encouraging. Warnock had fallen out with Blackwell after finding out in the papers that he was leaving for Leeds, and we'd discussed our mutual dislike for him. Funnily enough, I bumped into Warnock shortly afterwards and he confirmed the ominous feeling that I had about my future.

"Fucking hell," he said, "When I heard he got the job, the first thing I thought about was you."

He knew it meant trouble. This wasn't going to end well.

(24)

Lighting The Fuse

MANY drinks had been taken when I first lifted my phone to send an anonymous, abusive text message to Kevin Blackwell. I kept it simple.

"How's the small man syndrome going?"

It felt damn good, when it delivered. And, even though there was no reply, I decided it wouldn't be the last time that I punched his number in at an uncivilised hour.

Childish? Definitely. But I have so little respect for the man that I can't say that I regret it. My Sheffield United career was over when I sunk to those depths. Truth be told, it was effectively finished when he walked in the door. He picked a striker, Jon Stead, on the right wing for his first match, and directed me to the stands. I didn't start another competitive game for the club.

Of course, I was never going to like a man that clearly didn't rate me. But it's not the rejection that makes Blackwell the worst boss I've ever worked under. It was his style of management, that at times I felt just amounted to abusing and belittling people. I sent him that message because to me he was a living version of that character in the Harry Enfield sketch show, the short man always looking to pick a fight because he's insecure about his size. Maybe that's unfair. Blackwell's paranoia might have just come from his lack of standing in the game. He was a low-grade player who had done well to manage at this level but, from what I could see, his people skills were deplorable.

Put simply, I saw him as a bully. Like most people who have that label attached, he picked his battles. Certain senior respected players like Gary Speed and James Beattie never felt his wrath. The younger lads seemed fair game. We had a guy called David Cotterill on loan from Wigan, a talented lad who Robbo had brought in to compete with me on the right side. He was treated disgracefully. Blackwell seemed to spend every minute roaring abuse at Cotts, be it on the training ground or in a match. One time, a defender smashed a clearance straight at Cotts, who was completely blameless, but Blackwell tore into him. Cotts just stood there, shaking his head, asking "how is it my fault?"

My longest appearance under Blackwell was at Southampton on the final day of the season, when he was caning Cotts from the outset and lost the plot so much that he took him off before half-time and sent me on. The long walk to the sideline when you've been subbed that early in a game is the ultimate humiliation for a footballer, but Cotts still chose to make his deal permanent in the summer. I could never understand that.

Billy Sharp was another to get it in the neck. When there was a problem with the front line, Billy was singled out, even when Beattie was contributing nothing. Ugo Ehiogu, a defender who'd been around the block, could see through it. We shared the same view. Blackwell behaved like he was intimidated by the big-name players, perhaps even threatened by them. It was easier to have a go at Billy. When I did sit on the bench, I couldn't believe the extent of it. Andy Leaning, the goalkeeping coach, would look at me and roll his eyes.

Andy was a good guy to be around, unlike some other members of the backroom staff, the 'yes' men who were appointed to back up the weak general. Blackwell brought Sam Ellis from Leeds as assistant, the same man who'd been in my ear at Cheltenham two years previously saying what a mistake it was not to offer me a contract. When the shit was hitting the fan in the manager's office one day, I brought that up, and Sam denied it point blank, probably in an attempt to cover himself. That just about summed Sam up.

I never trusted him. Sam's main role at the club seemed to be policing a fines system at our training ground, Shirecliffe, that developed from a bit of fun into a pain in the arse. He was a timekeeper, standing by the dressing room door, giving a running commentary on everyone's arrival. 'Oh, you're lucky, you've just made it' or 'Oh, you're late, that's a £5 fine'. He'd be lurking around the showers. 'Have you got flip flops on? No. That's another £2'. 'Whose loose top is this? Number 22? Is that you? Well that's a fiver.' I'd be thinking, 'You're fucking assistant manager, have you nothing else better to do?'

Mark Smith, the reserve team manager, reminded me of Blackwell. His sessions mostly consisted of the same repetitive drill. There wasn't much encouragement on offer and the atmosphere was dreadful. Dean Riddle, the fitness coach, was an okay bloke but, like Smith, he had an inflated sense of his own authority. Blackwell even supported me in a row with Riddle once, when he approached myself and Dave Carney – an Aussie who was also out of favour – towards the end of training and told us if we did a quick running session with him, we could have the afternoon off. The senior pros were never in after lunch, so I told him where to go. It kicked off, and Blackwell had to intervene to invite me to his office. "I've told Dean under no circumstances will you ever be training again in the afternoon," he said. He told Smith the same thing when he tried a similar stunt.

That was a rare instance where I wondered if I was too harsh on Blackwell. Another came towards the end of that season where he took over, he turned around in the dying stages of a game against Leicester. "Are you on appearance money?" he asked. "Yes, I am gaffer." A couple of minutes later, I was running on to earn an easy £3,000. I didn't think he was such a bad bloke that night, and considered the possibility that I was just bitter because I couldn't get near the team. I was also on a decent contract and didn't want to go anywhere, so I went through a phase of thinking I should give him a chance. By the time I'd spent a summer with the man, however, our relationship was a ticking time-bomb.

A pre-season tour in Hungary was the tipping point. Sheffield United had built a relationship with their top club, Ferencvaros, through our chairman Kevin McCabe's business interests, so we travelled there to continue preparations. I could already see how the squad was shaping up, and became increasingly certain that I wouldn't be in contention for a starting place whatever happened. Blackwell was unbearable, really getting under my skin. Even when he tried to be one of the lads, it was annoying. I didn't see the point in being civil to him any more.

His idea of injecting fun into a session was introducing forfeits. We played piggy in the middle, with two lads in the centre of a circle trying to block passes from the group, and the worst pair were to be punished. I was in there with Stephen Quinn, a young lad from Dublin, and when the lads called for handball when I'd stopped a pass with my chest, Blackwell sided with them. "Right, let's continue from where we were," he said. "25 passes so far." It was only five or six. Nobody laughed. "Hang on," I shouted. "Can we just stop for a minute and laugh at the manager who thinks he's so fucking funny." Gary Speed was in stitches, and that embarrassed Blackwell. He didn't like being undermined – especially in front of Speedo.

A few days later, he split us into twos, saying that if neither one of a duo could chip the ball onto the crossbar from a certain distance, the penalty would be running for the rest of training. "C'mon Bestie, join in," he said. I was sure he wanted the pleasure of seeing me do laps. So, with Quinny as my partner again, I jogged up and struck the bar perfectly with my first attempt, celebrating with a fist pumping fuck-you salute in Blackwell's direction that didn't go down well.

We had passed the point of no return. The niggling continued, a smart comment here and there, so the season kicked off as I expected. I would report for an away trip, count the number of other lads on the bus, and realise before the key turned in the ignition that I'd be lucky to make the bench. I would more than likely spend the game in the stands. Blackwell would have been better off taking young lads for experience, but I suspected that he quite liked bringing me around the country for nowt. The best I could hope for was a few minutes as sub, a happy alternative to doing shuttle runs on the pitch after the match with nobody but the cleaners there to watch you. Other bosses would at least allow the outcasts and reserves to do their exercise beforehand but this was a regime that placed little value on player satisfaction.

The inevitable blow up came in September, when I was brought to Norwich and stuck on the bench. Already, I was in bad enough form after they'd rushed me back from international duty for training a week earlier only to tell me I could do 15 minutes on the bike and go home. So, I finally flipped when, with six minutes left and the game scoreless, Blackwell took off Cotts and replaced him with our teenage full-back, Kyle Naughton. He was putting a 19-year-old defender in my position instead of me.

"Fucking wanker," I screamed. The lads on the bench looked to see who I was addressing.

I pointed at Blackwell.

He turned around and put a finger to his lip and shushed me. "NO, YOU BE FUCKING QUIET, YOU FUCKING WANKER."

Norwich scored a last-minute winner. I stormed down the tunnel ready to have it out, and marched into the dressing room where I swiped a plate of sandwiches off the bench. It smashed into pieces. Blackwell walked in. Most of the players were still on the pitch.

"Fucking grow up," he shouted.

On the run: Battling it out for Blackburn Rovers against Manchester United, trying to get the better of Mikael Silvestre. I often found myself exiled during my time at Ewood Park

Rover time: There was a good bunch of lads at Blackburn. I always enjoyed a laugh with Garry Flitcroft. Here we are celebrating against United in 2001. Above: Enjoying another goal – this time with Dwight Yorke

Silver lining: Getting a winner's medal at last with victory in the Worthington Cup Final of 2002. The boss, Graeme Souness, had us well prepared for the challenge of Tottenham

La Manga nightmare: Facing the cameras after leaving Sangonera Prison, which wasn't as intimidating as I feared it would be. Some of the inmates were actually supportive of our plight

Innocent men: The focus of attention at Alicante airport with Frank Sinclair and Paul Dickov. We were greeted by a British media scrum as we checked in for a flight back to the UK

All eyes on us: Back home and the cameras were even there at a Leicester reserve game to get a picture of me and Paul

A losing battle: Cristiano Ronaldo and United were 1-0 winners in April, 2004. We would soon be relegated after one season in the top flight

Of to a flier: In action against Iceland in 2001. I responded to a dressing down from boss Sammy McIlroy in Heathrow Airport to turn in one of my best performances for my country

Famous scalp: The 1-0 win over England at Windsor Park in September, 2005, will live with me forever. Here I am coming up against Rio Ferdinand.

Standing together: I join boss Lawrie Sanchez in saluting the amazing travelling support against England at Old Trafford. In the end, I was disappointed to see Sanchez call time on his reign

Spanish highs: Celebrating with my good mate David Healy after our 3-2 win over Spain in September, 2006. We underestimated the victory at the time – Spain would go on to dominate the international scene

Beginning of the end: Feeling glum during a defeat to Slovenia in 2008. I made my last appearance for my country against Hungary (right) later that year

Blade runner: Back in the Premier League with Sheffield United. I scored one of my best ever goals against Charlton (left) but getting sent off during a wage dispute sparked a row with Neil Warnock

That sinking feeling: The heartbreak of relegation. Things soon got much worse for me at Sheffield United and a loan move to Charlton (right) provided a welcome escape from my problems

Sad day: At the funeral of Alan McDonald (inset below). I never expected to be saying goodbye to him so soon. Big Mac was always someone I looked up to as a guiding influence

Reunion: The man joking behind the camera is the one and only Tino Asprilla. Together again for a charity event, we reminisced about the good times we had at Newcastle

Still playing: Pulling on a black and white shirt again for The Entertainers Charity Match against a Liverpool Legends XI in 2011

The most important people: Enjoying being a dad with (top, left) Madison, newly-born Nico (right) and (above left) Lexie. Above right: Coming full circle – signing for Longford Town

The future:
Who knows
what it holds…

"Grow up? I've had bigger and better managers than you, and they haven't treated me like this."

"You had a big-name manager last year and look what happened."

I didn't appreciate the dig at Robbo. By now, he was right in my face, so I stood up and went head-to-head, egging him on to hit me. He was always telling this story about how he'd knocked out Stan Ternent in a row years earlier.

"Go on, tell us the Stan Ternent story again," I said. By now, the majority of the others were present. Speedo came in and pulled us apart. Blackwell was shaking with rage. It got silly.

"That cunt over there," he said, pointing at me.

"Fuck off you cunt."

"You're a fucking cunt."

"You fucking egg."

"You're a fucking egg."

Speedo looked in my direction. "Fucking shut up". The manager kept shouting, so Speedo turned to him. "You can fucking shut up too." Blackwell did what he was told. He wasn't going to take on the real authority of the dressing room.

I was punished with a two-week fine for my outburst and indefinitely sent to the reserves. Anyone who associated with me was in trouble. I felt particularly sorry for Ben Rome, one of the masseurs who had the misfortune to live beside me in Harrogate. This became a problem for Ben when my fast driving landed me in the dock. I'd spent six months off the road when I was at Blackburn for reaching 12 penalty points, and didn't learn the lesson. My £120,000 Aston Martin always seemed to be going quicker than I realised. I hit 12 points again, and another six-month ban was the punishment. Ben heard and kindly offered me a daily lift into training. Strangely, management started demanding that he report for work at 9am while the other members of staff swanned in afterwards. Blackwell and Ellis would tear strips off Ben if he was late, and it had a big effect on him; he'd be a nervous wreck in his car, fidgeting and constantly looking at his watch if there was a delay, fearing he'd get the sack. The players didn't arrive until 9.30am or 10am, so having a masseur in earlier didn't make any sense. He was put under undue stress for his generosity, and that made me angrier. I was hating every minute around the place and, after a blazing argument with Ellis, they suspended me for a week. Ellis notified me by letter, claiming that they were trying to do me a favour.

"It is quite clear there is still resentment towards our relationship," he wrote. "We have no wish to keep taking your wages, so we have decided to suspend you for one week starting Monday September 29th. After this week there is a two-week international break... we hope that your attitude has changed when you report back to training at 11am on Monday, October 20th, 2008."

Nothing was going to change though. November provided a temporary escape. I was sitting at home one afternoon when the new Charlton boss Phil Parkinson rang to say they wanted me on loan; I'd come up in discussion after the game and they'd enquired about my whereabouts.

The chance to get away for a month was a no-brainer, and I enjoyed my time there. I looked forward to getting out of bed in the morning again and, football wise, it went okay, without being spectacular. I set my heart on a full-time move somewhere in January. Sheffield United recalled me at the beginning of the month, saying they were short of bodies for an FA Cup tie at Leyton Orient. Another wasted journey. Typical.

I sunk into the background again, all the time asking Phil if there was anything he could do. But I did have one worry, an ongoing back problem that might have been an obstacle to a move. I played a practice match at the start of the week before the window shut, and the pain was still there. Sam approached me after.

"You're playing for the reserves tomorrow night," he said.

"No, I'm not. It's the last week of the transfer window and I'm not going out to play in a game where I might do myself no favours."

"Right, you're in this afternoon then."

I explained that Dennis Pettitt, the physio, was managing the problem. Dennis was an ex-RAF serviceman who was retiring at the end of the season. He knew his stuff, and also didn't seem to enjoy working with Blackwell. Some bosses recognise their limits when it comes to the medical side of things, but our gaffer was the interfering type. Dennis might recommend one course of recovery for a player, and then Blackwell would step in and dictate another plan. So, clearly, anything Dennis had to say about my back was going to be ignored by management. He was telling me to be careful, and advised against sticking around for the afternoon in case I overdid it. I showered, changed and was ready for home when Sam, as busy as ever, appeared over my shoulder in the dressing room.

"Just go down and get yourself a bit of lunch and come up and get a bit of treatment," he chirped.

He wasn't listening to a word I was saying. I flipped, and

looked for something to kick. The bin was all I could see, so I sprinted across the room and volleyed it against the wall.

"Will you fucking leave me alone?" I screamed.

I grabbed my bag, and headed for the door with Dave Carney who was giving me a lift to the train station. Sam had little to say. "Just have a word with him, Dave," he muttered. I shot back. "I'm fucking not injured, I'm not training, I'm going home." And that was that.

Mick McGuire from the PFA called that evening. "Go in and have the problem assessed tomorrow," he said. I'd calmed down by then, and agreed. It was a Wednesday, so the first-teamers were off. The only other lads around were those carrying knocks, so Derek Geary and a young lad, Nicky Travis, were there. Dennis performed a few basic checks and said it would be too risky for me to play a match. He told me to go and soak in the bath while he called Blackwell to get the all-clear.

I was lying there when he sheepishly approached me with his response. "I've spoken to the manager and he says that under no circumstances are you leaving until 5pm." This was 11am. No chance. I rang Blackwell.

"Why the hell are you keeping me in?"

"Keith, if I say you're in until five o'clock, you're in til five o'clock."

"No, you're keeping me in and it's out of order. You're trying to bully me."

He hung up. I rang back

"Why the fuck did you put the phone down?"

"I'm with my Dad here."

So I called Sam instead. I threatened to report the pair of

them to the PFA. I brought up Blackwell's dismissal of Bryan Robson in the dressing room at Carrow Road. "How would Bryan Robson, a legend, feel about getting caned by some fucker who played 40 times for Boston and Scarborough?" I said. Sam was suddenly defensive. "Ah, there's no need to do all of that." I put the phone down.

The PFA sent Simon Barker, the ex-QPR midfielder, to Sheffield the following day.

We met at the training ground for tea and toast before he went into speak with the management duo and Terry Robinson. He came out with good news. The club told Simon they wanted to sack me but wouldn't do it if the PFA could sort me with a transfer before the end of the season. It was a stupid thing to say. They couldn't give the union an ultimatum like that. 'Find a club or you're sacked?' That wouldn't stand up if we had taken the case to court. Simon reckoned we had them by the balls – if they wanted rid of me, they would have to pay me off. So, Phil was called and went in to thrash out a severance package with the powers that be. On January 30, 2009, the Compromise Agreement was signed. Sheffield United paid me £87,000, and I officially became a free agent.

Despite my departure, I did keep in contact with Blackwell in my own, unique, late night, anonymous way. It was how I channelled the frustration.

My exit had slipped under the radar because, somehow, the team was doing quite well. The nicest thing I can say about Blackwell is that for all his personality flaws, he was technically quite a good coach. He was also given funds to strengthen the squad and played the loan market well, constructing a team with a balance of youth and experience. They put a run together to finish third in the league, and then reached the play-off final where Burnley, a team with modest resources in comparison, proved too good. Blackwell was slaughtered for getting the tactics wrong and going with a 4-5-1.

I wanted to send a message but he had switched to a new number. To be fair, I can understand why he changed it.

My actions would catch up on me. As part of the deal with Ferencvaros, Craig Short had moved there as assistant to their manager, Bobby Davison. They were doing some pre-season work at Shirecliffe and I was invited along. Craig grew up in the same area as Blackwell, so they spoke quite a bit. He approached me after one of the sessions. "Blackie wants a word with you," he said.

I wasn't sure what it was about, but thought I'd go and hear him out. He wore a familiar expression when I found him waiting for me, pacing around with a phone in his hand.

"Was this you?" he said, showing me the small man syndrome message.

"That's not my number," I lied.

He showed me another text.

'Congratulations on making history.'

I'd sent that one in February, on the night that Sheffield Wednesday had won the derby to do the double over United for the first time in 95 years. Again, I pleaded ignorance, and butted in before he produced another.

"Look, I know who's ringing you, but I'm not prepared to say."

I was aware of another person who liked to dial Blackwell late at night. My Northern Ireland team-mate Warren Feeney hated him even more than I did. Blackwell was appointed Luton manager on the day that Warren had agreed to leave the club and join Cardiff. He went into the dressing room to say goodbye to the lads and Blackwell caused a scene. "We don't want any traitors in here," he said. Warren couldn't forgive that and started ringing Blackwell in the early hours, roaring abuse down the phone. Blackwell's wife would sometimes answer. "Stop ringing my Kevin," she'd say.

I didn't grass Warren up as my 'chat' with Blackwell became a full-blown argument. "I'll decide whether you go to Ferencvaros or not," he shouted. "I can fuck you up."

Somehow, we ended up discussing his credentials as a boss. He didn't like his ability being questioned.

"I'm not just a good manager. I'm a top manager. I've been to three play-off finals in the last six years."

"Yeah, but you've fucking lost them all."

"That makes no odds. I'm a top manager."

From a man who'd won nothing in the game, the arrogance was astounding (And he'd only been assistant to Warnock in one of those finals). But he did appear to enjoy one victory that summer. The Ferencvaros deal didn't happen. I couldn't be absolutely sure that it was down to him but after our conversation, how could I not have thought that? One way or another, 18 months after his appointment, he had succeeded in fucking my career up. I was staring into the abyss, finished in the upper echelons of English football.

There was no happy ending for Blackwell either. The players stopped responding to his confidence-sapping methods. They didn't make the play-offs the following season, and he left by 'mutual consent' at the start of the 2010/11 campaign after a thrashing at the hands of a QPR side managed by none other than Neil Warnock.

Luckily I happened to have his latest number, and sent my commiserations. For some reason, I had the name of a non-league club stuck in my head.

'Braintree are looking for a new manager,' I started. 'A good experienced manager. Do you know of anyone?'

It took him two years to find a job, at my old haunt Bury, who were too broke to find a quality alternative. He announced his arrival by calling his new players 'garbage', and then led them to relegation. They have my sympathies.

(25)

We Can Be Heroes

IT'S the worst training session of my career. Three days before
a World Cup qualifier with Wales, I am watching a young full-
back from Wolves, Mark Clyde, pump long diagonal balls from
the halfway line towards the edge of the penalty box where our
goalkeeper Roy Carroll is comfortably gathering every ball.

"Cherries!" shouts Roy, as he rises to collect another punt
under no pressure. When a keeper calls that, he's basically saying that it's too easy. This is ridiculous. It happens again and
again. But Mark is just following the instructions of the new
Northern Ireland boss. "That's exactly what I want," bellows
Lawrie Sanchez, the man who the IFA had selected as Sammy
McIlroy's replacement. My first impression was negative, and
on that morning, seven months after our initial meeting, I was
even more convinced that it was a terrible decision.

The previous night, we'd lost his competitive debut 3-0 to Poland at Windsor Park. Lawrie's finest moment as a player was scoring the winning goal for Wimbledon in the 1988 FA Cup final, a side famous for its direct approach, so he clearly wanted to bring that style to Northern Ireland. But some of his drills just weren't making any sense, particularly this one. I couldn't believe what I was seeing or hearing. "Are you for fucking real?" I shout, in response to his approval for Roy's latest catch.

Lawrie looked at me, shook his head and continued as before.

I didn't make the bench for the game in Wales. No big surprise considering I was an unused sub in the Polish thrashing, and the obvious evidence that my relationship with Lawrie was rapidly deteriorating. I'd already predicted what would happen when Gerry Armstrong, who was back as part of the coaching staff, interrupted my card school on the afternoon of the game in Cardiff. The boys who aren't going to get a jersey generally find out before we go to the stadium. Gary Hamilton knew he had no chance. "Gary, can Lawrie have a word?" Gerry asked. "Ah, it's alright, I know what it's about," Gary replied, barely looking up. "Keith, Lawrie would like to see you too," Gerry said. I decided to go and hear the predictable news.

There was a patio outside the hotel lobby which overlooked some water. Lawrie was sitting there with a free chair beside him. I sat down. "You're not going to be involved tonight," he said. "Okay, cheers" I replied, while hopping up and walking off before he could react. I saw his reflection in the glass door as I went back inside and he looked a little taken aback, as though he was preparing for a chat. But I had no intention of spending any more time with him than necessary.

The boys drew 2-2 that night, and Lawrie must have been

satisfied with the performance of his chosen players. When he named the squad for the following month's double-header with Azerbaijan and Austria, I missed the cut.

There was more to it than just one training session. Quite literally, I had started off on the wrong foot with Lawrie. In his first friendly match against Norway in February 2004, the goal famine still hung over our heads. We kept missing chances and were 3-0 down when David Healy finally ended our misery just before the hour mark. From the restart, all I could think about was getting another one, and I did – at our end of the pitch. I was buzzed up and sprinted back to help the defence, just in time to divert a Norwegian cross past Maik Taylor.

The next game, a friendly in Estonia, was a fortnight after I came home from La Manga. I found out on Sky that I wasn't a part of the squad. So I rang Lawrie, who said he wanted to look at fringe players which was fair enough, but I found it strange that he didn't call me beforehand. That was Lawrie though, he didn't really have much personality. He may have been part of Wimbledon's Crazy Gang, but from his dour opening speech it was obvious he was never going to provide any laughs. The entertainment came from his support staff. His assistant, Terry Gibson, and goalkeeping coach, Dave Beasant, were also members of the '88 FA Cup team and they seriously lightened the mood. Big Bes was a brilliant character, who'd always join the team on our nights out, and was trusted by the lads.

Lawrie did try to change the social culture though. He'd won three caps under Billy Bingham – he was born in London but his mother was Northern Irish – and knew all the stories about our drinking escapades. Clearly, it bugged him. When all the senior lads were brought back in for a friendly with Serbia, he called us into a meeting. "What should we do?" he said. "Should we just ban drink for all trips?" That idea didn't get very far. Michael Hughes spoke up and objected, arguing that we were professional enough to drink at the right time. I backed his comments and, with no dissenting voices, it was knocked on the head. Lawrie was asking the question, and had received his answer.

When it came to the beloved summer tours, however, the lines were again blurred on what constituted drinking at the right time. Lawrie's first such trip in charge was a comical tour of the Caribbean for games with Barbados, St Kitts & Nevis and Trinidad & Tobago. It sounded great for a holiday, but it was a pain in the arse at the end of a long stressful season. CONCACAF, the local ruling body, had invited the IFA and offered to pay all their costs, although I believe there were a few problems from that end of things when it came to the crunch. Not that we paid much attention. All we knew is that we had to turn up because Lawrie made it clear that, unless a good reason was given for pulling out, any no-shows would miss out on the World Cup qualifiers. Considering we'd just been drawn in a group with England, that was a big threat, but it didn't prevent some withdrawals.

The itinerary was crazy. I think we had to take four different flights to get from Barbados to St Kitts, so the stopovers in the airport bars were the only thing that stopped us from completely losing our minds. And it was the banter that kept us going between the games. Lawrie was getting on everyone's nerves. In the first game with Barbados, which was played on a cow field, he was intent on introducing his new tactics. The defenders were encouraged to go long every time. I was dropping short to look for the ball and it was just sent over the top for someone to chase. In scorching heat, the strategy didn't make sense and I let him know my feelings.

Still, apart from the football, the trip was quite enjoyable. Lawrie seemed to think it was too enjoyable. After we brushed aside St Kitts, he laid down some ground rules before the final match with Trinidad & Tobago. Going out was banned. So was afternoon drinking. We were training in the evenings because of the heat, and quite a few of us had taken to relaxing with a few beers in the middle of the day. I suppose I could see where Lawrie was coming from on that one. But the nights were different and when I bumped into Dwight Yorke two days before our game, and he mentioned showing me around his home patch, there was no chance of me staying in. Later that evening, I sneaked out with Gary Hamilton and Andy Smith to go and meet Yorkey. Unfortunately, his chosen club was also where Gerry Armstrong, Big Bes and a few of the backroom staff had ended up on their night out. Gerry came over and told us to go home, but I refused. My attitude was that we were in trouble whatever happened, so we might as well enjoy the night. It was a bloody stupid trip anyway.

Lawrie left me out of the team for the game, and I flipped when he told us on the training ground. Okay, so I had stepped out of line, but he'd selected Phil Mulryne, a lad who was a few years behind me at Manchester United, even though he'd turned up at training drunk the day before I broke curfew. "That's a joke Lawrie," I said. We stood away from the group and had it out for a good 30 minutes. He admitted he knew about Phil and, convinced I was being made the scapegoat, I stormed away, telling him to leave me off the bench. I only changed my mind when Terry Gibson came to my hotel room and talked me out of it. That was the start of the slippery slope with Lawrie. He thought I was argumentative and I was, but only because of how much he wound me up with his inconsistent decisions and rubbish tactics. We didn't have much to say to each other after that. Two or three word conversations at most, one or two words fewer than his chats with the others, many of whom shared my view. I reached breaking point in September when Michael Hughes got the nod ahead of me for the Polish game. Hughesy didn't go to the Caribbean, despite the manager's warning. More bullshit. That's why I had no interest in a discussion on that patio in Wales. I had no time for the man.

That could have been the end of international football for me but, a year later, I tasted my greatest moment in a green jersey. The night we beat England at Windsor Park. It's an occasion that will live with me forever. Lawrie masterminded the success. My view of his approach had turned full circle.

There's no big secret about how I got into his good books. Sometimes, in football, it's quite straightforward. I was dropped for that trip to Azerbaijan and looked to be in serious trouble. But then a few bodies dropped out of the game, the call was extended my way, and I accepted it. Perhaps Lawrie thought I wouldn't fancy an unglamorous 8,000-kilometre round trip to Baku, but I reported for duty, played the game, did a reasonably good job and stayed in his team after that. Simple. No heart-to-heart chat was required.

The game in Azerbaijan was a dull draw, but I gradually began to understand the method behind his strategy. He just thought we needed to compromise for our lack of options by keeping it simple and getting the ball forward as quickly as possible, and trying to pick up second balls here and there to see what happens. He focused on stats and set pieces, and always produced the figures of how many crosses we were getting into the box. It was repetitive and often boring but, over time, we became more effective. Certainly, it didn't change overnight. Lawrie was slow to win over the public and had running battles with the press. We drew with Austria, and then lost 4-0 to England at Old Trafford, a game that was memorable for the fantastic travelling support. The fact that we were level at the break gave some hope for encouragement. Still, a defeat in Poland meant we were still searching for a victory going into the double-header with Azerbaijan and England in September, 2005.

If there was a real turning point for Lawrie, it was a friendly with Malta a month earlier. It finished 1-1 and I was sent off by the English ref, Mike Riley, for a silly scrap with one of their lads. They were a poor side so it was another dismal result and Lawrie tore into us afterwards. He made it clear that the two games in Belfast were vital, although the message obviously didn't hit home with everyone. A team meeting was scheduled on the Sunday, the beginning of the week leading up to the Azerbaijan match. Mulryne and Jeff Whitley didn't show. They'd arrived in Belfast, mad to go for a drink. I knew because they rang me but, for once, I stayed put, especially as I was so relieved to be available – my first thought when Riley flashed the red card in Malta was that I'd be suspended but it only carried into the next friendly game.

Lawrie kicked Phil and Jeff out of the camp. It was a big statement, particularly at a time when his own position didn't appear to be that strong. A couple more bad results might have spelled the end for him. But it worked. The focus was good and we brushed Azerbaijan aside 2-0, our first competitive win in almost four years.

Then came England. Victory gave us some momentum, but they were naturally clear favourites when we met in Belfast on Wednesday, September 7, 2005. They had Rooney, Gerrard, Beckham, Ferdinand, Lampard, a squad packed with Premier League talent. We had a mixture of lads from up and down the divisions in England and Scotland. All of us had tasted some kind of rejection in our careers, and this was a chance to make a statement. Before our game in Manchester, The Sun ran a sweepstake for their readers with a range of possible final scores. It went all the way up to a 14-0 win for England, really taking the piss. And that was in my mind before the return match. We knew a massive audience was watching, and it was a chance to show we were better than they thought. Lawrie's pre-match team-talks rarely lived long in the memory, but he got the tone right. As we were standing up to leave the dressing room, he played the David Bowie song, 'Heroes' on the stereo. You know the words. 'We can be heroes, just for one day...'

And this was our day. The atmosphere was incredible, just like the special nights in the '80s that I spent with Dad on the Kop. Our first objective was making it to half-time scoreless, and we managed to do that relatively comfortably. The English lads were frustrated. In fact, I probably could have got Wayne Rooney sent off. He jumped for a header and caught me with his elbow. I didn't make a meal of it and the ref produced a yellow. Wayne thanked me on the way to the tunnel. But Becks was having a right go, telling him to calm down. It was just

what we wanted. They were rattled. Lawrie told us to start playing the match in their half, getting the ball forward as quickly
as possible. All the training ground work was built towards this.
In the 73rd minute, it paid off. We pegged them back, and their
keeper, Paul Robinson, hoofed the ball towards the halfway
line. Steve Davis judged the flight better than Lampard, and
found the space to chip David Healy into space. He did the
rest, right in front of the Kop. I was the closest to him and will
never forget the sound of that celebration, or the noise at the
final whistle after we held out for the win. We were heroes, and
stayed on the pitch to do a lap of honour.

England were gracious in defeat. Becks clapped the Kop and
was very complimentary. Their manager, Sven Goran Eriksson,
popped his head into the dressing room to say well done on his
way up to get a grilling from the press, which spoke volumes
for his character. I leaned back against the wall, mentally and
physically drained by the experience. Just like after the Barca
game back in '97, I didn't go out that night. So, I went back to
Mum's and sat up and watched the video of the game, remind-
ing myself what had just happened.

I'd be lying if I said that everybody had grown to love Lawrie.
We never looked forward to his meetings. "Not another fucking
one!" someone would say. They were regular affairs, and often
quite strange.

A year after the England win, he called us together before
the Euro 2008 qualifiers. Expectations were higher, although
we'd landed another tricky group with Spain, Denmark, and
Sweden. Lawrie presented us with a projection of how the table
might look at the end of the campaign. He had predicted the

possible results for all games, not just who would win or lose, but also the goals for and against. As he went through it in nerdy detail, there were a few raised eyebrows. It was extremely bizarre. In his scenario, we would finish second, behind Spain. I guess he wanted us to believe in that vision, but we had to come to realise that the oddness was just part of his personality. The main thing was that, football wise, he was bringing us on the right way.

Still, his crystal ball theory was out the window after the first game, the visit of Iceland to Windsor Park. Lawrie had it down as a home win. We were three down at half-time and that was that. They beat us fair and square, and it hurt. It was a terrible afternoon, and I went into town that evening with Healy and Roy Carroll to get it out of the system. We had more than a couple. The following day it was back to work. Spain were coming to town as the second part of the double header. It was an odd build-up. Lawrie always had his issues with the local press and wasn't talking to them now, so a few of us were sent out in his place on the Monday. Then, on the morning of the game, the Northern Irish edition of The Sun splashed with a front page picture of myself, Healy and Roy on the town after the Iceland match.

The implication was that we didn't care. Roy had bought a bottle of champagne, which added to the story. Lawrie knew we were out, so it wasn't like we had breached discipline. Typically, they had waited until the morning of the game to put it out but if the intention was to turn people against us, then it backfired. It was the dawn of another famous day.

We knew at the time that turning Spain over was a big deal. For a small nation like ours, beating a major nation is always going to be huge. But looking back now, it was an even better result than we realised. They were building a team that would go on to dominate international football for six years, winning two European Championships and a World Cup. Xavi, Iker Casillas, David Villa, Xabi Alonso, Fernando Torres and Carles Puyol started, with Cesc Fabregas and Andres Iniesta on the bench. But this was another night where Healy looked like the world beater. Xavi scored, he equalised. Villa scored, and he levelled again. Ten minutes from time, he completed his hat-trick in front of the Kop, lobbing Casillas from 25 yards. It was backs to the wall then and Jonny Evans, another young Northern Irish lad coming through at Manchester United, was outstanding at left-back on his debut. At the final whistle, 14,500 voices let out a roar to rival the English celebration.

It was a magic time to be a Northern Ireland player. From a situation a few years previous where only 3,000-4,000 people were attending games, we could have sold the ground three or four times over. And everyone was starting to believe. Lawrie might have got the specific results wrong, but a top-two finish in the group – and automatic qualification for Euro 2008 – began to look very possible. We drew in Denmark with the backing of our biggest away support in over 20 years, and then took full points from Latvia at home and Liechtenstein away, before another famous win at Windsor against Sweden put us top of the group.

Everything was going right. We had a really balanced side that didn't give much away, while Healy was in simply unbelievable form. His club career could never reach the heights of his international form. At that time, he was playing for a poor Leeds side in the Championship, yet he still managed to become the highest ever scorer in a European qualifying campaign. Not just in Northern Irish history. I mean, across the entire continent.

It was inevitable that our exploits would draw attention. People in England were beginning to wonder about the secret of our success. Lawrie's profile soared, and it was to our cost. His contract was small money.

With five games left in the 2006/07 Premier League season, Fulham needed a manager to fight the drop and the IFA allowed Lawrie to take over on a caretaker basis. We feared the worst when he managed to keep them up.

There was a campaign for him to stay, because it was such a critical point in the Euros race. But we all understood why the Fulham job was going to be too attractive when they offered it on a full-time basis. It was a chance to manage at the top level and multiply his salary. Football is a selfish game and for those reasons, the lads didn't want Lawrie to leave. But it's also why we couldn't begrudge his decision to walk away. I'd imagine most of us would have done the same.

I was genuinely disappointed. It turned out the IFA had made a brilliant call to appoint him, and the really sad thing is that his departure didn't work out well for either party. A little over six months later, Lawrie was out of a job, and our dreams of qualifying for a major tournament were dead.

26

Down The Ladder

MY texting didn't always lead to trouble.

When my final fling with Frances finished, I waited for time to pass and then made contact with Vikki again. It'd been ages since we had spoken, but she was still on my mind, and I knew the feeling was mutual when I received a prompt response to my message. After a steady flow of SMS traffic, I decided to go and see her in London and, from there, it escalated. The distance apart remained a problem, so she made the big decision to pack her bags and move to Hartlepool, just after I got promoted with Sheffield United.

And then it became even more serious. We decided to try for a baby. Vikki had suffered a couple of miscarriages so we kept the celebrations in check when she fell pregnant in the spring of 2007. But there was no need to be nervous. On October

27, I became the father of a beautiful baby girl. We called her Madison. A couple of months later, I suddenly realised the significance of the birthday; it was the 12th anniversary of Black Friday. I guess I was due a bit of luck on that date.

I'd always been pretty good with my sisters' kids, so becoming a father didn't terrify me. Quite the opposite, actually. I reckoned that, at 32, it was time I took on responsibility. I wasn't a very mature person, but Madison reminded me, however briefly, that I had to take stock of where I was going.

We'd moved to Harrogate just two months before her arrival. With a new contract and a supportive manager in Robbo, everything was set up nicely, but the bliss didn't last for long. Madison was the only bright light of the Blackwell era. I'd come home from training, pissed off with the world, and her greeting would cheer me up in an instant.

I always knew that I would have to drop down the football ladder eventually, but I was unprepared for the speed of my fall. After Sheff U, the only way was down. Heck, I nearly ended up Down Under. We'd talked about a move to Australia before the severance package was agreed. They had a partnership with a club there called Central Coast Mariners, but the deadline was tight, the deal came up short of expectations, and moving to the other side of the world with a one-year-old just didn't seem like the right thing to do.

So, I took my chances as a free agent, and my first port of call was another trial at Leeds, who were now in League One and managed by a former colleague from Blackburn, Simon Grayson. Like my first visit, it was a waste of time. My fitness wasn't where it should have been, but it would have improved with games. But this was mid-season, so the opportunities weren't there. Going on trial can be a humiliating experience, especially when you're quite a well-known player. I knew a few lads in the dressing room, guys who I'd played against before, or looked down on from a higher level. They were turning up for work, training and preparing for games. I joined in with their sessions for two weeks and left without the offer of a contract.

I ended up at Bradford, in League Two, the bottom tier of league football. Their manager, Stuart McCall, had been assistant to Warnock, and lived in Harrogate so he knew my story. Considering I was still off the road, I needed somewhere local. Paul Arnison, a lad who lived further north, picked me up on the way to training.

The deal at Bradford was £1,000 a week until the end of the season, and I knew pretty quickly that I wouldn't be staying any longer. I found the whole package difficult to adjust to. The people at the club were nice, but that couldn't paper over the cracks of the lifestyle. Our training pitch was bumpy, well below the standards at Sheffield. And the games were a chore for a winger. League Two is better suited to the rough and ready. The ball spends most of the time in the air, and you're up against lads who have spent their careers at that level for a reason. It's physical, a battle, and I wasn't up for it. I just couldn't find the motivation. The fall to earth had demoralised me completely, and I think Stuart could see it. I made three appearances, none of which lasted for 90 minutes, and that was the end of that.

I reached a crossroads in the summer of 2009. Two years earlier, I'd been playing in the Premier League. Now, there was nobody in the four divisions willing to give me a shot. As much as I disliked the League Two experience, I couldn't afford to ignore anybody's call, but the phone didn't ring. Managers talk, and I'm sure that the manner of my departure from Sheffield United had affixed a 'Do Not Touch' label to my name once and for all. I still felt I had plenty to offer, but it mattered little. Desperation time. With nothing else to do, I spent my days running around The Stray, a grassland area which surrounds Harrogate. Sometimes, Ben Rome, my old chaffeur, would come out to train with me. I didn't know who or what I was preparing for, but I had to keep going, even though every passing day confirmed that, in England at least, there was no room in any inn. The Ferencvaros deal that Blackwell screwed up was the only glimmer.

This was the backdrop in which I married Vikki. Just like with Frances, there was no grand proposal. Once the divorce came through, we thought it was the logical step, especially with Madison in our lives. We were very much in love, and wanted to cement our relationship. There was no dodging the big occasion this time around, though. We had a small ceremony in the registry office on Friday, June 5, 2009. Then, on the Sunday, 100 family and friends toasted our union in Rudding Park, a luxury hotel just outside Harrogate. Jim was the best man, and made a brilliant speech about his childhood memories. It was a fantastic day, but there would be no happily ever after.

Our love was the real thing, but I don't think Vikki was prepared for what was coming down the tracks. Everything was changing. I had to go where work brought me and, increasingly, it became clear that a return to Northern Ireland was the only option. Gary Hamilton had called earlier in the year to see if I'd be interested in joining his club Glentoran, one of Belfast's traditional Big Two, on a short-term arrangement, but I'd already given my word to Bradford. So after another lost day on The Stray, I asked Phil to make an enquiry and see if the interest was still there. It helped that their manager was Alan McDonald, my first Northern Ireland skipper, who Phil was familiar with through his QPR connection.

Big Mac's stature made it an easier decision. He rang with one question. "Do you definitely want to come and play for us?" We both knew that once I packed up for home, chances are I wouldn't ever properly come back to England in a playing capacity. This was a switch to a part-time league, a drastic change in circumstances. But, there were reasons why it appealed. Some were more obvious than others.

After 18 years away, it presented a chance to come home and build a new life. Glentoran attracted decent crowds, and had pipped their arch rivals, Linfield, to the title on the last day of the previous season, so there was a good buzz around the club. And I liked the gaffer, and was good mates with their main striker, Gary, meaning I had nothing to fear in the dressing room. I told Big Mac and Phil to make it happen.

With the help of a sponsor they came up with the cash, and I was officially unveiled at their famous old ground, The Oval, on August 19, before a derby game with Linfield. It was a big story in Northern Ireland, a novelty really considering that it was rare for ex-internationals to come back to their local league. The attention and the warm welcome was a contrast from the solo runs around a field in Yorkshire.

For Vikki, a lot had happened in a short space of time, and then she found out that another child was on the way. It added another layer to her struggle to adapt to life in Bangor. She was a city girl, and moving from London in the first place was a challenge. Now, she was pregnant in an unfamiliar country, a plane ride away from her friends and family. Mum and my sisters were delighted to have me around, and tried their best to make Vikki feel welcome, but it didn't feel like home to her.

My lifestyle didn't make things easier. With the other lads having day jobs, training was scheduled for the evenings, and I had the unusual feeling of being free every morning. Angela's husband, Davy, invited me into a golf society with a gang of his mates, and I launched myself into that, while striking up friendships with the other lads. Vikki didn't have that outlet. I'd be packing my clubs into the car while she complained about being stuck at home as a childminder again, taking no consolation when I pointed out that I was still spending far more time around the house than a bloke in a 9-5 job could. There was similar grief when I went for a few drinks with the lads.

Our second amazing daughter, Lexie, was born in the Ulster Hospital in Dundonald on March 8, 2010, and she temporarily shelved our tensions. But the strain was always there, lingering in the background. I resented her complaints, believing she could have made more of an effort to give Bangor a chance. She thought I didn't care about her concerns. We chipped away at each other, arguing for days at a time.

The real problem was gnawing away at me, a headache that I couldn't avoid any longer. Call it the elephant in the postbox. Cash was the other driving force in coming home. Moving into the five-bedroom house in Bangor I'd bought in 2006, saved me the expense of the £3,000 a month rent in Harrogate, and I was beginning to grasp the necessity of budgeting. Numbers were suddenly a major part of my life. I even wore the 33 shirt at Glentoran because the sponsors stumping up my wage were a taxi company, Fonacab, whose hotline ended with those digits. That commitment was a potential deal breaker, or else there'd be no £1,000 a week contract.

I couldn't afford to say no. The letters that were arriving with alarming frequency reminded me of that. I knew what they were about – I could see through the envelope. It all stemmed back to that meeting in that room in London, introducing the film scheme, the opportunity for a quick buck that I'd discarded to the back of my mind, along with all the warnings about the future which I hadn't really listened to.

It was the unspoken reason for coming home to Northern Ireland. My toughest opponent, a pursuer that I simply could not escape. The Inland Revenue were on my case, and nothing could ever be the same again.

(27)

Broke

'YOUR account has insufficient funds for this transaction'

The first time I read those words on an ATM screen, I didn't panic. Truth be told, I had an inkling it was coming. In my fraught final 18 months at Sheffield United, the expenditures were adding up, and there was little appearance money coming my way given my standing with Blackwell. My gross earnings were £26,000 a month. Subtract £10,000 for the taxman, and £3,000 for rent and you're left with a balance of £13,000 which didn't go very far with a child to look after and a gambling habit to feed.

Still, I didn't worry too much about the current account because I had money put away. Not that I had any real idea where it was, but I knew there were investments somewhere.

Paperwork was another person's job; my friend from Bangor looked after that. We first met all those years ago when I scored the goal for Manchester United against Newcastle; he was a golfing acquaintance of Jim, and became a part of my social circle from that night onwards. He worked as a financial advisor and was always offering to take over my affairs. Frances never took to him but as soon as she was off the scene, there was no dissenting voice. I gave him control of my books, believing he would divert cash in the right direction.

I signed whatever forms he put in front of me without paying too much attention, although it wasn't a very sophisticated system. Often, he would present me with handwritten notes, hardly the secure paper trail. But he was a pal, we spoke most days, and I really didn't feel there was anything untoward going on. And, besides, there was always enough money pouring into my account to deal with the bills that came my way.

That changed in 2007, with a letter from chartered accountants Hanna Thompson, which laid out the tax implications of the film syndicate I'd signed up to back in 2001. Five full years had passed, and now the little details which I had previously ignored were suddenly very relevant. I vaguely recalled the references to tax bills kicking in after year five.

My understanding was basic.

I was still paying off the £1.3 million loan registered in my name with an income stream that showed up in my tax forms every year. By the declaration of that loan as a trading loss, I'd pocketed the £500,000 tax relief, and blown the majority of it.

The missive from Hanna Thompson detailed that the tax liability due on the Film Partnership Profits was £436,000 spread out over ten years. The figure was calculated as a taxable percentage of the 'Profit from Partnership' – the income stream – which showed up annually in my assessment forms. A bank had a charge on that income as security for the original loan. In other words, I didn't see any of it; it was cancelling out the £1.3 million. All I inherited was the tax arising from that transaction.

Let me give you an example. In my assessment form for 2006/07, the 'Profit for Partnership' figure was £128,528. Subtracting the interest charge of £51,624 left taxable profit of £76, 941. Therefore, the tax due for that period was 40 per cent of that figure – a bill of £30,776.

Every year, those figures would incrementally increase.

Circa £33,000 in 2008...

£36,000 in 2009...

£39,000 in 2010...

You get the picture.

For 2016, the final year of the arrangement, the tax due was £70,618.

It brought home the insanity of the scheme which I'd signed up to. We, the footballers who signed up in 2001, were naturally going to see our earnings decrease as we hit our mid-thirties and beyond, unless we landed a seriously lucrative managing role. But it's only a minority who enjoy that good fortune. La Manga chopped into my income. The fall-out from Sheffield United decimated it.

Another example. My tax assessment form for 2008/09, the season I started with Sheffield United and ended at Bradford:

Gross earnings from employment? £402,686

Tax due on the film scheme? £36,141

Now, let's move onto 2010, the season at Glentoran:

Gross earnings from employment? £43,875
Tax due on the film scheme? £38,995.

Once my Glentoran wage was taxed at 40 per cent, I was left with net earnings of just over £26,000 – almost £13,000 short of what I need to cover my film syndicate bill. And that's before I dipped into my pocket to buy a pack of smokes and a loaf of bread.

That deficit was set to widen year on year, driving me further and further into debt.

But wait a minute.

What about the films our syndicate had financed? That was one element I remembered from the meeting; the prospect of a bonus on top of the tax relief if our monies went towards a blockbuster. Our partnership was called Castle Media Film Partnership and there was a rumour that the investment had played a significant part in the creation of Band of Brothers, a smash-hit TV mini series which boasted Steven Spielberg and Tom Hanks as executive co-producers.

I set Phil on the case and he made contact with a representative from Scotts, the firm who oversaw our partnership, who said that the interest in Band of Brothers was owned by another syndicate. We had learned there were hundreds of similar partnerships in football, including prominent internationals who had ploughed cash into film leasing. Sir Alex Ferguson had invested into one called Eclipse 35. Why the confusion over Band of Brothers? Because the interest belonged to a syndicate called Castle Media Partnership II – the sequel to our scheme.

The Data Protection Act prevented Phil from gaining access to their list of members. We desperately wanted to see it, but permission was denied.

Instead, the man from Scotts told us what belonged to Castle Media Partnership I. He listed three productions. 'The Glass', 'Starhunter' and 'Bride of the Wind'.

No, I've never heard of them either.

Their legacy is the tax bills that drove me into bankruptcy.

When I tell people that story, two obvious questions arise. The first is straightforward. Why didn't I put the £500,000 away to prepare for a rainy day? A fair point, but I never had a long-term attitude to cash. In a battle between stocks and shares, and the 1.30 at Pontefract, there was only going to be one winner. The bookies. But I was convinced to save some, and pooled it with the contributions from my bumper contract at Blackburn to divert funds with a view to the long term, to mature in my mid-thirties.

All of which leads to the second question. What happened to those investments?

I started to make enquiries as the fruitless visits to the ATM grew in frequency, and the letters from Hanna Thompson gathered dust. Where had my fallback money gone?

With the help of my sister Angela, who works in a bank and has a good head for figures, I uncovered a mess which spelled out the seriousness of my situation. If I'd involved her in my personal finances from the start, then I could be telling a different tale. I should have brought Phil in too, and it was too late when he learned the full story. I genuinely thought that my pal was acting in my best interests and boy, did it cost me.

All I have to show for those investments are stacks of documents and a trail of emails that make little sense to me. Angela sifted through the wreckage, lifting up streams of correspondence. "What does this mean?" "What does that mean?" I'd shrug my shoulders. No answers.

Things were run by me and I'd agree without paying too much attention to the detail. It turned out that this involved cashing in a lot of investments previously recommended to me; some policies and bonds that were maturing nicely, including a 10-year one that was 11 months away from completion, and putting the money into other avenues, primarily into property.

One evening, my new financial advisor introduced me to a small grey-haired man, a sharply dressed smooth talker who was his brother-in-law. He was a property developer; and I got to know him better through a couple of games of golf and a few beers. He talked the talk, and I was urged to go into business with him. I agreed and invested £60,000 in a property in Bangor. I was given a note which guaranteed a return of £90,000 in 12 months time but by the time it came around it transpired that the cash had been moved to another property. That was the first of the warning signs that I stupidly ignored. When I pressed for a return on two other investments and was sent a £50,000 cheque which bounced, it was another red flag. They quickly came back with a cheque for £15,000 which I cashed and was enough to keep me happy for a while.

The really big venture was a property in Spain which Phil still refers to as the only holiday home in Spain that's nowhere near the sea. I thought I was buying it off plan for £300,000, with £60,000 up front and a mortgage of £240,000. Angela was on holiday there when she opened my post and read a statement which said the mortgage was £300,000. It then became apparent that I hadn't bought the house off plan – instead, I'd bought it off a business partner of the property developer, a fact I learned when I found out that £56,000 of my money had been directed towards him. The property developer then promptly disappeared to Spain. I was made promises that I would get my money back but it didn't materialise. I took legal action but it didn't do me any good. It just cost another £10,000 in legal fees. The property developer, it emerged, had been driven into bankruptcy.

I kept listening to my golfing pal advisor, though. Regardless of what anyone else said, I was always taken in by his persuasive tone, his apparent conviction, so we embarked on another route. His idea was to get involved in more property deals with a Bangor-based businessman.

Together, we invested money to buy some land across the border in Republic of Ireland, in the rural county of Cavan, a bright idea which turned into a complete disaster. We had 25 acres (when I say 'we', I mean the partnership that my cash had been placed into. I learned about all this retrospectively). An initial offer of £3 million came in for the first seven acres, in order to build a shopping precinct. If it had been accepted, it would have covered all the costs, and guaranteed profit on whatever we did with the remaining acres – building houses was the likely call. But Ireland was booming, so the proprietor greedily refused the £3 million, and demanded more. Big mistake. In 2008, the global economy crashed, Ireland fell into recession, and the land was practically worthless. Similar projects around Bangor went the same way. £60,000 here. £200,000 there. All frittered away.

This was all playing out like a day in the bookies. Whatever the loss, there was always another race, a chance to make it right. I was told we had found the solution in the form of an extremely promising deal in Glasgow. It would prove the final straw.

From an investment of £200,000, I assumed a 12 per cent share in a development. As Phil, who was oblivious to my dealings at the time, later pointed out, that didn't really add up when the paper trail showed that another fella had invested £90,000 for a 27 per cent share, and a third character appeared to have a 29 per cent share from putting in nothing at all. "You're the only bloody person who invested in these things, Keith," he said.

I'd been told the land would make us millions, for it was needed for the hosting of the Commonwealth Games in 2014. We had evidence to believe we were onto a good thing. One developer had received £17 million from the local authorities for a contract which was only worth £8 million at the time of purchase. Our people expected a comparable windfall. Instead, the city council, who were under pressure after taking flak for some of the earlier deals, exercised Compulsory Purchase powers that were afforded to them by the Scottish government. It drove the price down rapidly, and reduced the bargaining wriggle room. I ended up with a dividend in the region of £380,000, another sizeable entry in my tax assessment form, but a misleading figure when you broke down the sums.

I'd invested £200,000 in the first place, and then the tax on the so-called profits ate into my share of the pot. And then there was my financial advisor's cut. When it came to distributing the Glasgow cash, I was informed of a two per cent introducers fee.

I believed this to be two per cent of the profit, the £380,000, which would be a return of around £7,600. That wasn't the case. Instead, I was told it was two per cent of my 12 per cent share. This didn't make sense to me but to cut a long story short, I was landed with a demand for £50,000.

Somehow, I'd come out making a loss on the Glasgow deal. Angela, by now further immersed in my financial affairs, couldn't believe what I'd done.

"Please tell me you didn't pay him 50 grand?"

"Yeah…"

A difficult phone call between Angela and my financial advisor marked the end of our working arrangement, and the start of a painstaking legal process. She called in outside help to try and make sense of what had unfolded.

All I knew was that my problems ran deeper than the insufficent funds message on the ATM screen. I didn't have the cash to cope with the mounting tax bills from the film scheme. There was an inevitability about what came next.

In the final months at Glentoran, the slide towards the exposure of my struggles gathered pace. I put on a brave face, and reverted to the familiar post-Black Friday defence mode. Deny everything. Mum and Vikki nagged about replying to the stream of letters, believing it was a typical case of me being too laid-back. In truth, I was resigned to my fate. I couldn't treat the Revenue like Mickey Arnott and ring up to fob them off with a few grand here and there. This creditor was an entirely different animal.

The gambling had to stop. That decision was made once I landed back in Northern Ireland. I just didn't have the cash to follow the horses anymore. Even at Bradford, I could find a spare £500 in the wallet to squander in the bookies. Those days were gone.

It was a big change, especially as my interest in the horses had extended to co-ownership, in tandem with Gary McCausland, a pal from Belfast. Our first venture, Jurado's Honour, broke a leg at Navan, which was a pretty grim experience. They put the screens around him, and the next thing we heard was a gunshot. Luckily, we had him insured, and put it towards a horse called First Row, who proved a much better purchase. He won a few races and was good enough to run at Cheltenham in 2006, where he finished ninth in the Triumph Hurdle. Injury halted his progress, but he was a good servant. And moving in racing circles exposed me to information. First Row's trainer, Dessie Hughes, is the father of the flat jockey, Richard, who provided the tip that led to my biggest ever individual bet. He told us that a horse of Aiden O'Brien's, George Washington, had a great chance of winning the 2,000 Guineas at Newmarket in 2006. I staked £7,000 on him at 15/8 and he cruised home in front. A tidy win. The problem was that the winnings were soon splurged on horses I knew nothing about. That brief run of luck during Robbo's time at Sheffield United was the exception to the rule. I followed it up with a lengthy losing streak.

Phil, who had stepped back from being a football agent to concentrate on his thriving construction business, paired up with Gary to buy some more horses, and they've still got almost a dozen. I had to step back from the game, and find a new hobby. Golf. Table quizzes. Fantasy football. Anything.

I stopped answering my phone. The few letters from Hanna Thompson which I did open all kicked off the same way.

"Dear Keith... Unfortunately we have been unable to reach you by telephone regarding various issues."

I just didn't see the point in talking. They presumed I had the means to sign a form and send a cheque to cover my unpaid tax. But I couldn't and, once I slipped behind in payments, I knew that each fresh envelope or missed call meant that either another instalment was due, or there was further interest accruing on the arrears.

In the summer of 2010, I parted company with Glentoran because they didn't have the money to keep me on. By then, my tax bill exceeded £137,000. The petition for bankruptcy was filed in August, and granted in September. Then it hit the papers, and my plight was out in the open.

With Vikki, it was all over bar even more shouting.

The final straw came that winter, when I was offered a route back to England with Darlington in the Blue Square Premier – my first taste of non league-football – on a short-term deal. I couldn't justify the cost of renting anywhere for the family, so I bunked in with Jim in Hartlepool and left Vikki and the girls at home. I flew back when I could, but the tone of the phonecalls reflected the awkwardness of the situation. The paperwork at Darlington took ages to go through, and I was training without playing, which was hard to explain. And then when the clearance came, the North-East was brought to a standstill by heavy snowfall, so games and training were cancelled. I lined up a couple of times, but it came to nothing, and they let me go before Christmas.

I needed to get home. My head was gone.

Our marriage had reached rock bottom. As much as I tried

to put on a front, I was hurting. I was in bad form most of the time, unable to show her any affection. I couldn't put my finger on what was wrong; it was just there in the pit of my stomach the whole time, a drag that was holding me back and making me impossible to be around. I couldn't find the motivation to do anything about our problems. It hinted at something more serious, but I didn't grasp it at the time.

She started spending more and more time back in England visiting her family, and it was clear our futures lay apart – a conclusion that everyone around us had long since reached. I think we stretched it out for the sake of the kids but, by trying to stay together for them, we were making things worse.

Madison and Lexie deserved better than to grow up in a house with their parents arguing all the time. So we separated. Vikki relocated to London with the girls, and we set about working an arrangement where they could visit often. In the meantime, I had to find a way to support them.

Angela knew what I had to do, and where I needed to go. She came along in the car to talk me through it.

Our destination?

Bangor's Social Security office.

The purpose of the trip?

To register for Jobseeker's Allowance.

At the age of 35, I was going on the dole.

28

Bowing Out

FUNERALS. You know you're getting older when you start going to more of them.

But I never expected to be saying goodbye to former teammates, to guys from my generation, at this stage in life.

I remember the last time I saw Alan McDonald. He was outside his trophy shop in Bangor and looking well, which was good news because when Big Mac left Glentoran before the end of my season there, I worried for his health. He was taking so much grief from the supporters that he just had to escape. It turned really nasty after we lost 6-0 at the Oval to Coleraine, a mediocre side, and the fans waited outside to voice their disapproval. Big Mac had to stay in the club, waiting for them to go home, so he could get out to his car. When he decided to resign in March 2010, it was the best resolution for all parties.

It allowed him to get on with his life.

But he didn't have very much time left. The League of Ireland plays through the summer months so when the rest of the football world had their eyes on the knockout stages of Euro 2012, I was in the north west of Ireland in Ballybofey, Co. Donegal, preparing for an away game with Finn Harps. As I packed the car the day before, I spotted a black tie that I'd worn to the funeral of a family friend a couple of weeks earlier. "I hope I won't be needing that soon," I said to myself. The stream of messages into my phone that Saturday lunchtime told me that I would. Big Mac had suffered a heart attack on Temple Park golf course, and passed away. It numbed me. He was a strong man, a fearless captain, a solid pal. That he should be taken away like that didn't seem right.

With all that was going on off the park, people might be surprised when I say that I enjoyed my year in Glentoran, but I did, and Big Mac was a major factor. When I landed into the Northern Ireland squad as a teenager, I looked up to him as a guiding influence, and that first impression stuck. Even when results were poor, and the fans were on his back, it didn't lesson his standing in my eyes. He was a legend. There's a famous clip of Alan giving an interview to the BBC after the draw with England in 1985 that booked our country's place in the World Cup in Mexico. The result suited both teams, but it was a full blooded game, and Alan looked straight into the camera and said: "Anyone who says that's a fix, can come and see me." I watched it again after I'd heard he died, and what struck me was that he was only 22 and winning his second cap, but he spoke with the authority of a veteran. That's the man I would like to remember.

The abuse at Glentoran hurt him terribly. I met his assistant, George Neill, at the service, and he only had one thought on his mind. "The bastards got what they wanted, Keith."

Big Mac made over 400 appearances for QPR and represented his country 52 times, but the mob showed no respect when the results turned. A man of his decency deserved better. Big Mac didn't have an ego. He led by example that way.

When I came home, I was conscious of coming across like someone who thought he was too good for the Irish League, where some of the stadiums and facilities would be well below what I'd experienced in Bradford, never mind in the Premier League.

The other boys at the club told me there was a lad called Colin Coates, who played for another Belfast club Crusaders, that had been drafted in to plug the gaps for Northern Ireland on a few summer tours and used to taunt opponents by asking them how many caps they'd got. I wouldn't mind, but all he could bloody do was head the ball. The lads were laughing about what would happen if he said it to me. I couldn't help myself when he deliberately miscontrolled the ball to delay taking a free-kick in the 92nd minute when it was scoreless. "International, my arse," I shouted. But otherwise, I kept my mouth shut, and received very little back in return, aside from a deliberate elbow from one chap at Cliftonville that left me requiring 14 stitches. The ref didn't even give us a free-kick.

Naturally, some opposition supporters dished it out, especially away at Linfield, who play at Windsor Park, so there were boys on the Kop calling me a waste of money as I walked off the pitch. I responded by applauding them. The same lads were probably cheering me when I was lining up for Northern

Ireland, so the last thing I wanted to do was damage my relationship with them by reacting.

For Big Mac, however, the shouts from the terraces were only the tip of the iceberg.

His own fans were the chief tormentors, and he received threatening messages and phonecalls. Collectively, the team just weren't good enough, but he bore the brunt of it.

His funeral allowed us to reflect on better times. There was a huge turnout of my old Northern Ireland team-mates, and his colleagues from QPR. Jackie Fullerton, the popular BBC commentator, gave a brilliant speech that centred around Big Mac's relationship with Jimmy Quinn. It's strange, but I actually didn't know Jimmy was a Catholic until Jackie spoke, even though I'd briefly played alongside him. Big Mac and Jimmy used to sit five or six rows apart on the bus, roaring silly abuse at each other that managed to entertain everyone else. Many more stories were recounted, and there were lots of laughs, but the mood changed as the coffin went out to the sound of the Battle Hymn of the Republic. Our fans have adapted that tune with their own words, a simple chorus of "We're not Brazil, we're Northern Ireland," and when the congregation started singing that version, it really hit me. Big Mac was gone.

Nigel Worthington was at the funeral. We didn't speak. He'd ended my international career and it hurt.

After Lawrie left for Fulham, the IFA brought Nigel in as a temporary replacement. He was a man I knew well. Following my antics in Canada back in '95, Bryan Hamilton roomed us together, believing that our silver-haired full-back could be a calming influence. I saw the logic. Nigel was an outsider in the group, a responsible senior player who didn't approve of the drinking. I remember him going toe to toe with Jim Magilton in the dressing room over that very topic. Nigel hailed from Ballymena, just 15 minutes away from where we used to stay, and preferred to spend time with his family or just sit in the hotel lobby with some of the backroom staff, sipping a Baileys, while the rest of us headed out on the tear. He was a bit of a mystery to us.

I welcomed his appointment though. He was a familiar face to the group and, considering we had a great chance of qualifying for Euro '08 after our flying start under Lawrie, we didn't want major upheaval. A handy win over Liechtenstein provided a smooth landing, but an away double header in Latvia and Iceland presented his first major test. We travelled in control of our destiny, aware that two wins would put us within touching distance, and four points would leave us in a strong position too. Nigel didn't change very much in the preparations. There was no need seeing as Lawrie's solid 4-4-2 had worked well. So he took a backseat on the training ground and let his likeable assistant, Glynn Snodin, run the sessions.

It was a different story on match day. Nigel baffled us in Riga. At half-time, it was 0-0 and we'd played reasonably poorly, but there was time to turn it around. Nigel burst into the dressing room, livid, and announced that if we didn't buck up our ideas, then we wouldn't be allowed to go for a drink that night. What kind of thing was that to say at half-time in an international? I was stunned. Maybe he'd been waiting for years to use that line.

Nigel obviously had his own views on the drinking culture, but he really didn't understand us if he thought that was going to provide motivation at half-time in a big qualifier, especially in that campaign. We emerged for the second half none the wiser about how to escape from this situation. Chris Baird scored an own goal, and our position of strength in the group was gone. And yes, we ended up having a few drinks that night anyway, looseners before the journey to Iceland which had suddenly taken on extra relevance.

Nigel called a meeting for the next day. I'd mentioned to a few of the boys that I would stand up and state our unhappiness with the half-time speech. They agreed with the sentiment, and a few said they'd back me up. So, I raised my hand, and said my piece. "We're not here for the jolly-up," I said, waiting for other voices to chime in. Silence. They'd bottled it. Thanks lads. Nigel didn't seem aggrieved. "I take your point," he said, and later on he pulled me aside and genuinely thanked me for raising the issue. All very amicable, and pretty bloody ironic considering what happened a couple of days later. The Iceland trip turned into a fiasco which backed up the stereotypical view of our team.

Away double-headers can test the patience at the best of times, but this was particularly shit. The hotel was in the middle of nowhere. There was a horrible stench off the water (I know there's a geographical reason for that, but try explaining it to a bunch of restless footballers). And we were simply bored off our tree. So bored, in fact, that there wasn't even enough enthusiasm for a proper game of cards. Myself, Healy, and our mutual friend, the West Ham defender George McCartney, played a couple of hands. The rest were on their Playstations.

That frustrated vibe carried over into the game. It shouldn't have, given the significance, but perhaps the expectation was bogging us down. Riga had checked the momentum, and we couldn't raise the intensity to the required level in the first half. Iceland, who had nothing to lose, led at the break. Nigel spoke to us like adults this time around, and we rose from our slumber. Healy levelled from the spot – his 12th of the campaign – and, roared on by a big travelling support, we piled forward in search of the three points. But, in classic Northern Ireland style, disaster struck. With two minutes left, we gifted the Icelandics a comical winner. I should know, I bloody scored it. After an error from Steve Jones, Iceland countered, Gretar Steinsson crossed and, as I raced back to cover, the speed of the ball took me my surprise, bounced off my shin and past Maik Taylor. Another own goal, another loss.

We'd blown it.

Few words were spoken on our way back to the hotel, where we reacted in the only way we knew – by drowning our sorrows in the bar. We had time to burn until a 5am departure to the airport and lying in bed, staring at the ceiling would have killed me.

So a gang of us drank right through, in the company of some American plane engineers, finding that each sip eased the agony of defeat.

I'd had more than a couple when I boarded the coach, and I wasn't the only one. Jonny Evans' passport was being tossed around like a rugby ball, and by the time we'd reached the airport, it had disappeared. I stayed behind on the bus helping Jonny look for it while the first group of lads ploughed ahead and checked in. David Currie from the IFA, who was getting impatient, came back to us. "George McCartney says you have it, Keith." Did I hell. We eventually found it stuffed down the back of a seat, but David's accusation had pissed me off.

I stormed into the airport determined to have a row with George, who was standing at the front at the queue while I stood at the back, hurling abuse in his direction. Typical 5am stuff. "What the fuck did you say I had the passport for?"

I didn't see him again until I boarded the plane. We always travelled on scheduled flights and IFA never booked us together in blocks, so the players were spread all over the place. On the way to my seat, I walked past the edge of the row where George was sitting..

"Why the fuck did you say that?" I repeated.

"But you fucking did have it," he said.

Anger coursed through my veins. It was a combination of everything, the drink, the shitty result, the own goal. The red mist returned, and I went for him. He grabbed me back, and then it's all a blur. Healy pulling us apart and leading me to my seat, where I sat back and drifted into oblivion, sleeping all the way to Heathrow. I don't remember the goodbyes. All I recall is sitting in a lounge for three hours, hungover and alone, waiting for a connecting flight up north, when Ulster Television called. The story of a fight on the plane had broken, and it was big news. And it carried on into the weekend, with a scrap developing into a brawl with every telling, like a public game of Chinese whispers. The Sunday World printed an extremely dramatic version of a fist-fight, and I tried suing them until they settled out of court. It helped that I had the testimony of Kate Hoey, a Labour MP from Belfast and a former Minister for Sport, who travelled to all our games, and wrote to me to say she was sitting a few rows back and could vouch for the truth.

But I'd been through enough controversy to know that the 'Fight on the Flight' tales would outlive any clarification. And, deep down, I realised that my behaviour was out of order. The IFA launched an internal investigation. Nigel and the CEO Howard Wells came to Sheffield United and told me they'd be giving my match fee to charity. I didn't protest. They went to see George too and, rightly, decided against punishing him. There was no problem between us and it was back to normal the next time we met up. I just wanted to forget about the whole incident, the whole crappy trip. There wouldn't have been any hassle if we'd won the game. I'm sure of that.

We'd let the fans down by passing up an unbelievable opportunity. True to form, we finished the group strongly in underdog mode. A draw in Sweden, an epic home win over Denmark, and a brave 1-0 loss in Spain on the final night where we needed a victory and a couple of miraculous results elsewhere. Sweden grabbed the second automatic spot; we wound up third in the group, six points back. Iceland's only two wins in that campaign came against us. That was the difference, and that's before you consider Riga. Our country will never have a better chance.

On 19 November, 2008, I won my 86th, and final, cap for Northern Ireland. The occasion was a 2-0 friendly loss to Hungary at Windsor Park. As low key as it gets.

I didn't know that was the end. Perhaps Nigel did. The strong finish to the Euros group had secured him the job on a long-term basis and I was happy with that. Iceland didn't sour our relationship. In fact, when he came to Sheffield United that time, he'd spoken about how he wanted me to reach the 100-cap mark. So, I started the World Cup campaign in the starting XI, despite my deterioriating situation with Blackwell, and received the man of the match for a draw with the Czechs in Belfast, a game that was sandwiched between disappointing defeats in Slovakia and Slovenia. We thrashed San Marino in October, my final competitive outing, and the return was scheduled for February, with that Hungary match in between. That winter, I had other things on my mind, with the shit hitting the fan at the club. Still, San Marino were the worst team I'd ever encountered, and I presumed I'd be involved. I learned otherwise by turning on Sky Sports News, where Nigel was talking about leaving me out, and claiming he'd unsuccessfully tried to contact me for the past 12 days.

Sure, I had changed phone networks because I was having some reception problems in my house, but my number was the same and I could access voicemail. If Nigel was calling, he could have left a message, or asked someone at the IFA to make contact. I put down the remote and dialled his number straight away. Choice words were exchanged. He said he'd been speaking to Sam Ellis, which was never going to work in my favour. Still, he concluded by promising I was still in his plans, provided I got back playing regularly somewhere again.

I always had Northern Ireland in my thoughts when I picked a club. Nigel called me when I was at Bradford, and I told him I'd be moving on at the end of the season, and he seemed fine with that. Then, I joined Glentoran. There were a few lads from the Irish League around his squad, so I hoped that door could open again for me.

A week after I signed, I was in the car with Davy and my nephew Luke when Nigel rang. He asked how the move was going, and then progressed from the small talk to his real question.

"I'm getting a lot of hassle from the press about putting you back in the squad," he said. "How do you want to work it?"

"That's up to you," I replied.

"Well, I'm not going to involve you in any more squads. What way do you want to work that in the press?"

"I don't have anything to say to the press."

"Well, I'm getting a bit of hassle. Do you want to come out and announce your retirement?"

The cheeky bastard. I bit my lip, and the conversation ended. I was raging that he wanted me to come out and do the hard work for him. As manager, it was his duty to make a decision and deal with the consequences. There was no way I was going to quit, none at all. A year later, when questions were being asked about David Healy, Nigel claimed that he would never ask a player to retire. Well, he'd obviously forgotten our little discussion.

I've since heard other reasons for his decision to axe me. Apparently, he thought I was a bad influence on Jonny Evans. That surprised me. Jonny wouldn't strike me as a person that would idolise anyone. But maybe Nigel viewed it as a chance to change the atmosphere that he never belonged in.

He was bringing a lot of English voices into the set-up. He sacked his old team-mate, Mal Donaghy, and brought in a guy called Steve Beaglehole to run the U19 and U21 sides. And then he put the kibosh on Tommy Wright – another former colleague – helping out with the U21 side.

Around the hotel, he started calling meetings with just the English staff. The likes of the physio, Terry Hayes, and the kitman, Derek McKinley, weren't invited. He'd also stopped Terry and Derek from having a drink in the hotel lobby on the days before games so they ended up sitting in their room with a bottle of wine; I used to go in and see them. It wasn't right. They were grown men who felt like they were in captivity. Northern Ireland teams always have a chance when the spirit is good, and that means socialising and doing everything together. Nigel couldn't grasp that.

The results speak for themselves. He took the team backwards, and undid Lawrie's good work. I went to watch the key World Cup qualifier at home to Slovakia, and there were four centre-backs in defence and four central midfielders in front of them. We had no width, but he blamed the players for losing. The Euro 2012 campaign was a joke, and deservedly cost him his job.

I am bitter towards him. I don't deny it. In the car that day, the first thing Davy said was that it shouldn't have ended that way. It should have been at Windsor Park, in front of the Kop, and the fans that I always had such a good relationship with. I'd have loved a proper chance to say goodbye, and the way it was handled left a real sour taste in the mouth. Football clubs can be ruthless when they're showing you the door, but I always thought it would be different with my country. Instead it was far worse, and Nigel kicked me when I was down. The press asked him about my exclusion. "Keith's had his fling," he replied. A fling? Is that what you call 15 years and 86 caps?

For that comment, I can never forgive him.

(29)

Justice

IT was like a scene from a TV show. Four people converging on the surreal backdrop of the public car park of Crawsfordburn Country Park outside Bangor for an unofficial business meeting. Crawsfordburn is a scenic retreat, with two beaches, walking trails, and all sorts of tourist facilities, and on this typical summer's day, the place was buzzing with families coming and going.

There was nothing relaxing about my visit, however. I was standing face to face with the financial advisor who I used to call my friend.

The niceties didn't last for long, and the discussion grew heated. The purpose of the meeting was to discuss the £50,000 I'd paid for the Commonwealth Games deal in Glasgow, but the underlying tension was about everything in our shambolic arrangement. I wanted a chunky refund, but our negotiations were going nowhere.

The meeting in Crawsfordburn was tense, but it belatedly achieved something. I was sent a cheque for £20,000, but that was never going to be the end of the affair.

The lines of combat were drawn. There was no interest in reconciliation. Maybe I simply wasn't useful to him anymore. After that I saw him once, on the opposite fairway of a golf course, and we both kept our heads down. Solicitors would conduct our future discussions. I had a legal case and, in my financial state, pursuing it was the only option.

I'd started the process in England, with a solicitor who I paid £10,000 to be told that they could do nothing for me and I should deal with a practice in Northern Ireland. I shelled out another £5,000 to a firm in Belfast they recommended, which was more money down the drain once I was declared bankrupt and the accounting firm, Grant Thornton, became trustees of my bankruptcy. I was £15,000 down already. An ominous start.

They appointed A&L Goodbody as my solicitors, setting the wheels in motion for a court case. It was recommended that we pursue an indemnity insurance claim of £1,050,000.

Meanwhile, with the help of Phil again, I was trying to get myself back on my feet. I came out of bankruptcy in October 2011.

It's a dirty word but it had some positive implications as it allowed me to escape the film scheme. Phil told the guys who ran the film partnership that I wouldn't be making any more payments; otherwise I'd simply go straight back into bankruptcy again. They tried to play hardball at first, and suggested there would be repercussions, but as Phil asked more questions about the basis of their scheme, the correspondence dried up and they went away.

The claim I had made had already protected my main possessions, basically the house and my car, as Grant Thornton had classified my case as an asset given the likelihood that the outcome would satisfy my creditors. Technically, they could have gone after my house but while it probably appreciated in value by £150,000 to £250,000 in the three years after I bought it, the recession had removed the equity and it would have been hard for them to find a seller.

Still, while I had a roof over my head, there was nothing to occupy my time, and the Jobseeker's Allowance couldn't look after two kids.

On a trip to Dublin to watch an Ireland-England Six Nations game, Phil floated an idea. His company, Munnelly Support Services, who specialise in logistics and waste management for the construction industry, was expanding, and he saw an opening there which would keep me playing football. Phil sponsored Longford Town, a semi-professional club, in the second tier of the League of Ireland, and he'd devised an arrangement which would involve me playing for them as well as doing some marketing work for Munnellys in England from time to time. I jumped at the chance to get off the dole, and back in the game.

The travel involved was the downside. Initially, I didn't realise it would take me three hours to reach every home game, and two and a half hours to every training session in Dublin, where most of the lads live and work in their day jobs. The manager, Tony Cousins, agreed to a compromise where I came down once a week for training, and do the rest of my fitness work at home. He understands my circumstances, particularly when the away matches add to the logistical headache. While the Premier Division is dominated by Dublin sides, our league is made up of regional teams from far flung parts of the Republic. The 100-mile trip to Finn Harps in Donegal, the north-west, is the closest thing I have to a 'home' game.

The odd smart arse will chide me for dropping down to that level, and it's true that running out in front of a couple of hundreds spectactors came as a culture shock.

The crowds are so sparse that you hear every taunt. I stand at the post, waiting to defend a corner and some bloke will shout, "Have you got a bet on the match tonight, Keith?" I look over and smile. I've heard that one a million times, and yet some guys seem to think they're the first genius to crack that joke.

But it was a chance to stay in the game and bring in some money. And my responsibilities were about to grow.

In the summer of 2011, not long after I'd signed for Longford, I was ordering a drink in Cafe Ceol, a popular spot in Bangor, when my eyes were drawn to a gorgeous dark haired girl across the bar. As I stared, she stuck out her tongue in my general direction. I presumed it was at somebody else. The following week, I spotted her again and, this time, it led to a conversation where I learned that Claire Munn, a local girl almost 10 years my junior, who normally did her socialising in Belfast, was actually trying to respond to me. We had a connection from the outset. I learned she had a fashion degree, and did some modelling to supplement her job in the civil service. She's a football fan, a witty girl who recognised me and knew a fair bit about my eventful past. But taking it further was a challenge.

Small towns can be strange places and when she mentioned

to people that we'd met, she was told to steer well clear and refused to meet me. I asked her what the rumour mill was saying. Some guy in her work claimed that I'd headbutted a friend of his in a bar in Belfast, and then hit him with a snooker cue. I don't even know if I've ever been in a bar in Belfast with a snooker cue. Someone else had told her that I'd been thrown through the window of Piccolos, the kebab shop next to Cafe Ceol. I tried to explain to her that if this was true, it'd have been in the papers, but at first she was having none of it. It took a fair bit of persuasion over the phone to convince her to finally go for a drink.

I told her I was no angel, that many of the stories she was aware of from my past were true, but the latest dispatches she were hearing were complete nonsense, pure and simple lies. She listened, and gave me the benefit of the doubt. I didn't intend to get into another serious relationship so soon after Vikki, but I had a good feeling about this girl. And, like myself, Claire has an impulsive streak. We ran with it.

Things moved quicker than we ever could have imagined and we became inseparable. Within four months, we received unexpected news; she was pregnant. I invited her to move in with me, so we could learn more about each other as we prepared for parenthood.

I'm not sure if she realised the complicated nature of my life when she came into it. Plenty would have run a mile. Vikki wasn't long gone and things were bad between us; the constant sniping continued. But for the sake of the girls we had to try and work it out. When they left Northern Ireland, Madison was old enough to know me, but Lexie had just turned one, and I worried she would forget my face. We arranged for them to come and stay with me in Northern Ireland once a month, and that required a fair bit of talking out. Claire was, understandably, uneasy when I was spending time on the phone with Vikki, considering we'd only recently split, and it would cause arguments. And I suppose it was strange for Vikki when she heard Claire was on the scene and expecting. The juggling was taking its toll, and I had to try and make a living as well, which meant that I had sometimes had to leave the girls behind with Mum or Claire while I travelled to Longford or beyond.

Our beautiful baby boy, Nico, entered the world on July 17, 2012. He's got his mother's looks. We'd heard the name a few months earlier and, for some reason, it just sounded right for us. Claire would admit that when we first met, she wouldn't have viewed herself as the maternal type. But she's an amazing mum. She's with Nico practically every moment of every day and, after coming through so much in a short space of time, she deserved better support from me. But I had other things on my mind, issues that I couldn't avoid and feelings I couldn't explain. And a court date that I hoped would make everything better.

I didn't have any friends in Grant Thornton or A & L Goodbody. That's the weird thing about the fight to retrieve the lost thousands. I was relying on strangers to undo the damage done by my so-called pals.

The case was my incentive to be positive. When I did interviews about my situation, particularly when I joined Longford, I tread carefully when speaking about finances. I always referred to legal matters that I couldn't talk about just yet.

My dealings with the solicitors were semi-regular over the

space of a couple of years, with emails going forward and back and occasional meetings in their office in Belfast. We met a barrister who said I had a strong case and wouldn't be advising me to go to court otherwise. But there was a procedure to go through before we reached the dock.

Our documents were filed. Then there was the discovery phase, which gave the other side the chance to respond with their documentation before a date for a hearing was set. They had to hand their files over to solicitors, a requirement which I always felt would work in my favour. The advice I had been given would surely speak for itself, even if his handwritten notes system was quite sloppy.

The lengthy process was originally building towards October 2012, and a High Court date in Belfast. The local media would have a field day, but that was only a passing concern. I wanted some of this out in the open, as it would prove there was more to my bankruptcy than bad betting.

But it never made it to court. Instead, I was given the impression this would be solved by mediation. Initially, this seemed promising; out of court settlements are often designed to save face and I thought they would come to us with a good offer. I never thought we'd get the full £1,050,000 but I always believed I could recover a significant percentage.

As the summer trickled into autumn with sparing updates, my optimism began to wane.

No news was bad news.

The bright-side-up attitude that had sustained me through La Manga was replaced by negativity, a fear of the worst as it dragged on. Claire, who had enough to worry about with Nico arriving, bore the brunt of the anxiety.

The problem was I didn't really know who was in my corner and that left me with an uneasy feeling. I was out of my comfort zone, and my fate rested in the hands of others. After all, Grant Thornton's primary purpose was to sort out the creditors in my bankruptcy.

It was on a Friday at the start of December that a man from A & L delivered some firm news. Mediation was set for the following Tuesday. I had one question. "Are they going to settle with a figure there and then or will there an ongoing process?" "Grant Thornton have a duty of care to you as well," he said.

That provided encouragement. I'd always been under the impression that mediation would not be concluded without my approval, and this appeared to confirm it. So I waited until the Wednesday, and called the solicitors to find out how talks had gone. No response. The same on Thursday. I was sitting in Costa Coffee on the Friday when I got through to A&L.

"What's going on?"

"You'll have to speak to Grant Thornton."

On Monday, I buzzed their offices in London, introduced myself, and asked to be put through to someone relevant. After a time, I was connected to another faceless woman with a knowledge of my case. Her tone was matter of fact. The words were like a punch to the stomach.

At the mediation, a settlement of £250,000 had been reached. They discovered that the other side's indemnity insurance had a limit of £500,000. So we were basically down to £500,000 to start with. The legal cost of my financial advisor's representatives came to £120,000, bringing the pot down to £380,000. That's where the bartering started. "They started at £75,000," she said. "We worked them up to £250,000."

I asked how the £250,000 would be divided. She said that legal costs for my side came to around £60,000, and the balance of £190,000 was roughly what I owed to creditors, mostly the Inland Revenue. They'd had a meeting to distribute the funds.

"Are you telling me now that I won't be seeing a penny?"

"No... nothing"

"Can you fucking explain why it's taken me six days to get a hold of you to explain this to me?"

She fell silent. I vented. How did it take them so long to realise their Indemnity Insurance was capped? What would have happened if the other side's legal costs were bigger? Why was I the last person to find out the conclusion?

Angela thought we should approach an Ombudsman. Phil, who I had been slow to involve, laid out his grievances. He wrapped it up in his own, inimitable style. The advisor who had cost me a fortune on investments was still able to trade. His brother-in-law, who had fled the country, had escaped punishment and could do the same. The Inland Revenue had received full payment including investment. The solicitors on both sides had been richly compensated.

And me?

I received nothing.

The case was supposed to be my light at the end of the tunnel. But it only succeeded in bringing darkness like I'd never known.

(30)

Pills

"CLAIRE, I don't want to get out of bed today."

In the autumn of 2012, I started to spend entire days in my bedroom, a voluntary inmate between the four walls. The growing anxiety that I wouldn't be getting any of my money back, which was duly confirmed, had sapped my spirit. I'd wake in the morning with no interest in moving, nor desire to interact with anyone. The phone was ignored or switched off. I didn't see the point in stirring to have a shower or face the day. Instead, I'd lie back, switch on the TV and mindlessly flick through the channels.

For Claire, who was coming to terms with life as a first-time mother, it was difficult as I withdrew further into my shell. She would try and gee me up, get me to do something. "Go and play some golf, Keith." I couldn't be arsed.

Occasionally, I would find some motivation. Until November, there was training once a week and a match at the weekend to give me a little focus, or else the odd trip to England to earn a few quid. They gave me a distraction from whatever was draining my enthusiasm the rest of the time. Claire was barely sleeping because she'd be up breast-feeding Nico during the night and, sometimes, when I was having an off day, she would lie in bed next to me, with our infant son beside us, as the hours ticked by and evening drew in. Mum would drive by, see the blinds down in our bedroom and realise there was no point in calling because I wouldn't be talkative. If Claire couldn't get anything from me, nobody else stood a chance. It was no way to live. I had to seek help, for the sake of Claire and Nico as much as myself.

Depression. It's a scary word. I don't think I have the authority to explain what it is and what it means fully. I'm still trying to discover more about it and know that the journey is going to take a while.

My family saw the warning signs before I did. They knew there was something up, realised I wasn't myself. It was the moody behaviour, the snappy comments, the lack of heart for anything. I'd spent a lifetime telling everyone I was fine, even as things appeared to be going wrong. It's a recurring chain of events. Shit happens – people worry – I say I'm alright. Done. Whatever the strife, my stock response was consistent.

"I'm fine... I don't want to talk about it."

"Keith, you need to go and sit with someone."

"No I don't. That's silly. You're being silly."

Maybe that's how I convinced myself I was okay as well.

It changed that autumn. Everything seemed to come together

at once, from the likelihood I wouldn't be getting any cash back, to the distance from my girls, and the pressures of having a child in a new relationship. It snowballed to the point where the emotions I was bottling up were more than I could deal with. I heard the same questions again.

"Is everything okay, Keith? Do you want to talk about it?" and this time, I knew that I had to give in and find out the reasons I was feeling this way. Without Claire, I'd never have done it; she was the catalyst. We fought tooth and nail about it as I tried to resist and continued with the denial but, over time, she broke down the walls I had built up and made me see sense.

What do you do? Where do you go?

My first port of call was my local GP in Bangor, a man who I've known for years. He listened to my problems, made some recommendations and referred me to the hospital in Newtownards, where an appointment was made with a man in the Mental Health Assessment Centre.

Mental health? It sounded a bit dramatic to me. I associated the words with lunatics going around screaming and pounding the walls. I suppose I was guilty of buying in to that stereotype. It was recommended for Claire to come along too and we kept a low profile, taking the seats closest to the waiting room door where my name was called immediately before anyone had a chance to recognise me. I was taken into a room where a consultant, an African guy, was waiting to assess me. I can always tell if someone knows who I am – their eyes give it away – but I don't think he had any idea. We talked for an hour. I went through my feelings while he jotted down notes. Claire offered her thoughts. He concluded that I was suffering from mild depression. Claire wasn't satisfied and made it clear on the walk back to the car. "Mild?" she said, shaking her head. "It's gone further than that." She called my GP to make her point.

"How can you determine someone's state in the space of one hour?"

In the meantime, he had arranged for me to see an occupational therapist who ran a clinic in his office once a week. She was a friendly woman in her fifties with blondey greying hair and a warm smile. I went on my own and she instantly made me feel at ease. I felt we had a productive hour and was given the opportunity to come back the following Wednesday. But the timing didn't suit, the following week was the same and, then, in typical fashion, I just let it slide.

After all, I had my tablets. They'd been prescribed by my GP at the outset. I brought my happy pills everywhere, the green and gold capsules in a tin-foil package. Fluoexetine. Or, Prozac, as it's commonly known. I read an article recently which said it's been prescribed to 54 million worldwide. 54 million! That's one way of realising you're not alone.

I started with one-a-night and the dose was doubled on the advice of the doctor who did my medical ahead of the 2013 season with Longford. I take them at night, with a glass of water, and I suppose they must be having some impact. I've forgotten to take them and the next day, I can feel something's not right, which probably isn't a good sign. They say you can become addicted. My doc ran through the science of it with me at the start, explaining how the tablets tackle the chemical imbalance in my brain that apparently makes me feel this way. But I didn't take in enough to be able to give a presentation on the mechanics. I just had one question really: 'Will these make me feel better?'

When Gary Speed took his own life on a miserable Sunday in November 2011, the mental health of footballers became a talking point, but the bigger picture stuff from the talking heads on the television passed me by. I was too numbed by the fact that Speedo was dead. I really couldn't think about anything beyond that.

It's such a typical, predictable thing to say, but he's the last person I'd have expected to take that option. From the outside, his life looked perfect. After taking over as manager of Wales, results had improved dramatically, and I know that would have made him proud. When I shared a dressing room with Speedo at Newcastle and Sheffield United, his patriotism shone through. We all heard about it when the Welsh rugby boys were on fire.

I was at the final game he attended, the meeting of my old clubs, Manchester United and Newcastle United, at Old Trafford, but our paths didn't cross. I thought it was some kind of sick joke when the news broke the following morning that his wife, Louise, had found him in the garage of their family home.

It just didn't make any sense. I'd socialised plenty of times with Speedo, and he never displayed any hint of unhappiness. There was so much crappy speculation afterwards that I tried to ignore, because all I remembered was my own experience. Yet you could sense that the shock amongst those who knew him well, like Alan Shearer, was totally genuine.

Speedo was such a bright fella, the definition of a good character to have around the dressing room. Blackwell's deference towards him spoke volumes. He was the manager in waiting, and so it proved. Then, the seamless manner in which he slotted into the Welsh job marked him out as a candidate to reach the very top but there was obviously something deeper going on. It just goes to show, you never know what's going on behind closed doors.

I've heard Stan Collymore speak powerfully and impressively about his own problems with depression since then and I can relate to it but I'm still wary of generalising when I discuss Speedo. He didn't fit into any obvious category. Sometimes, there just isn't any explanation.

After he died, there was a big drive for the PFA to raise awareness. I don't ever remember receiving any material through the post about depression or mental health issues in the run of my career but then I wasn't a great man for opening letters and, even if I had come across something, I probably would have folded it up and tossed it in the bin.

Footballers aren't superhuman, much as we might like to think we are. But we're not really taught to open up about our feelings either, nor do many of us feel comfortable doing that. When I started taking medication, the last thing I was going to do was tell my team-mates at Longford about it. I certainly had no intention of letting anyone know beyond my immediate family. Phil only found out when Claire told him. It's wrong to think in these terms, but I suppose I didn't want to admit any weakness considering I'd been pretending to cope so well for so long. Heck, I'd been pretending to myself.

Pride is a strange thing because I'd like to think I would never let it get in the way of anything. I wouldn't have gone on the dole if I was precious. My time on Jobseeker's Allowance lasted for six weeks. There were a few puzzled looks from others in the Social Security office but that wasn't going to deter me from doing what was necessary to survive and look after the kids. I'm aware of ex-pros that are in a bad way and too embarrassed to admit it in case the wider world finds out. Other guys involved in the film schemes are doing whatever it takes to meet their payments. Phil and I invited a mutual friend, a former high profile Premier League player, to Old Trafford last year, and he refused as he was driving a van for a living and couldn't justify the expense of taking a day off and travelling. It's a glum existence when you've spent half your life in a bubble.

In the midst of my self-imposed isolation, I did open myself up to cyber scrutiny by signing up to Twitter, the social media website, to see what it was all about. Most people are nice, but you get the odd idiot who has a go. Against all advice, I do react; I can't abide grown men in their 40s who just go on Twitter to hurl abuse at people. We all have our issues, but those lads need help too. What pisses me off is guys talking as if they know me. One fella wrote that I used to go around Newcastle thinking I was the top dog, which has never been my way. When I went there first, I always used to stand in 50-deep queues for nightclubs, and the bouncers walking down the line would double take and ask what the hell I was doing there when I could stroll in anywhere I wanted. I always hated doing that because I knew there'd be guys looking, thinking, 'who the fuck does he think he is?'

But the presumptions come with the territory on Twitter. I even had a player from one of Longford's promotion rivals, Mervue United, talking shit about me, claiming I was at the centre of a match-fixing investigation which actually revolved around one of my team-mates. I confronted the coward when we played them and, unsurprisingly, he wasn't as brave in person.

The silver lining of my slide down the ranks was finding out who my real friends are. I spend more time now with people from other professions, like Davy, who is a builder, and the boys in the golf society, whose jobs range from the civil service to kitchen fitting. It was the same when I lived in Hartlepool. My social life then was a 'Tuesday Club' with Jim and his mates. There was a policeman, a solicitor, a butcher, an estate agent, a plasterer, and a surgeon. Good guys. It's the same now. Everywhere I go, 99 per cent of people are positive. I've made appearances at legends dos in Newcastle and Manchester and all over Northern Ireland and the response is great. People are sincere, slapping you on the back and wanting to know how you're doing and I say that I'm good. It's the safest answer, but it's not always the truth.

I need to get off these pills though. I can't spend the rest of my life relying on antidepressants. It's delaying a solution, not finding one. Claire stuck to her guns on the mild depression verdict and made sure that another trip to the Mental Health Assessment Centre, to see the same guy, was arranged. I opened up more the second time, gave a fuller picture of the moods, the stifling lows that trapped me in the bedroom for days. What I really wanted was to be referred to a clinical psychologist, so that I could receive proper treatment for my condition instead of just upping my Prozac dosage. After a productive chat, I received a letter from the Clinical Psychology Department of the hospital to say I would be given an appointment within three months. It came up sooner than that, and the first step was routine, another assessment with a view to breaking down the barriers. I'm hopeful I can stay on this path.

I'm perfectly capable of closing myself off to people I care about, never mind complete strangers, so I don't expect an overnight miracle. But these psychologists are experienced in what they do. They can dig deeper and draw things out, help me embrace the discussions I avoid, and find the strength to become a more open person. I'm not a great communicator and, by the end of this process, I want that to have changed, so I can become a better person for everyone that needs me. I've buried my head in the sand for too long. You can't find answers if you don't allow the questions.

31

The Other Side

"WHAT'S your gameplan, Keith?"

Phil often sits me down over a pint and steers discussion that way. I shrug my shoulders.

As an active businessman who always has something on the go, I don't think he really understands my approach to things.

My lack of direction was the motive behind getting me involved with his company, Munnellys. I couldn't run away from the offer, because it was all I had. So I found myself in London on a December morning, showering and shaving and putting on a shirt and tie instead of a tracksuit. The uniform for an alien world.

Over the winter of 2011, I spent a couple of days each week in their head office in the suburban borough of Harrow, gaining an insight into a real job. Phil invited me to meetings, where experts in their field talked about the finer points of the construction industry. I didn't really know what I was supposed to say or do, so concentrated on looking busy. The lingo went straight over my head. I just hoped that nobody noticed my blank expression.

The whole experience was strange. It's not that I disliked it. I did find it interesting to watch a successful business in full flow, and the boys in the office really made me feel welcome. And I reckon they were glad to have me around for their annual football tournament with other companies from around the UK. Their new recruit played a significant part in a glorious victory.

But the problem, really, is that the 9-5 existence is just so different to the working environment I grew up in. I can't adjust.

I remember sitting at a Christmas party, listening to a guy complaining about the fact that he was paying his secretary £32,000 a year, and all I could think about was the contrast in the discussion from my old Christmas bashes. Some of the flashier lads might have spent £32,000 on a round of drinks.

It wasn't the life for me; I was a duck out of water. As I sunk into depression, I didn't have the fire in the belly to keep it up, even though Phil was paying a decent wage to keep me focused.

When he set up a new international recruitment company, City Calling, at the start of 2013, he called me into the promotional drive. I wound up at a jobs expo in Dublin, watching Phil's son James sign people up with a view to helping them find work around the world. I listened to the 'roll up, roll up' pitch he was giving every potential customer and was encouraged to join in. As the crowds increased, I was on the coalface, taking people's details, explaining the procedure. At one stage, I was signing up a new person every 27 seconds. We took in 2,000 people in two days. It was more up my street and there could be a future in that, I suppose, but I'd be lying if I said it with any certainty.

I realise the prospect of living without the structure of football is scary, but all things must come to an end. That's why the news that Sir Alex Ferguson was retiring from Manchester United really struck a chord with me. Even he had to accept there's a time to say goodbye.

Phil and I decided at the start of 2013 that I'd hang up my boots at the end of the year; we timed the announcement for the day of the sponsorship launch which saw the City Calling name take over Longford's jersey and stadium. I only told the manager, Tony, on the day itself. I'm not really sure I thought it through properly. My body still felt good; the aches and pains were minimal. The new defensive midfield role is kinder on the limbs – I sit while the younger lads do most of the running – but it emerged a couple of months into the season that I'm suffering from a knee cartilage problem that makes it the percentage call to quit. Injections will get me through to the chequered flag.

A few of the lads at Big Mac's funeral raised their eyebrows when they heard where I was playing these days, but the boys who've gone into management, like Michael O'Neill and Steve Lomas, they understand that nothing compares to the buzz of playing when you consider the pressures on the other side. Regardless of what else is going on in my life, I still love having a game to look forward to at the weekend. If I go through with the retirement, there'll be a huge void, I know this, and that could be dangerous for someone with my personality. I have to prepare myself for that challenge.

What will I do?

There's punditry, I've dabbled in a bit of that, some radio, some TV. I'm getting the hang of it. It's all about getting your foot in the door in the right places really. Dave Bassett has encouraged me to go into the after-dinner speaking circuit. Some of my old pals, like Jason McAteer, have adapted to that scene perfectly. Me? I think I'd need to sink a couple to find the confidence to address a group of pissed-up strangers.

Then there's the old boys circuit, the charity track. One of my first housemates, Colin Telford, organises legends games, which brings you up against retired lads from other big clubs, and they are worth a few quid. I'm a bit fitter than some of my peers, so I seem to get invited back. It's taken me to Brunei and Malaysia and places I'd never dreamed of visiting otherwise.

The Manchester United connection still opens doors. Their TV station, MUTV, followed me for a week as part of the documentary to mark the 20-year anniversary of the 'Class of 92', and I actually enjoyed it. Self promotion doesn't sit easy, but to stay in the picture, and keep bringing in cash, I have to put myself out there. My links to Newcastle also help; I've done a few gigs back in the North East, including a lively reunion with Tino Asprilla. Blackburn has also thrown up opportunities to catch up with friendly faces. These gatherings follow a similar pattern. We briefly talk about the present and then revert to storytelling mode and delve into the past. The hours fly by.

I signed up to do my coaching badges; it seemed the natural step and Mum and Claire are very keen for me to go down that route, but the experience of the 'B' Licence gave me second thoughts. Parts of it were tedious. We'd sit in a classroom, studying what kind of a warm-up should take place every morning before a particular type of session, and I struggled to see the relevance. I've worked under some brilliant coaches, and this regimented, boring process didn't tally with the way I was raised at the Cliff. The top guys, like Brian Kidd, naturally knew how to vary sessions so as to keep players interested. It was instinctive, rather than by a book. People in football have said to me that securing the right coaching qualifications is a bit like the process for a driving licence; you get through it in a particular way and then practice your own ideas.

At Big Mac's funeral, Ian Stewart from the IFA gave me a pep talk, telling me that we needed more ex-internationals in the system. I said I'd think about it. I guess it's a bit like the after dinner stuff. You wonder if you have the right personality for it. I've seen lads who weren't the most obvious candidates going into management. Gary Hamilton, my regular drinking partner, surprised everyone by taking a job as player-manager with Glenavon in the Irish League. For his first game, he stood on the sidelines wearing a pair of jeans, doing things his own way. The one thing about dropping down the levels is that it makes you appreciate the experience you've gleaned from mixing it with the best. At Longford, I see lads with raw ability making bad decisions, trying a Hollywood pass when a simple ball would do and I think, yeah, the benefit of my experience could bring something. Other days, I think a break from the game would be for the best.

For every retiree that goes into management or media, there's another who goes off the rails. I hear tales about the exploits of my old team-mates which really make me wonder. By far the most bizarre is Phil Mulryne joining the priesthood. I associate Phil with chaos, the boozing in the West Indies and the no-show before the England game that led to Lawrie throwing him out.

Knowing what he was like on nights out, it's hard to imagine him standing on an altar, preaching to an audience, but that's the path he's chosen and good luck to him. He's found happiness. Many of us never do.

Sometimes, when Madison and Lexie visit, they order me to turn on Sky Plus and go to into my saved programmes. They're always looking for the same thing, a recording of a goal I scored for Sheffield United against Manchester United, a header past Edwin van der Sar in the relegation season. Every single time, they go crazy around the room, screaming as the camera pans in on my celebration.

I hope they'll still be as proud of their Dad when they're older.

Things are better with Vikki now. She appreciates what Claire does with the girls when they're in Northern Ireland and she's invited her to come over to England with Nico and me for a visit. Madison and Lexie love their little brother too; it's great that everybody can get along, so I don't have that pressure of worrying about the phonecalls, thinking that I want to ring the girls but feel Claire won't like to hear me speaking to Vikki. Now, I can sit and have a chat with Vikki with Claire sitting next to me. It's eased a lot of the pressure.

I still have bad days, where I think it would be so much easier if I had the means to live more comfortably. The logistics of getting the girls over to Northern Ireland can be hard if it's around a Longford match. I've got to fly over, pick them up, get a flight back with them and then, after a week, go through the reverse journey. The schedule seems to mean I'm always on the red-eye flights; it's cheaper. Here's a typical example:

I had a game down in Wexford, in the south-east of the

Republic, on a Friday night, when the girls were due back in England on the Saturday morning. I was sent off which didn't help my mood, and then by the time I made it back to Bangor, it was 2.30am. I was up at 4.30am to get the girls dressed and ready for the airport and a 6.15am flight. The only option available for my return was at 6.55pm in the evening so, after Vikki picked Madison and Lexie up, I retired to the airport terminal for an 11-hour wait. If you ever need advice on a good place to sleep in Stansted Airport, I'm your man. The evening flight always goes from the same gate, which is deserted during the day, so I make my way down there and stretch out, waiting for the time to pass. I bring a book sometimes, I've become a fan of the author Stephen Leather, who specialises in crime thrillers. I read them between naps in my own little prison, as the minutes towards departure slowly tick down. There was more to do in Sangonera.

I feel guilty for complaining because I love every minute with the girls. When I set eyes on them after a break, and Lexie runs towards me with a smile and hug, I forget everything that's wrong. What I hate is losing quality time from their trips because of the stress of making sure everything runs smoothly. Sometimes, we fly from Dublin because quite often the easyJet fares from Belfast are impossible to justify with my cashflow. With another mouth to feed, I have to shop around for value. Every penny counts.

I don't have time to gamble anymore; I flick through the racing pages now.

On Saturdays, I still like to do a football accumulator and maybe a few quid on the golf as well, but it's only small money. I never received any treatment for my betting habit, so I can't describe myself as a reformed gambler. I just grew out of the madness; it's unsustainable. Claire will never allow me to go down that road again.

I have to do the right thing by my kids now, and that's going to colour all my future decisions. There's plenty of people around me to help; Mum, Dad, Angela and Heather all live within a two-mile radius and Claire's family are close by too. As much as I like being based in Northern Ireland, I can't say for certain that I'm going to live there forever. I'll have to go wherever the work is. But for Nico's sake, it would be good to have stability. Before I know it, he'll be old enough to pose questions too, wondering about what his Daddy used to do.

People assume that I'm weighed down with regrets, and it might sound like a contradiction when I say that I'm not. Heck, I've made so many mistakes, done so many stupid things. Trusted the wrong people, ignored the right ones. And I've still got a lot of talking to do to sort my head out. I've mastered the art of self deprecation; I can go on a stage and talk about how my big money move to Newcastle was good news for me and better news for the bookies and people laugh. If that's how I'm to be remembered, then so be it.

I am proud of my football career though. I'll tell Nico that. I was able pull on the shirt of some huge clubs, alongside great players, under a selection of the biggest names and best managers the game has ever seen.

Maybe I didn't meet other people's expectations but when I was kicking a ball around Northern Ireland as a kid, I didn't have any. I just wanted to play.

Life's easy when you're running around a field with a ball at your feet. Figuring out what I'm going to do without it will be tough, but I've got to find a way. The most important people in my life are depending on it.

I'm not there yet. There's no simple way of signing off this story. Phil can keep me asking the same question the same day of the week. Chances are, I'll give him a different response every time.

The gameplan?

Don't have one. Not sure that I ever did.

What happens now?

Honestly, I haven't got a clue.

Index

Statistics

Club Career

Manchester United	July 1991-January 1995
Wigan Athletic (loan)	September-November 1993
Newcastle United	January 1995-December 1998
Blackburn Rovers	December 1998-July 2003
Wigan Athletic (loan)	December 2000-January 2001
Leicester City	July 2003-August 2005
Sheffield United	August 2005-January 2009
Charlton Athletic (loan)	November 2008-January 2009
Bradford City	March-May 2009
Glentoran	August 2009-June 2010
Darlington	November 2010-March 2011
Longford Town	March 2011-

Professional League Career

Season	Club	Appearances* (Goals)
1992-93	Manchester United	2 (1)
1993-94	Wigan Athletic	10 (4)
1994-95	Manchester United	12 (1)
1994-95	Newcastle United	20 (4)
1995-96	Newcastle United	32 (5)
1996-97	Newcastle United	44 (1)
1997-98	Newcastle United	43 (4)
1998-99	Newcastle United	8 (0)
1998-99	Blackburn Rovers	20 (2)
1999-00	Blackburn Rovers	25 (2)
2000-01	Blackburn Rovers	20 (0)

KEITH **GILLESPIE**

2000-01	Wigan Athletic	7 (0)
2001-02	Blackburn Rovers	39 (3)
2002-03	Blackburn Rovers	34 (0)
2003-04	Leicester City	13 (0)
2004-05	Leicester City	35 (2)
2005-06	Sheffield United	33 (0)
2006-07	Sheffield United	31 (2)
2007-08	Sheffield United	38 (2)
2008-09	Sheffield United	1 (0)
2008-09	Charlton Athletic	6 (0)
2008-09	Bradford City	3 (0)

* Appearances include League, FA Cup, League Cup, Football League Trophy, Champions League, UEFA Cup, FA Charity Shield

Northern Ireland (86 caps, 2 goals)

1994-95	8 (1)
1995-96	4 (0)
1996-97	5 (0)
1997-98	4 (0)
1998-99	5 (0)
1999-00	6 (0)
2000-01	4 (0)
2001-02	5 (0)
2002-03	6 (0)
2003-04	8 (0)
2004-05	7 (0)
2005-06	6 (1)
2006-07	8 (0)
2007-08	5 (0)
2008-09	5 (0)

Landmarks

05/01/93: First-team debut.
Manchester United 2-0 Bury (FA Cup) – 1 goal
07/09/94: International debut. Northern Ireland 1-2 Portugal
21/09/94: League Cup debut.
Port Vale 1-2 Manchester United
08/10/94: Premier League debut.
Sheffield Wednesday 1-0 Manchester United
12/10/94: First Northern Ireland goal.
Austria 1-2 Northern Ireland
29/10/94: First Premier League goal.
Manchester United 2-0 Newcastle United
21/01/95: Newcastle United debut.
Sheffield Wednesday 0-0 Newcastle United
19/02/95: First Newcastle United goal.
Newcastle United 3-1 Manchester City (FA Cup) – 2
10/09/96: European debut. Newcastle United 4-0 Halmstads
13/08/97: CL debut. Newcastle United 2-1 NK Croatia
11/10/03: 50th Northern Ireland cap.
Greece 1-0 Northern Ireland – captain
19/11/08: Final Northern Ireland cap.
Northern Ireland 0-2 Hungary

Individual Honours

1991/92 FA Youth Cup
1994/95 FA Charity Shield
1996/97 FA Charity Shield runner-up
2001/02 League Cup
2009/10 Irish League Cup
2012 PFAI First Division Team Of The Year

HOW **NOT** TO BE A
FOOTBALL
MILLIONAIRE

KEITH GILLESPIE

MY AUTOBIOGRAPHY